Cosmopolitanism

Cosmopolitanism

A Philosophy for Global Ethics

Stan van Hooft

McGill-Queen's University Press
Montreal & Kingston • Ithaca

ISBN: 978-0-7735-3643-2 (bound)
ISBN: 978-0-7735-3644-9 (pbk.)

Legal deposit third quarter 2009
Bibliothèque nationale du Québec

Published simultaneously in the United Kingdom by Acumen Publishing Limited
and in North America by McGill-Queen's University Press

Library and Archives Canada Cataloguing in Publication

Hooft, Stan van, 1945-
Cosmopolitanism : a philosophy of global ethics / Stan van Hooft.

Includes bibliographical references and index.
ISBN 978-0-7735-3643-2 (bound).--ISBN 978-0-7735-3644-9 (pbk.)

1. Cosmopolitanism. 2. Globalization--Moral and ethical aspects.
3. International relations--Moral and ethical aspects. I. Title.

JZ1308.H66 2009 172'.4 C2009-902271-0

Typeset in Warnock Pro.
Printed in the UK by the MPG Books Group.

Contents

Introduction

Ethical challenges of globalization

> The basic fact that human experiential space is being subtly changed through an opening to cosmopolitanization should not lead us to assume that we are all becoming cosmopolitans. Even the most positive conceivable development – an erosion of frontiers between cultural horizons and a growing sensitivity towards unfamiliar geographies of life and coexistence – does not necessarily demand a sense of cosmopolitan responsibility. The question of how such a sense might become even a possibility has up to now scarcely been posed, let alone investigated. (Beck 2004: 154)

The world is facing crises in global politics and international relations that have only recently begun to be discussed in the philosophical literature. There is a crisis in peace highlighted by the so-called war on terror (Sterba 2003b). There is a refugee crisis with people moving around the globe in unprecedented numbers driven by war, persecution, famine and economic hardship (Carens 1987; Goodin 1992; Boswell 2005). There is a crisis of global justice with entire populations in underdeveloped parts of the world facing the threat of starvation owing to avoidable poverty.[1] There is a global environmental crisis, of which climate change is only the most widely debated consequence (Jonas 1984; Crocker & Linden 1998; Newton 2003). There is a crisis in the global economy with the high social costs of globalization and trade as well as threats to supplies of energy resources (Sen 1999). There is a crisis in human rights with many regimes unwilling to honour the requirements of human dignity (Vincent 1992; Campbell 2006; Churchill 2006). And there is the so-called "clash of civilizations" in which major world religions and political ideologies are implicated in global tensions (Huntington 1996; Caputo 2001). Because of globalization we all have a part to play in addressing problems of global governance, management of the environment, maintenance of peace, equitable global distribution of social goods and resources, humanitarian assistance, intercultural tolerance and understanding, and the protection of human dignity around the world. Accordingly, it could be claimed that we are "global citizens" and that we should develop a "global ethics" through which we can articulate and exercise our global responsibilities as such citizens. The aim of this book is to articulate, explicate and develop a normative philosophical framework for global ethics and international relations that has recently become widely discussed under the term "cosmopolitanism".[2]

International relations is an academic discipline that is relatively well established while global ethics is an emerging field in applied ethics, one that provides a meeting point between theorists of international law, political science, political philosophy, economics and development studies, as well as international relations itself (Dower 1998, 2003; Amstutz 1999; Rawls 1999; O'Neill 2000; Singer 2002). It is, however, inadequate to approach the scholarly study of global ethics as if it were a form of applied ethics seeking to embody the moral theories developed in the Western philosophical tradition (Pollis & Schwab 1979; Commers *et al.* 2008). Global ethics must not just be an application of our Western way of thinking to global problems, but must be a form of ethical thinking that is itself global in its resonance and appeal. It must be an ethics founded on a moral framework that all thinkers and policy-makers in the world can accept. Accordingly, it must transcend the particular cultural traditions of those thinkers and policy-makers and appeal to norms inherent in humanity itself (Gaita 1999). We need not only an ethics for a global society, but also a globally valid ethics.

Globalization

The process of globalization has had immeasurable impacts on our daily lives and on international politics. Globalization includes the following set of processes and changes:

- The world economic system has become highly complex and interdependent. Many nation-states are unable to control effectively their own economic policies in their national interests. Many smaller states that depend on agriculture are no longer able to be self-sufficient in feeding their populations because they have largely replaced food crops for their own populations with cash crops grown for the international market. Multinational corporations, some of which have budgets larger than small nation-states, are able to situate manufacturing and service centres anywhere in the world where labour is cheapest, regulations and taxes least onerous and access to markets most effective. Terms of trade between nations are dictated by the more powerful states.

- International diplomacy has been transformed from bilateral relationships centred on disputes over territory or resources to a multitude of multilateral arrangements and agreements relating to everything from management of the Antarctic to the structures of international financial institutions. This has given rise to systems of international politics of great complexity involving issues of global governance through such bodies as the United Nations (UN) that require the creation and policing of international law.
- There has been a greater realization that disasters and risks in one country can have global effects. This is most obviously true in relation to the environment and global warming, but it also applies to poverty, oppression and injustice, all of which result in cross-border flows of refugees. The HIV/AIDS epidemic is also an international scourge that does not respect borders.
- War has ceased to be a relatively limited form of international conflict between specific states but has become a global phenomenon in several senses. First, there were the two "world wars" in which a great many nations were involved. Secondly, there was the "cold war" during which the world was divided into two mutually antagonistic armed camps that pitted capitalism against communism. Thirdly, there is the almost constant presence in the contemporary world of armed conflicts at a more local level, ranging from civil wars, violent political struggles and ethnic cleansing to humanitarian interventions. These conflicts become the concern of the world community through the UN, which is charged with maintaining peace globally.
- As a result of the terrorist attacks in the USA of 11 September 2001 and the growth of terrorism more generally, there has been a greater realization of the impacts of culture on world politics. Whether this is understood as a conflict between "civilizations" (Huntington 1996) or as a clash between religions (Armstrong 2000), the world is increasingly seen as divided between modern liberal societies and traditional theocracies. Whatever the accuracy of this analysis, it is clear that global conflict is based on more than economic or territorial rivalries and that cultural differences between civilizations can have volatile effects. The so-called "war on terror" has forced many people to become more aware of the conditions in which people live in other parts of the world.
- International travel is fast and available to anyone with the funds for the relatively cheap fares. Whether through tourism or more purposeful travel, most people in the richer parts of the world are able to experience

countries and cultures different from their own by visiting them at some time in their lives.

- Communication is now so speedy that events anywhere in the world can be brought into our living rooms during the evening news. The internet and new forms of mobile telephony make it possible to communicate instantly with family, friends or business colleagues no matter where they are located.
- As a result of these changes, a global culture has emerged that corresponds to the global market, with many brands being recognizable anywhere in the world and with television programmes and films being seen in most parts of the world simultaneously. Modern cities around the world are becoming architecturally indistinguishable from one another and even popular music is becoming homogenized. A counter-movement is the interest being shown in local and regional cultures and artistic productions on the part of affluent consumers in metropolitan centres.
- Many political, charitable or advocacy groups, such as aid organizations, feminists, environmentalists and peace activists, have responded to these changes by giving their campaigns a global scope and by establishing international non-governmental organizations (NGOs) to pursue their goals internationally.
- As a result of all these changes, a new realization is emerging that we live in a world community as well as in our own countries. We are not citizens just of specific nation-states, but are also citizens of the world. We should be concerned not just for our compatriots but for all human beings, especially those who are suffering from poverty, war, religious intolerance or injustice.

Cosmopolitanism

It is this last claim that will be the focus of this book. This claim articulates what is meant by the term "cosmopolitanism". Cosmopolitanism is the view that the moral standing of all peoples and of each individual person around the globe is equal.[3] Individuals should not give moral preference to their compatriots, their co-religionists or fellow members of their demographic identity groups. The famous words of the American Declaration of Independence to the effect that "all men are created equal" also highlight the centrality of this notion of equality. Thomas Pogge has described cosmopolitanism in this way:

> Three elements are shared by all cosmopolitan positions. First, *individualism*: the ultimate units of concern are *human beings*, or *persons* – rather

> than, say, family lines, tribes, ethnic, cultural, or religious communities, nations, or states. The latter may be units of concern only indirectly, in virtue of their individual members or citizens. Second, *universality*: the status of ultimate unit of concern attaches to *every* living human being *equally* – not merely to some sub-set, such as men, aristocrats, Aryans, whites, or Muslims. Third, *generality*: this special status has global force. Persons are ultimate units of concern for *everyone* – not only for their compatriots, fellow religionists, or such like. (1992: 48)

But cosmopolitanism is not just another name for egalitarianism or liberal humanism. What it targets are forms of discrimination that arise from the victim's being of a different nationality, ethnicity, religion, language, race or any other form of identity that is used to classify people into discrete groups. When commentators speak of a "clash of civilizations" or of a clash of cultures, they may not be using national boundaries in order to define the groups that are said to be clashing, but they are alluding to sources of identity, including nationality, religion and ethnicity, that serve to define a community as distinct from another. Such definitions can then become the basis for prejudice or exploitation. Although debates about human rights often refer to them, gender, age and sexual preference do not usually constitute group memberships in this way. Gender, age and sexual preference are certainly possible sources of prejudice and exploitation but they fall under a different heading. They do not categorize people into definable national, ethnic or cultural groups. Rather, it is national, ethnic or cultural groups that differentially define the normative status of gender, age and sexual preference in various communities around the world. It is identity as established by national, ethnic or cultural groups that is the more basic. As a result, it is the divisions between people that are created primarily by religion, race, nationality and ethnicity that are of central concern to cosmopolitanism. Moreover, such divisions often provide the historical, demographic and geographic bases of nation-states so that they too are subject to cosmopolitan scrutiny.

The view that all human beings have equal moral standing despite their group identifications might be called a negative characterization of cosmopolitanism: one that urges us not to discriminate on inappropriate grounds. A more positive conception of cosmopolitanism would be one that urges us to accord all people equal respect. Once again, this does not imply that we should ignore the differences between people on the bases of which it is legitimate to discriminate between them, such as their accomplishments, but it does suggest that even the least deserving should be given a level of respect that rules out, for example, exploitation or neglect. Another way in which these ideas have been formulated is by using the language of human rights. The claim that everyone has inalienable and basic human rights can be interpreted in the negative sense that no one should be discriminated against, and in the positive sense that everyone should be accorded a basic level of respect. The idea that everyone enjoys, and should be acknowledged as having, what is called "human dignity" also captures this idea. Yet another way of expressing these intuitions is to speak of "global humanism", which is the view that we all share a quality called "humanity" and should respect each other's rights or meet each other's needs on that basis. Lastly, cosmopolitanism may be expressed as the view that there exists a global community of which all people, by virtue of their humanity, are members. If such a community could be said to exist, then membership of it would ground both responsibilities and expectations between members of such a community.

In contrast, Kwame Anthony Appiah (2006) has described cosmopolitanism as primarily an openness to, and tolerance of, the cultural and historical differences that constitute the identities of different peoples. For him a cosmopolitan is one who takes a keen interest in the cultures and ways of life of other peoples as well as taking their interests to heart. A cosmopolitan does not just tolerate cultural differences, but acknowledges them and is prepared to enter into respectful dialogue with them (Shapcott 2001). If political progress is to be made in international relations and if debates to that end are to be engaged in by appealing to readily acceptable understandings of the human condition, then cosmopolitans, with their interest in, and knowledge of, the cultures of the world, will be uniquely placed to contribute to such debates.

Historically, the most important contrasting position to cosmopolitanism was a mixture of nationalism and racism. It was a deep form of racism that made both slavery and colonialism possible because it allowed people to think of the victims of those practices as inherently inferior to their masters. Failure to respect the religious beliefs and cultural practices of foreign peoples encouraged the more powerful societies to exploit those peoples. Empires everywhere have depended on denigrating the human status of those whom they conquer. Inextricable from such forms of racism was nationalism. Nationalism holds that national interests may override the universal humanitarian demands of cosmopolitanism. It affirms the rights that stem from state sovereignty. While this can sometimes be a crude form of political "realism" – the view that rejects the influence of any moral considerations within international politics – more sophisticated anti-cosmopolitan positions highlight the local moral and cultural traditions that shape people's attitudes and moral commitments in order to suggest that the individualism inherent in cosmopolitanism is inappropriate for global ethics.

This "communitarian" position would insist that respect should be shown to those cultures in which the autonomy of the individual is not a regulative ideal and that cosmopolitanism hides an imposition of Western liberal cultural hegemony. The rights of societies to maintain their sometimes non-liberal traditions and identities must also be respected (Walzer 1983; Taylor & Gutman 1994; Rawls 1999). This critique argues that cosmopolitanism is a form of global liberalism that seeks to apply globally the stress on individual liberty, political rights and individual conceptions of the good life that are the hallmarks of Western liberal thought. Charles Beitz (1999b) takes individual liberty to be a central value in this way, and Kok-Chor Tan (2000) espouses a "comprehensive liberalism" that takes autonomy as a central value and as the benchmark against which cultural practices and political arrangements around the world are to be judged. However, along with many others, Bernard Williams (2005) has noticed that this is a case of cultural imperialism. It seeks to impose the value of autonomy universally and asserts that any practices in other cultures that reduce autonomy are not to be tolerated. The problem with this position is that comprehensive liberalism is not value-neutral. Even a procedural form of liberalism such as that of John Rawls (1972) or Jürgen Habermas (1973), while it attempts to withhold allegiance to any core value apart from fair procedures or uncoerced communication, still ends up espousing autonomy. It has to be said, of course, that for anyone thinking within a post-Enlightenment culture, this is unavoidable. We moderns simply do give high regard to autonomy. However, it must not be assumed that other cultures will think this way or that they would welcome this value being imposed on them. Autonomy, it might be argued, is a concept that belongs to a self-assertive and individualistic culture and is, like liberalism itself, tied to capitalism, free-market ideology and a consumerism that valorizes choice.

It ought to be possible, however, to develop a conception of cosmopolitanism that is not simply a projection of Western liberal and modernist political thought. We should not imperialistically impose our own commitments as if they were universally valid. But nor should we accept that the evils that foreigners do is of no concern to us on the basis of a pluralist stance that sees moral norms as deriving only from local traditions. In this book, reflecting on the basics of human life and the essential requirements of human dignity will serve to avoid conceiving of cosmopolitanism as a form of Western ideology.

While many moral philosophers discuss cosmopolitanism from the point of view of the individual so as to identify and expand the range of moral responsibilities that an individual bears towards others (Singer 1972; Chatterjee 2004), thinkers in the fields of international relations and global politics see cosmopolitanism as especially relevant to the actions of states and of national and international leaders and to the design of international institutions (Beitz 1979; Shue 1996). Such thinkers argue that the traditional presumption that the national interest should trump international or global concerns such as the environment, global justice or world peace must be called into question in our globalized world. The first of these strands of thought has been called "ethical cosmopolitanism", while the second is "political cosmopolitanism".[4] In either case, it will be clear that cosmopolitanism is a demanding moral position. It urges us, whether as citizens or as occupants of positions of political leadership, to embrace the whole world into our moral concerns and to apply the standards of impartiality and equity across boundaries of nationality, race, religion or ethnicity in a way that would have been unheard of even fifty years ago.

The focus of this book will be on ethical cosmopolitanism and it will discuss international, political and institutional structures and norms only as extensions of the personal responsibilities of individuals. The distinction between ethical and political cosmopolitanism cannot be sharp. Many cosmopolitan responsibilities of individual citizens can be exercised through political action. In democratic states the minimum requirement is that citizens vote so as to influence their governments in the pursuit of the good. More active participation in political processes such as joining political parties or engaging in public debate is also called for. A newer form of political and social participation has emerged through the emergence of "civil society", which comprises a great many NGOs ranging from trade unions, business organizations, charitable societies, international networks, activist networks and lobby groups of various kinds, churches and so on. All of these provide opportunities for influencing the policies of decision-makers and require ethically informed participation. Citizenship is a concept that is both far-reaching and ethically demanding at the national level, and global citizenship is even more so. Moreover, global ethical awareness is necessary not just for citizens, but also for individuals who work in business. Business organizations that operate in the global context need to be willing to accept arrangements about working conditions, social justice and human rights even when they threaten profits. In the absence of sanctions, such a willingness must be motivated by moral commitments.

Accordingly, cosmopolitanism is a moral position applicable to several fields of concern. It speaks to us individually of our duties to others by arguing that demographic, national or cultural identity does not constitute, of itself, a morally valid basis for making moral distinctions between people. And it suggests a range of virtues that the cosmopolitan individual should display: virtues such as tolerance, justice, pity, righteous indignation at injustice, generosity towards the poor and starving, care for the global environment and a willingness to take responsibility for change on a global scale (van Hooft 2007; see also Turner 2000). This is the field of individual ethics and of the existential commitments that individuals and their communities make towards the world at large. Cosmopolitanism is a virtue.

But cosmopolitanism does not speak only to the ethical lives of individual world citizens. It also speaks to the moral stances that, arguably, should be adopted by politicians, business leaders, governments and organizations that operate across borders. People who have power in our globalized world cannot avoid facing such questions as: do states have a responsibility to pursue global justice and to assist in the development of poorer nations? Do states have an obligation to help people in other states who suffer from man-made or natural disasters such as famine or earthquake? What controls if any should be placed on multinational corporations as they exploit natural resources and poorly paid and policed working conditions in developing nations? Should the human rights record of a state be considered relevant to the shaping of bilateral relationships with that state? When is it appropriate to intervene in the domestic affairs of another sovereign state? When is war justified and how should it be waged? What roles should states play in global governance and international law? These are moral questions that differ from individual and existential questions in their scope and in the moral agent to which the question is being addressed. They are addressed to collective bodies such as nation-states, business corporations or international NGOs. But it is still individual persons who have the responsibility to answer them.

Putative cosmopolitan practices

Accordingly, this book will understand cosmopolitanism in terms of the moral outlooks that it embodies rather than in terms of the practices, institutions and customs that contingently overcome any normative division between one's own people and "others". Such practices have occurred from time to time in human history and some scholars have described them as "cosmopolitan". So, for example, it has been argued that cosmopolitanism was a form of life in the medieval period in Islamic Spain. At this time, when the Moors ruled large tracts of that country, there was considerable contact been Muslims, Jews and Christians, and their respective communities lived side by side in harmony. Thinkers such as the Muslim scholar Ibn Rushd (Averroës) (1126–98) and the Jewish philosopher Moses Maimonides (1135–1204), along with notable Christian theologians, engaged in debates and discussions on matters of faith and morals. Tolerance was also a feature of the rule of some Mogul emperors on the Indian subcontinent, such as Jalaluddin Muhammad Akbar, who allowed Hindu and other religious communities to enjoy the same rights within their states as their co-religionists (Sen 2006: ch. 4). In later centuries such mutual tolerance and rapport existed among intellectual elites in the Ottoman Empire: in Istanbul, Cairo and Alexandria, in which cafes and other urban spaces provided a setting for the influx of European ideas (Zubaida 2002). While tolerance of the cultural, religious and practical traditions of other peoples is a virtue central to the cosmopolitan stance, it is remarkable how fragile the historical instances of such tolerance have been. The completion of the Reconquista with the conquest of Granada in 1492, marking the end of Muslim rule in the Iberian peninsula, put a brutal end to such forms of coexistence there, while contemporary Islamists regard the kind of urban and urbane cosmopolitanism enjoyed by the elites of the Ottoman Empire as a corruption of the purity of their faith (Armstrong 2000). Deep divisions among Hindus and Muslims on the Indian subcontinent led to the partition of India and Pakistan amid horrific bloodshed in 1947.

Another form that cosmopolitanism has taken is the sharing of common languages. Examples would include the spread of Latin in early Europe and the use of Sanskrit throughout south Asia. The first occurred because of the spread of the Roman Empire, while the second was a more voluntary adoption of a literary vehicle on the part of the intellectual elites in countries surrounding the Indian subcontinent (Pollock 2002). The widespread use of English in the world today would be a contemporary example. However, one could ask of this last example whether it occurred because of a newly emerging sense of global solidarity and cultural understanding or whether it arose because of the hegemony of English-speaking peoples in the world. It is clear that the earlier spread of Latin was associated with the spread of Roman power. It is interesting to note that many nationalist movements or struggles to maintain the identities and cultures of oppressed peoples focus on the restoration and maintenance of their vernacular languages. Perhaps the only language that is genuinely cosmopolitan in spirit is Esperanto, which is an artificial tongue developed in the late nineteenth century in an attempt to overcome the language-based divisions between European peoples and is now used only by a small group of aficionados.

Another practice that both encourages the outward gaze of a people and serves to define what cosmopolitanism is for some modern commentators is trade. If the only contact that a particular people has with another is based on conflict – if all that one group does in relation to another is raid it for its goods or its women – then the people of the two communities concerned are indeed likely to see each other as barbarians and as threats. And if the languages, customs and even physical appearances of the two peoples are different, this seems only to deepen the distrust between them. On the other hand, if the two peoples trade with each other they will derive mutual benefit from their relationship. Traders and merchants, rather than soldiers, will travel from one community to the other and establish contact. Knowledge of one another will grow and, while one community may still find the customs of the other strange or even repugnant, their relationship, being based on mutual advantage and cooperation, will enhance understanding and tolerance. The philosopher and economist Adam Smith (1723–90) was neither the first nor the last to point out that free trade had this humanizing advantage, even though his focus was on the commercial value of such trade (Smith 1976: bk 4).

Indeed, more recent thinkers in the tradition of Smith have urged that cosmopolitanism should be thought of primarily in economic terms. Rather than concerning ourselves with the role that governments should play in international relations and in regulating international trade through tariffs and trade rules, they urge that the globalized market is the best and most efficient means whereby international commerce can be encouraged and thus cooperative relations between peoples established. While this represents an attempt to rob cosmopolitanism of its moral content, there is no doubt that a great deal of international cooperation has emerged in the wake of global trade and other pragmatic relationships between peoples. As a result, international norms already exist in a great variety of mundane fields. International financial rules, standards of measurement and electronic connectivity, the international date line, aviation rules, laws of the sea and many more such instruments are all global normative arrangements that resulted from international agreements. However, these norms express forms of "internationalism" rather than cosmopolitanism in that they are entered into by, and are binding on, nation-states.

Even colonialism has been described as cosmopolitan. As distinct from empire, in which one powerful nation conquers and assimilates another politically, colonialism imposes rule by a foreign power while leaving a great deal of the local cultural and political infrastructure in place. So long as economic advantage can be secured, the social and political hierarchies of the colonized people can be left untouched. Many European colonial powers in the nineteenth century differed in the degree to which they replaced local political structures with their own, but if we take as an example the case of British colonialism in India, we can see that local systems of rule were largely protected even as they were subsumed within a British military and economic command structure. The way in which such systems of rule could be said to be cosmopolitan – at least in the eyes of the colonizer – is that they involved superimposing a wider, allegedly global culture on more local cultural practices. This was often justified as an attempt to bring civilization to the natives. A kind of ersatz benevolence was expressed in the rhetoric of the colonizers, in which the local populations were seen as more or less primitive savages in need of the benefits of Western civilization. The improvement of the lot of the natives was seen as "the white man's burden". In this way the Eurocentric outlooks of the colonizers were expanded to include a regard for the welfare of those who were "other" and foreign. Moreover, if cosmopolitanism is marked by a genuine curiosity about the ways of other peoples, it could be suggested that the science of anthropology, which flourished in the wake of colonialism, was an expression of a cosmopolitan impulse. In this context, a cosmopolitan is seen as the opposite of the parochial person in that he is open to, and sympathetic with, the otherness of exotic peoples, and interested in their ways of life (van der Veer 2002).

Another allegedly cosmopolitan practice is religious missionary activity, through which many religions seek to propagate themselves globally. This was much easier in the colonial period than it is now because then the missionaries were backed by the armed power of the colonizers. Moreover, given the apparent superior strength of the colonizers, colonized peoples were inclined to think that they too could acquire such power if only they converted to the ways of thought of their masters. However, even without the backing of colonial powers, most religions take themselves to have the mission of bringing others to their faiths. It seems endemic in the human condition that, if you have a deep moral or metaphysical conviction, you will want to share it with others. Whatever we might think of the appropriateness of acting on this impulse, there seems no doubt that the people who have it will feel themselves entitled to see it as cosmopolitan. It is a reaching out to others irrespective of their cultural and historical backgrounds in order to benevolently bring them the "good news" of whatever the missionary's particular prophet has announced. However, whether it be the attempt by Christian missionaries to bring exotic peoples to Christ or the attempt on the part of Islamists to establish a global caliphate, the missionary quests of most religions have the potential to bring them into conflict with each other and with the people they seek to proselytize. Accordingly, other religious thinkers take this notion of cosmopolitanism in a different direction. There have also been quests for a spirituality that transcends organized religion and seeks input from many faiths so as to give expression to what is thought to be common to all of them. Theosophy is an example of this, as is the form of yoga taught in the West in the nineteenth century by Swami Vivekananda.[5] Once again, these quests have been described as cosmopolitan.

The notion of cosmopolitanism has also been used as a pejorative term to describe people who are deemed to lack an appropriate degree of patriotism. In the nineteenth and twentieth centuries, young and urbane city dwellers were thought to be more interested in international cultural movements and fashions than in the national cultural traditions of their native countries. Their cafe-based lifestyles in the great urban centres of the West were all of a piece and paid scant regard to the links to the land and language of their forebears and elders. Jews, socialists and socialites were equally tarred with the brush of "cosmopolitanism" and their loyalty to country and tradition was called into question by their more conservative compatriots, Jews because they adhered to a "foreign" faith, socialists because they espoused international solidarity among the working classes and socialites because they felt equally at home in the salons of London, Berlin, Paris and New York. In 1931, a German intellectual, Werner Ackermann, created a short-lived "Cosmopolitan Union" comprising people who had voluntarily renounced their national citizenship and claimed the right to remain stateless (Ackermann 1931). Contemporary global entrepreneurs who work for multinational corporations or NGOs and think nothing of flying to several countries in a week are also deemed footloose and rootless in a way derided by the more patriotic, as are tourists who regard the whole world as their playground.

These "cosmopolitan" entrepreneurs and tourists are seen to represent the most visible form of the economic power of the countries from which they come: a power that is no less imperialistic in effect than are the conquering armies of previous centuries. These imperialistic trends within cosmopolitan practices are summed up by Timothy Brennan as follows:

> If we wished to capture the essence of cosmopolitanism in a single formula, it would be this. It is a discourse of the universal that is inherently local – a locality that's always surreptitiously imperial. Its covert appeal is most powerful when, in a double displacement, its political sense is expressed in cultural forms. Typically, cosmopolitanism constructs political utopias in aesthetic or ethical guise, so that they may more effectively play what often proves, on inspection, to be ultimately an economic role. (2003: 45)[6]

Critiques of this kind have given rise to a vigorous academic debate about the moral significance of cosmopolitanism. The contrasting position has been put by such writers as Seyla Benhabib, who remarks:

> Cosmopolitanism is not equivalent to a global ethic as such; nor is it adequate to characterize cosmopolitanism through cultural attitudes and choices alone. I follow the Kantian tradition in thinking of cosmopolitanism as the emergence of norms that ought to govern relations among individuals in a global civil society. (2006: 20)

In order to understand the terms of this debate and develop an ethically positive conception of cosmopolitanism, I would suggest that the use of the term "cosmopolitanism" to describe the practices listed above is inappropriate. I would suggest that the following phenomena, which have sometimes been called cosmopolitan, are not genuinely so:

- liberalization of global trade;
- colonialism and imperialism, whether through military conquest, cultural hegemony, neo-liberal trade policies or religious missionary activity;

- quest for a single global culture, language or religion;
- rejection of any state-based citizenship;
- following of international fashion trends in an urbane cafe society;
- growth in tourism and international travel;
- consumer interest in exotic products, clothes, world music and so on;
- Western liberalism with a global agenda;
- imposition of Western morality in the form of moral universalism;
- advocacy of a single world government.

I shall discuss the last three points on this list more deeply in the pages to come. For the moment I need to justify my rejection of the practices and outlooks on this list as genuine examples of cosmopolitanism. I do so by briefly exploring the etymology of the term "cosmopolitanism" and how the idea originated in the thinking of some ancient moralists, and then describing the central twentieth-century embodiment of the idea.

Stoic origins

Cosmopolitanism is a response to a number of ethical and social problems relating to strangers, foreign peoples and other countries. The default position in human existence, it might be argued, is one of local allegiance. In the distant past, because the opportunities for geographic exploration for most people in most places were extremely limited, the worldviews and the range of practical concerns for most people were confined to the village, the surrounding forests and seas, and those who could be reached with at most a few days' travel. Even as villages grew into cities, the range of a moral agent's concerns remained focused on what the ancient Greeks called the *polis*: the political community that was centred on the immediate social environment or city of that individual. The identity of a civilized person was shaped by the city or community of which he or she was a part and by the responsibilities of participation and contribution to which he or she was committed by virtue of birth or physical location. While many people were aware of other cities and lands and of the various customs and gods that were followed there, they identified themselves with their own *polis* and regarded strangers as people who were "other". When they were within the *polis*, strangers were embraced into the ethical category of guests and treated in accordance with the norms of hospitality. When they were outside the *polis*, they were regarded as barbarians who could be enslaved, conquered or exploited (Westermarck 1912: ch. 24). People from across the river or across the mountains were to be feared if one's own people were weak and attacked if one's own people were strong;

moreover, their beliefs and customs were often considered too strange to be given respect.

The first recorded use of the word "cosmopolitan" was when the philosopher Diogenes the Cynic in the fourth century BCE was asked where he came from. He replied that he was a citizen of the world (*kosmopolitēs*) (Diogenes Laertius VI 63). This reply could be interpreted as suggesting that Diogenes felt himself to owe no allegiance to the *polis* in which he was resident at the time, that he should give citizens of that *polis* no preference in his concerns or that he should take no part in the politics of that city. But it is more likely that, without being unmindful of local concerns, he took the universal concerns of humankind to be more important and binding than local concerns. His was a philosophical position rather than a political one, which implied that, however important they might be, the concerns of one's *polis* should be seen in the context of a more binding and universal set of values. Commenting on Diogenes' statement, Martha Nussbaum suggests: "Diogenes knew that the invitation to think as a world citizen was, in a sense, an invitation to be an exile from the comfort of patriotism and its easy sentiments, to see our own ways of life from the point of view of justice and the good" (1996a: 7).

The Stoic philosophers in ancient Greece and Rome are credited with being the first to develop this idea that a person might be a citizen of the whole world and hence that her concerns and responsibilities might extend to everyone irrespective of whether they were compatriots or strangers. The Greek historian Plutarch (*c.*45–125 CE), referring to a book by Zeno of Citium (*c.*335–262 BCE), describes it this way:

> Indeed, the much admired "Republic" of the founder of the Stoic sect, Zeno, is all directed towards this one summary point: that we ought not to dwell in cities or in districts, dividing ourselves up into local systems of justice, but instead come to think of all human beings as fellow citizens of the same district, making a single life in this single cosmos, like a herd that pastures together and is ruled in common by a common law.
> (*De Alexandri fortuna aut virtute*, quoted in Brennan 2005: 162)

Although the word "citizen" will not be exactly right in this context since there is no world state of which one is a citizen, it seeks to capture the idea that the kinds of allegiance, loyalty and solidarity that mark a person's relationship to the *polis* should now extend to the whole world. Indeed, the word "world" is not quite right either since it was not just all the known lands to which this new form of identity related itself, but the universe itself. For the Stoics, the universe was an entity of considerable moral significance. The universe was that overarching reality that established the forms of order in accordance with which we were to live our lives so as to live them ethically. The ethical task of each individual, according to the Stoics, was to live in accordance with "Nature". By this they meant that we were to live in accordance with the rational order, which marked the forms and cycles of the universe as a whole: forms and cycles that had been established by the gods and expressed their wisdom and love of justice. It is this idea that later gave rise to the concept of natural law: a moral law that was not dependent on the established law or customs of a given community for its normativity or for its applicability to us. Accordingly, the identity and range of responsibilities of an individual were seen as no longer dependent on the historical and regional contingencies of a particular *polis*, but rather on the eternal and global necessities of the universe itself. For a cosmopolitan, the *cosmos* was the *polis*.

The Roman philosopher Cicero (106–43 BCE) summed up the theoretical position in this way:

> Since reason exists both in people and God, the first common possession of human beings and God is reason. But those who have reason in common must also have right reason in common. And since right reason is Law, we must believe that people have Law also in common with the Gods. Further, those who share Law must also share Justice, and those who share these are to be regarded as members of the same commonwealth.
>
> (*On the Laws*, Bk 1)

From the Stoics, then, we have acquired the idea of cosmopolitanism as a stance of personal virtue grounded in a metaphysical conception of human beings as all equally under the sway of a universal moral order ordained by the gods. This stance entailed a devaluing of local loyalties so as to leave room for a benevolent regard for other people no matter what their national, ethnic, religious or cultural backgrounds might be. Anyone who acknowledged and followed natural law in this universal sense became part of a global community of right-thinking people.

Twentieth-century developments

The tendency of people to identify themselves with their nations conquered cosmopolitanism to such an extent during the nineteenth century that we can today think of it as a newly emerging tendency despite its venerable history. However, the resurgence of cosmopolitanism today is not due to philosophical developments or the advocacy of ethical thinkers in various parts of the world. Cosmopolitanism today has emerged in the form of political and institutional arrangements that reflect a global pursuit of lasting peace, human rights and global community. During the twentieth century cosmopolitan concepts have become embodied in international institutions and declarations.

After the horrors of two world wars, many nations came to see that peace and human rights could only be secured by forms of international cooperation that were institutionalized and grounded in law. The first attempt at establishing such institutions was the creation of the League of Nations in 1919 after the First World War. However, despite some successes in settling disputes between states involved in regional conflicts, it soon became clear that the most powerful nations – those that had won in the conflict of 1914–18 – were able to act without restraints or sanctions despite the league. Accordingly, after its failure to prevent the Second World War had been tragically demonstrated, the final meeting of the league was held in Geneva on 18 April 1946. It was replaced by the UN, which was established in 1945 and today embraces as members all the nation-states in the world that are recognized as such. The primary task of the UN is to establish and maintain world peace. This task is pursued through the establishment of a forum for member states to forge international agreements. In this respect the UN is not a cosmopolitan institution that focuses on the needs of individuals, but an internationalist institution that presupposes the existence and sovereignty of nation-states.

However, the nations of the world that established the UN gave it the further task of protecting human rights. This new kind of mandate for international institutions arose from a wholly unprecedented situation after the allied victory over Germany and its allies in 1945. In the course of the conquest of Germany's territory, the allies discovered the death camps and their horribly emaciated survivors, and realized that they were faced with a situation that went beyond that of war crimes. A war crime occurs when soldiers flout the rules of war by killing prisoners, looting cities or attacking non-combatants. There had been numerous such crimes on both sides of the war that had just ended. But the crimes that were evidenced by the death camps were of a different order. They were seen as attempts to wipe out entire groups of people because of who they were. The most notable of these was the attempt to eradicate all Jews from the lands that the Nazis had occupied. This gave rise to the new notion of "crimes against humanity" used in the trials of many Nazis in Nuremberg from 1945 to 1949. These trials treated the accused not as soldiers charged with departures from the rules of war but as common criminals. They were not heroes who had overstepped the bounds of soldierly behaviour and whose deeds might yet be mythologized, but ordinary people who had committed horrific and inexcusable crimes. Later thinkers saw that it was important that the trials not be seen to be applying "victor's justice" by imposing the moral convictions solely of those who had won the war (Arendt 1968; see also Habermas 1997). The trials were to be seen as representative of humanity itself upholding its standards of decent behaviour. Crimes against humanity were cosmopolitan crimes that were to be tried by cosmopolitan courts upholding values and norms that were universal in scope. Further, it was important that the perpetrators be held personally accountable and not be allowed to plead innocence on the basis that they were obeying orders. This too expresses the cosmopolitan nature of the thinking involved in conducting these trials. It would be assumed that any individual was sufficiently autonomous and responsible for his or her actions that any plea to the effect that only higher-level authorities should bear responsibility would be rejected. No claim that group loyalty or membership of a larger collective could lessen an individual's responsibility would be entertained. Even if a nation were at war in accordance with international law, its soldiers could be held personally liable for any crimes they might commit in the course of fighting such a war. Indeed the context of war was not essential. Crimes against humanity could be committed even where no state of war was in existence. Subsequent examples of ethnic cleansing or genocide include cases where no state of international war existed but where the motivations towards violence were political, religious or racial.

In so far as the concept of crimes against humanity was distinguished from that of war crimes as defined by international law, the new concept was a first step towards what the philosopher Immanuel Kant (1724–1804) had called "cosmopolitan law". Such law transcends international law by appealing directly to universal human values and rights that are held by individuals and to universal norms and standards of behaviour that apply to individuals. These rights and standards are rights held by any human being no matter what their citizenship or membership of a defined community. Whereas international law binds states in their relationships with each other, cosmopolitan law binds individuals globally.

The international community, through the UN and other agencies, has enshrined these principles and practices in an International Court of Justice and, more recently, an International Criminal Court. While not every nation has cooperated with these institutions or supported them, the concept of crimes against humanity and the concepts of cosmopolitan law or human rights that underpin it are now widely accepted in the world, at least in operational terms. The most notable expression of these concepts is the Universal Declaration of Human Rights, which the UN proclaimed in December 1948. Subsequent work by the UN between 1966 and 1976 has resulted, after ratification by a sufficient number of individual states, in according binding status in international law to the International Bill of Human Rights, which consists of the Universal Declaration of Human Rights, the International Covenant on Economic, Social and Cultural Rights and the International Covenant on

Civil and Political Rights and its two Optional Protocols (Office of the High Commissioner for Human Rights 1996).

The moral or political theory required to give intellectual foundations to these concepts in a way that would be globally understandable may be lacking, but the institutional endorsement of those concepts through UN declarations and international courts is sufficient to give them operational legitimacy in the world today. Accordingly, cosmopolitanism is not just an ideal or an aspiration in the way that, for example, pacifism might be thought to be. It is a set of norms embodied in international institutions and in international law.

Plan for the book

In this book I shall focus not on the institutional forms that cosmopolitanism might take, or on the global institutions that might embody it, but on the ethical values and norms that it encapsulates. I shall argue that the following features mark the genuine outlook of ethical cosmopolitanism:

(1) measured endorsement of patriotism;
(2) opposition to nationalism and chauvinism;
(3) willingness to suspend narrow national interests in order to tackle global problems such as those of environmental degradation or global justice;
(4) respect for basic human rights as universally normative;
(5) acknowledging the moral equality of all peoples and individuals;
(6) respect for the peoples of the world as united by reason, sociability and a common humanity;
(7) belief in a globally acceptable concept of human dignity;
(8) benevolence to all others irrespective of race, caste, nationality, religion, ethnicity or location;
(9) willingness to come to the aid of those suffering from natural or man-made disasters, including extreme poverty;
(10) commitment to justice in the distribution of natural resources and wealth on a global scale;
(11) global solidarity with struggles for human rights and social justice;
(12) commitment to the liberalization of immigration and refugee policies;
(13) acknowledging the sovereignty of nation-states while insisting on limitations to that sovereignty in order to secure human rights and global justice;
(14) quest for lasting world peace;
(15) respect for the right to self-determination of peoples;
(16) preparedness to prosecute crimes against humanity internationally;

(17) acknowledging the rule of international law;
(18) commitment to open and participatory political processes globally;
(19) religious and cultural tolerance and an acceptance of global pluralism;
(20) dialogue and communication across cultural and national boundaries;
(21) seeing the world as a single polity and community.

It is the task of this book to explicate the features listed above. Chapter 1 will explicate the features 1–3, while Chapter 2 will deal with 4–7. I shall discuss features 8–12 in Chapter 3 and features 13–16 in Chapter 4. The last chapter will discuss features 17–21. What I hope will emerge from this analysis is a fully articulated conception of the ethics of cosmopolitanism to which anyone in the world can subscribe irrespective of their cultural, religious or moral background.

Chapter 1

Cosmopolitanism and patriotism

> Love of a particular liberty ... is not exclusive: love of the common liberty of one's people easily extends beyond national boundaries and translates into solidarity. (Viroli 1995: 12)

The first three features of cosmopolitanism that I identified at the conclusion of the Introduction were:

(1) measured endorsement of patriotism;
(2) opposition to nationalism and chauvinism;
(3) willingness to suspend narrow national interests in order to tackle global problems such as those of environmental degradation or global justice.

According to Ulrich Beck (2002), nationalism is one of the chief enemies of cosmopolitan societies. In order to explicate why this is so, we need to distinguish patriotism from nationalism, and to understand how they relate to each other and to cosmopolitanism.

The Nussbaum debate

Martha Nussbaum wrote an essay on patriotism, "Patriotism and Cosmopolitanism", that was published in the *Boston Review*, a widely read intellectual journal in the United States, and was later republished with a series of responses and replies (Nussbaum 1996a). It critiqued the perceived insularity of American education and accused it of failing to produce citizens who are knowledgeable about, and thus concerned for, the wider world and its peoples. The education that Nussbaum advocated would involve not only expanding the scope of students' interests to distant peoples, but also considering global justice and human dignity: values that have no borders. Nussbaum argued that students should be taught that they share the world with the whole of humanity and that their being American does not entitle them to a privileged position in the world. Such an education would allow students to learn more about their own way of life by seeing it compared to that of other cultures. It would allow them to see that many problems, such as global poverty and the despoliation of the environment, can be solved by international cooperation, and that the moral values they hold dear as Americans can and should be applied in other parts of the world. They would come to see that such values as human dignity, distributive justice and human rights should be realized globally. In a new introduction to the book that she wrote after the attack on the World Trade Center in 2001, Nussbaum also highlighted the role of compassion, which should extend to the whole of humanity.

Among the several authors that Nussbaum discusses in the essay is Richard Rorty. Rorty supports patriotism or nationalism on the grounds that it is preferable that Americans define themselves according to their national identity rather than in terms of their ethnic, religious or other more local allegiances. On this view, patriotism is a positive emotion because it enlarges its holders' outlooks from their religious, ethnic or other "tribal" identities to that of the nation. Rather than highlight the many differences between people within America, a nationalist sentiment serves to unite people into a common allegiance with common social aspirations. However, Nussbaum considers that this wider allegiance is still too local. It leaves out what we all share universally as human beings. A politics of nationalism still involves sectarian interests because it still says "America first", even if it does not say, for example, "Catholic first". Against any form of patriotism or nationalism, Nussbaum says: "Only the cosmopolitan stance ... has the promise of transcending these divisions, because only this stance asks us to give our first allegiance to what is morally good – and that which, being good, I can commend as such to all human beings" (1996b: 5).

The replies to Nussbaum's essay are written by a veritable who's who of authors who have written on multiculturalism, identity politics, pluralism and communitarianism. Most of them are critical of Nussbaum's position. For example, Benjamin Barber argues that cosmopolitanism is a "thin" commitment based purely on intellectual conviction and lacks the appeal to the heart that parochial allegiances do.[1] As developed by Kant, it is a commitment arrived at by "pure reason", which lacks the motivational pull of love of "home and hearth" or of nation. As developed by social contract theorists such as Thomas Hobbes (1588–1679), it conceives of individuals merely as rights-bearers able to enter into nothing more emotional than pragmatically constructed civic relationships with others. Accordingly he argues that "What we require are healthy, democratic forms of local community and civic patriotism rather than abstract universalism and the thin gruel of contract relations" (Barber 1996: 31). This point raises an issue that has been discussed ever since Kant developed his moral theory. Is morality a matter of purely intellectual conviction, or does it also involve the emotions? Kant rejects the emotions as irrelevant to morality on the grounds that they are unreliable, confused and inconsistent with the freedom of the will to act only on the deliverances of pure reason. Any moral theorist who rejects the moral relevance of the emotions will therefore also reject the emotion of patriotism. But they will then be left with a purely intellectual moral conviction centred on an abstract notion of persons as bearers of rights or holders of human dignity. Barber takes Nussbaum to be proposing such a purely intellectual commitment to the moral equality of all people.

But there is a tradition in moral theory that is an alternative to Kant's. This tradition stems from David Hume (1711–76), who highlighted what he called the "feelings of humanity". These included sympathy, compassion, the pleasure we feel when we see others flourish and the pity we feel when we see others suffer. Such feelings come upon us without deliberation – and so cannot be the object of moral imperatives – but they are morally laudable. They motivate us to act well. By highlighting compassion in her later introduction, Nussbaum places herself in this tradition. Many of her critics, including Barber, would see themselves as belonging to this tradition as well. For them the question is not whether emotions as such matter morally, but which ones do. For Nussbaum, compassion is a morally positive emotion, while patriotism is a morally negative emotion. In contrast, Barber, like Rorty, considers patriotism to be ethically positive.

Robert Pinsky (1996) also sees patriotism as a positive emotion. For him both patriotism and cosmopolitanism are states of love. They are commitments that arise from our insertion into specific cultural and historical contexts and reflect our positive responses to them. But, according to Pinsky, Nussbaum's cosmopolitanism is in fact parochial in that it is the ideology of the globally mobile managerial class. It grows out of a kind of rootlessness that lacks grounding in specific communities. To critique nationalism as a form of "jingoism" is to fail to see the love of place and of community that is expressed in it.

Another of Nussbaum's critics, Amy Gutmann, sees positive value in nationalism because we need the nation-state as a context for teaching students to pursue justice. It is only through the teaching of democratic citizenship in the largest community they are in – the state – that students can be taught the universal value of human rights. According to Gutmann (1996), the world is not a community in the relevant sense and the cosmopolitan focus on the world as such does not encourage a respect for justice in any concrete form. In a global context, the concept of justice becomes too abstract and intellectual to be motivational. We need the value debates that membership in a democratic political community encourages to teach us what justice is so that we can then take that lesson out beyond our nation's borders. Making a similar point, Gertrude Himmelfarb rejects cosmopolitanism on Aristotelian grounds. She argues that every person must belong to a "polity". We are inherently social beings and require a sense of belonging to a political community with which we can identify. She thinks cosmopolitanism is a dangerous illusion because, in positing a global form of citizenship, it neglects the situated and communitarian bonds of each individual. "What cosmopolitanism obscures, even denies, are the givens of life: parents, ancestors, family, race, religion, heritage, history, culture, tradition, community – and nationality. These are not 'accidental' attributes of the individual" (Himmelfarb 1996: 77).[2] For his part, Charles Taylor (1996) stresses the need for social and political solidarity in liberal states, in which the citizen's allegiance is to a common national enterprise of seeking a good life. Such enterprises ought to include concern for outsiders but it would not help to replace them altogether with a purely cosmopolitan vision.[3]

Appiah endorses cosmopolitanism but argues that there is also a place for nationalism. For Appiah, a nation is an appropriate object of moral commitment, allegiance and loyalty. He sees a nation in the way that Taylor does: as a body of people united by a collective social project and by national sentiments that arise when a people lives together in state-like arrangements. Such a nation could include people of differing ethnicities, religions and cultural backgrounds, provided they are united by the common project of living in a political community. "Loosely and unphilosophically defined, a nation is an 'imagined community' of culture or ancestry running beyond the scale of the face-to-face and seeking political expression" (Appiah 1996: 27). Many multicultural societies in the world today have difficulties in creating a nation with a single social project in this way. Moreover, since the state is an institution necessary for the ordering of social life and since it exercises coercive power that, at least in the case of liberal democratic societies, has moral justification, it is a moral good. Appiah (2005: ch. 6) thinks that states are actually more important than nations (where nations are defined by the common ethnicity or traditions of its members) because they are the embodiment of the political project of making laws and a common life and so demand our civic allegiance in a way that national or ethnic traditions do not.

A further critic, Michael W. McConnell, reminds us that moral education begins with love of parents and spreads out to specific others through emotions such as admiration. The heroes of a nation are concrete role models, our emotional attachment to whom allows us to grow in moral responsibility. He repeats Barber's claim that cosmopolitanism is too thin a conception to serve this educative role. He quotes the English social philosopher Edmund Burke

(1729–97): "To be attached to the subdivision, to love the little platoon we belong to in society, is the first principle (the germ as it were) of public affections. It is the first link in the series by which we proceed toward a love to our country and to mankind" (McConnell 1996: 79). Even while advocating universal concerns, it is necessary to invoke the values of one's national culture or religion. In liberal societies, these values should include tolerance and a respect for the differences in the cultures and traditions of other peoples. In contrast, McConnell argues that, as cosmopolitanism is a commitment to abstractions such as "global justice", "human rights" or "humanity", it can lead to moralism and intolerance. According to him, "The moralistic cosmopolitan, therefore, is not one who everywhere feels comfortable but who everywhere feels superior" (*ibid.*: 82).[4] This point expands Himmelfarb's warning that cosmopolitanism is a dangerous illusion by suggesting that it is an imperialistic attempt at imposing Western values on the rest of the world.

In her reply to these critics, Nussbaum returns to the question of how upbringing impacts on moral education. She addresses the claim that moral education and the moral outlook it produces should be understood on the analogy of an expanding circle.[5] This analogy suggests that one first learns to love and respect one's parents and one's family and only then can one learn to love the wider community. One learns to love and respect one's own co-religionists or the members of one's own ethnic, linguistic or cultural groups before one is able to love and respect one's nation and, finally, global humanity. Whether one thinks that the nation is the limit of one's moral affections or that moral concern for the whole of humanity is psychologically possible, the model used for theorizing the question is that of an expanding circle of moral concern in which moral education consists in the widening of this circle to its furthest limits.[6] This account of moral education assumes that the centre of the circle – the individual self – is already shaped as a moral agent with fully formed moral motivations lacking only an appropriate object for its moral concerns. Such an agent finds itself initially alone but complete, and then learns to attach itself to its mother, its family, its community and so on. If the expanding circles were drawn in illustrations as a set of concentric rings defining zones of moral concern – representing family, community, neighbourhood, nation and then humanity – the rings themselves would represent "and then" in a sequence of developmental stages. This is the model implicit in the critiques of Gutmann, Himmelfarb, Taylor and McConnell. Nussbaum, however, understands the matter differently.

Nussbaum reminds us that developmental psychologists describe the process of moral education as one in which the infant comes to recognize itself at the same time as it recognizes others. Its identity is not pre-established but develops as its relationships with others develop. It is the acknowledgement and love given it by its parents that help shape the infant into the moral agent it will become. Moreover, this process is not only positive. The infant experiences pain, hunger and distress and, as a result, forms deeply ambivalent bonds with its primary carers. It is needful and also angry at being left needful. It then seeks to atone for this anger by love. The expansion of its compassion to others is not driven by moral teaching or ethical exemplars but arises because the child can empathize with needfulness. A multitude of childhood experiences, including stories such as fairy tales – which, Nussbaum reminds us, are seldom geographically or nationally specific – shape the child into a being who can empathize with those others who are needful in the same way as it is. Accordingly, the circle of compassion does not expand, but is all-embracing from the very beginning. It is not an expanding circle but an unlimited one. Of course, it is confined to what the child is familiar with, but it does not entail an "other" that is not yet included in its scope. According to Nussbaum:

> All circles develop simultaneously, in a complex and interlacing movement. But surely the outer circle is not the last to form. Long before children have any acquaintance with the idea of nation, or even of one specific religion, they know hunger and loneliness. Long before they encounter patriotism, they have probably encountered death. Long before ideology interferes, they know something of humanity. (1996c: 142)

Nussbaum's point is that the love of humanity is not a further stage of moral development that comes after one learns to love one's family or community, but is always already present in love of parents, community, tribe, race or nation. All of these illustrate what it is to be human and constitute concrete forms of the love of humanity. One does not have to learn to love one's country in order thereby to learn to love humanity later. One learns to love humanity even as one learns to love family, community and country. In loving one's family, one's friends or one's community, one has been loving humanity all along. If there are people who think that others from outside their family or community are less worthy of moral respect it will be because they have been taught by an excessively insular or nationalistic education to think that way.

However, there are other issues raised by Nussbaum's critics. Is cosmopolitanism a "thin" commitment lacking the full-bodied and emotional attachments that typify love of family, community and country? Is patriotism a positive moral emotion? Can cosmopolitans also love the country in which they live? What is the role of the nation-state in the life of a cosmopolitan? Can it be a context in which global concerns are developed and expressed? Does a cosmopolitan's commitment to human rights and global justice make her blind to local differences and intolerant of unusual social and political practices? Can the whole world be considered a polity – if not a community – in which we can learn what justice requires of us and what love and compassion demand of us? To answer these questions, let us make a fresh beginning.

Patriotism

The following phenomena could be used to illustrate patriotism, nationalism, chauvinism or all of them combined:

(a) Each year, on 26 January, Australia celebrates a national holiday called Australia Day. The date marks the settlement of the continent by British forces who established a penal colony housing convicts sent from overcrowded prisons in Britain. The Australian nation has sprung from these humble beginnings.

(b) Each year, on 25 April, Australia celebrates a national holiday called Anzac Day. The day commemorates a defeat of Australian and New Zealand forces at the hands of Turkish troops during the First World War at Gallipoli in the Dardanelles. Australian and New Zealand soldiers were said to have earned the respect of the world for their courage during that doomed campaign.

(c) There is occasional debate in Australia as to whether it should sever its ties with the United Kingdom and become a republic, and whether the Union Jack (the flag of the United Kingdom) should be removed from Australia's flag.

(d) During a news broadcast, we are told that an Australian athlete won a silver medal at the Olympic Games. We are not told who won the gold.

(e) During a news broadcast, we are told that seventy people died in a plane crash in South Korea. We are told that one victim was an Australian but are told nothing about the other sixty-nine.

(f) At the annual beer festival in Munich, small but rowdy groups of inebriated men wearing green and gold outfits (Australia's national colours) are heard loudly singing the well-known Australian song "The pub with no beer".

(g) Like many small townships founded by German settlers in South Australia during the nineteenth century, the town of Hergott Springs changed its name during the First World War: Hergott Springs became "Marree".

(h) The national anthem is sung before major sporting events.

(i) On winning a gold medal at the 1994 Commonwealth Games, Kathy Freeman, an Australian athlete of Aboriginal heritage, carried an Australian and an Aboriginal flag during her lap of honour. As a result, she was heavily criticized by some commentators for disloyalty to Australia.

(j) A political party is formed with policies inimical to immigration and the rights of indigenous people which calls itself "The Australia First Party".
(k) Just prior to the Australian federal election in 2002, a Norwegian freighter picked up a number of asylum seekers from the Middle East in open waters off the north-western coast of Australia. The prime minister of the day refused them permission to land in Australia, saying, "We will decide who comes to this country and the circumstances in which they come" (Howard 2001). His party wins the election.
(l) In December 2005, riots involving over 5000 people broke out on the beach at Cronulla, near Sydney. The fighting was between Australian youths, some draped in Australian flags and shouting racist slogans, and youths from Lebanon and other parts of the Middle East. Sporadic skirmishes continued in the area for several days between youths of Middle Eastern appearance and youths of Anglo- or Celtic Australian heritage.
(m) Australian consumers are urged to "buy Australian" in order to support Australian farmers and manufacturers.
(n) During debates about global warming during 2006 and 2007, the then prime minister of Australia said that he would not enter into any international agreements to limit carbon emissions if this compromised the competitive advantage of Australia's coal industry.
(o) Australian soldiers serve alongside American forces, together with other members of the "coalition of the willing", in Iraq and in Afghanistan. Australian soldiers are also deployed in peacekeeping missions in East Timor and the Solomon Islands. They are praised as heroes and as patriots.
(p) Australian expatriate workers or emigrants feel nostalgia for home.
(q) Australian musicians, artists, writers and film-makers describe themselves as giving expression to an Australian sensibility and way of life through their art.
(r) Australia is described as having a civilizing and enlightening role in its geopolitical region by virtue of its heritage in British traditions of democracy and the rule of law.
(s) Australian egalitarian virtues such as "mateship" and "a fair go" are lauded as characteristics that distinguish Australians from others.
(t) Applicants for Australian citizenship are required to pass a "citizenship test" in which they are quizzed on Australian political processes and values, and also on the life of Australian cricketing great, Don Bradman.
(u) Politicians and other social commentators sometimes describe those with whom they disagree as "un-Australian".
(v) In February 2008, at the beginning of the first sitting of the new Federal Parliament after the election of 2007, the new prime minister of Australia

offered a formal apology to the Aboriginal people of Australia for past government policies that removed Aboriginal children from their families for racist reasons.

(w) The present author is Australian and all the examples offered above relate to Australia.

These examples range from what could be seen as cynical uses of nationalist jingoism to illustrations of the way in which many people think of patriotism: namely, as "love of one's country". In what follows I shall question the appropriateness of the concept of "love" and also highlight the ambiguity of the notion of "country" that occurs in such definitions of patriotism.

According to Stephen Nathanson, patriotism could be described as an attitude that involves:

- special affection for one's own country;
- a sense of personal identification with the country;
- special concern for the well-being of the country;
- willingness to sacrifice to promote the country's good. (1993: 34–5)

The first of these features suggests that patriotism is an emotion. It is a positive feeling of affection that we have for our country. Accordingly, some writers suggest that it is not rational or based on a considered judgement (MacIntyre 2002; Oldenquist 1982; see also Primoratz & Pavkovic 2007). We do not survey the countries of the world and make a judgement as to which of them is worthy of our allegiance or affection. If we have such a feeling, we simply find ourselves with it. Love is not a feeling that is rationally based. In a romantic context, we do not choose whom we might love, but find ourselves falling in love with them. If love were based on a rational appraisal of the beloved, we would be apt to change our affections if we met someone who fulfilled our criteria for romantic excellence more fully than the one we actually loved. But if we were inclined to do this we would not really be in love. If patriotism were a form of love it would also be irrational in this way. We would just find ourselves having such a feeling without any rational basis and without any judgement having been made by us about the worthiness of our country.

In all but the most unusual cases, the country that we have the feeling for is *our* country. For most people this will be the country of their birth, but for many it will be their adopted country or the country to which they have migrated. To explain the logical point that patriotism is love of *our* country, we can use the analogy of parental love. Parental love is love for the parent's own child. It is not a love of children generally that happens to be applied to one's own child. It is not love of childlike qualities such that because the parent happens to find them in their child they then focus their love on that child. It is the love of that particular child simply because that child is *their* child. In a similar way it is said that patriots love their country simply because it is *their* country. Using the parental love analogy shows that it is true by definition that the country a patriot loves is their own country. They might love or admire other countries for one reason or another but those loves are not cases of patriotism, just as loving another's child is not a case of parental love.

The explanation for parental love being necessarily directed on the parent's own child is clear. Most often it is based on blood ties and sometimes it is based on a bond that is created through adoption or a second marriage. If we endorse the theory that patriotism is a special case of love, and if we agree that there is no rational basis for such love, we might nevertheless give an account of how patriots come to love their country. If it is not on the basis of reasons, then it will be a causal and psychological matter. It seems to be a psychological fact about most people that, in the course of their upbringing, they come to love their countries. Most basically, this will be because their own country is the country that they are most familiar with. If their country is the country of their birth, their country will also typically be the place where their most formative and valuable experiences have taken place. It will be the country whose history they have studied in school and celebrated in public events and holidays. At school they will often have taken part in rituals such as saluting the flag. The achievements of their country's citizens will have been most celebrated in their news media. The communal values that they have acquired will be linked to the traditions of that country. Much of their experiences of art and entertainment will have come to them with a significance that speaks to them of their country. (This explains why some Australians think it important for new citizens to be aware of Don Bradman, even though such knowledge, along with knowledge of the game of cricket, seems very incidental to loyal and responsible citizenship.) In some countries they will have heard stories about ancient links between the people and the land: between the race and its ties to the very soil on which the country is based. In other countries they will have heard stories about settlers carving a new and civilized life out of the wilderness, or about the battles that were necessary to establish the nation in the face of opposition from invaders or internal threats.

For migrants, on the other hand, the experiences that lead to love of country might be different. In such cases, there will be stories of families saved from economic hardship, political oppression or religious persecution, and of how the new country has been a source of refuge or opportunity. Migrants tend to have split feelings about their countries. Many continue to feel links to, and take an interest in, the country of their birth, while also finding themselves with positive feelings towards the country in which they have settled. When they return to the country of their birth, whether to visit friends or enjoy a holiday, they often feel a special connection to their old country despite many years of separation. They might feel themselves torn when the football team of the old country meets the football team of the new. Whom will they support? One British politician is reported to have said that it should be part of an English citizenship test that migrants support England in such cases (Sen 2006: 153). The crucial point here is that we are talking about feelings and affections that cannot be artificially produced by rational decisions or certified by loyalty tests. They are a product of experiences that are inevitably embedded in a specific country.

As plausible as the social psychology account sketched here might be, I do wonder whether the picture of patriotism as love of one's country that it gives us is accurate. Is patriotism to be understood as an irrational and socially caused affection for one's country? Are the analogies with romantic love and parental love appropriate? One of the ethical implications of such analogies is that such a love should withstand negative judgements about the beloved. The love of a spouse should survive most misdemeanours that the spouse might commit or blemishes in beauty or character that the spouse might suffer from. Parents should not reject their children when they fail to fulfil expectations or even turn to crime, but must continue to support them out of their love for them. If love of country is like this, does it follow that patriots must continue to love and support their countries even if their governments abuse human rights or engage in unjustified wars? Is there no point at which a rational appraisal of one's country's moral and political status should counter the positive feelings that upbringing will have produced? If rationality plays no part in one's love of country, then it would seem not. Accordingly, if patriotism is a special affection for one's country, I doubt that we should call it "love" understood on analogy with such irrational forms as romantic or parental love.

Let us consider what is meant by the second clause above: "a sense of personal identification with the country". "Identification" is an important concept in this context. It refers to how persons understand themselves and what self-images they have. It refers to what persons will find important and to what they will give priority. It refers to the norms they internalize and how strongly they feel themselves to be bound by them. If persons identify themselves as Catholic, to use an example not directly linked to patriotism, they will see themselves as living a life dedicated to achieving salvation and union with God in heaven through participation in the sacramental life and theological beliefs of the Catholic Church. They will give priority to the rituals, observances and practices of the Church and think of themselves as Catholics to the extent that they fulfil those requirements. If they are in situations of ethical conflict, they will follow the guidelines of Catholic moral theology and will feel themselves to be sinners if they should fail to follow those norms. Their identification with their faith will lead them to hold very strongly to their moral convictions. Presented with an option or a temptation that is contrary to the norms of their faith, they will reject it, not only as a violation of those convictions but also as an affront to who they are. They will also take part in public demonstrations of their religious commitment, whether it be through processions in the city streets or participation in pilgrimages to places sacred to the faith. Moreover, they will relate themselves to the central stories of their religion, seeking to live a life that imitates that of Jesus in relevant respects.

How would what we have learnt about what it is to identify oneself with a group in the case of religion apply to patriotism? What would "a sense of personal identification with a country" amount to? What does it mean to understand oneself, or announce oneself to the world, as an Australian? It would seem to imply that one relates oneself to the story of Australia and that one would want to participate in the rituals that mark one as an Australian. The history of a country is an ongoing saga with a vast cast of participants. But there are some people who are participants and others who are not. In calling oneself an Australian one is saying that one is a participant in that story and not the story of some other country. In this way one can take pride in the achievements recounted in that story, feel shame at the wrongs that have been done in it, and be committed to the progressive continuation of that story into the future and to playing a positive role in it. One associates oneself with other Australians, whether it be sports heroes, stars of entertainment, successful business entrepreneurs or soldiers serving in other parts of the world. This is illustrated by the first two examples at the head of this section. Australia Day and Anzac Day are ritual reminders of Australia's past that celebrate the achievements of Australians' predecessors and that invite Australians to join them in the unfolding Australian story.

Whereas the theory that patriotism is love of one's country would say that the processes of psychological formation, including engagement with these rituals and memorials, create affection for one's country, I would say that what they produce is identification with one's country. If the story of one's country is predominantly a positive one, this identification will tend to produce in the patriot a feeling of pride. The processes through which a person comes to identify with his or her country produce, not love for, but pride in, their country. One can feel pride in one's country to the extent that one identifies with it and with its achievements. Of course, there is a negative side to this. The story of Australia also includes shameful episodes, especially in relation to the dispossession of the Aboriginal inhabitants and their subsequent treatment. While the ideological apparatus that seeks to create positive feelings for one's country will stress the positive achievements or will seek to turn even such defeats as that suffered at Gallipoli into a positive demonstration of the pluck and persistence of Australia's young fighting men, the negative episodes must also be dealt with. That is why example (v) above was so important. It allowed Australians to once again feel pride in their country because it had acknowledged and apologized for the wrongs that it had committed in the past.

We can interpret many of the other examples at the head of this section in terms of pride more readily than in terms of affection. Debates about whether Australia should sever its ties to the British monarchy mentioned in example (c) are about the image of Australia as an independent and mature nation no longer reliant on adherence to the ancient institution of the British Crown for the legitimation of its political system. Example (d) illustrates the way in which Australians will identify with, and take pride in, Australian athletic champions and sports heroes. The same applies to Australian high achievers in other endeavours, whether these be the arts, entertainment or business. Because the achievers are Australian, Australians identify with them and take pride in them. Their achievements are felt to enhance those of all Australians. Even in competitions centred on individual effort, such as a Grand Slam tennis tournament, the nationality of the individual tennis player will be mentioned and groups in the crowd will cover themselves in the national colours and support their compatriots. Sometimes the behaviour will become unpleasant, as in example (f). But here too we see the need that people apparently feel to gather in groups defined by nationality and then express what they consider to be the most notable – if not always admirable – national characteristics of that group. In this case it is national pride expressed in boorish behaviour, but it is pride nonetheless. Singing the national anthem at major sporting events would clearly be an expression of pride if the event is an international match of some kind, but it is sung even at the grand finals of national competitions. In such cases, I would interpret it as a ritual of identification in which not only pride in one's country is expressed but also a commitment to those of its values that relate especially to sport – values such as "mateship" and "a fair go" – along with such universal values as fair play and competitiveness.

Our identity is a framework from within which we see the rest of the world. I think about the world and my obligations within it as an Australian, as a male, as someone well-to-do, as an atheist, as a member of a specific family, as white, as "Western" and so on. Accordingly, when I am called on to assist others in need, the fact that one of the possible objects of my concern is an Australian has the effect of drawing my attention to that person in a way that it is not drawn to another. This is why in news reports, when seventy people are killed in a disaster, Australians have their attention drawn to the fact (or drawn *by* the fact) that one of them was Australian. This is clearly not a matter of justice, which ought to be impartial. But it is a matter of human psychology, which structures and expresses our identity in these and other ways.

If pride is a predominant expression of national identification in a self-confident country such as Australia, identification can take other forms in countries or communities that have been oppressed or humiliated in the course of their histories. Recent commentary on the causes of Islamist terrorism, and on religious fundamentalism more generally, has described the victim mentality that often grows out of stories of national defeat or religious persecution (Ali 2007: ch. 7; see also Armstrong 2000). To identify with a defeated people is often to court resentment and anger and to feel that only violence can restore the pride of one's people.

Interpreting love of one's country in terms of pride and identification helps to explain the very close link between patriotism and militarism. As a sociological fact there is no doubt that there are very strong and frequent links between the two. Soldiers march at almost all of the rituals and celebrations that forge the identification of Australians with their country and such events are a global phenomenon. Australian soldiers posted abroad are said to be serving their country even in cases where the foreign policies being pursued are ultimately those of the USA or when they are serving as part of a UN mandate. The bodies of war casualties and even of those who died by accident or friendly fire in foreign campaigns are brought home in coffins draped in the national flag. As mentioned in example (o), to be a soldier and to face danger in uniform is seen as the quintessential example of patriotism. The stories that constitute the historical lore of a nation will most often be stories of battles fought and won in order to establish and then defend the national borders. These stories invite contemporary compatriots to identify themselves with the brave soldiers whose past exploits have forged the nation and its national character. Soldiers put their lives at risk and those of us who sit comfortably at home readily identify with them in order to swell our pride. The sacrifices made by soldiers also highlight the fourth of Nathanson's explications of what love of country might mean: namely, "willingness to sacrifice to promote the country's good". Soldiers are seen as being willing to make the ultimate sacrifice, and many do. Whether they do so explicitly or self-consciously for the sake of their countries or whether their soldiering was just a way to escape unemployment or meaninglessness is immaterial. The rhetoric of patriotism will ensure that their deaths or wounds are interpreted as gifts to the nation with which their compatriots can identify.

Nathanson's third explication of what love of country might mean was "special concern for the well-being of the country". This might be thought to extend to a special concern for one's compatriots as exemplified in example (e). But it is mainly illustrated by examples (m) and (n). Here we see "the well-being of the country" being understood as the economic prosperity of the country. In the case of being urged to buy Australian products, the benefit is envisaged as flowing to the whole national community. It might begin by being the prosperity and profitability of the Australian companies whose goods are being favoured, but through secure employment and contributions to taxation in an equitable system of social welfare, this prosperity should flow through to the whole country.

Example (n) raises significant issues of balancing the national commercial interest against global responsibility. Global warming is a threat to Australia just as much as it is to the rest of the world, and a pursuit of the national interest should be prepared to make short-term economic sacrifices to gain long-term environmental advantages. Moreover, national governments should be prepared to suspend the pursuit of purely national interests in order to exercise global responsibilities. It was the Australian prime minister who framed the issue as one in which national interests were seen as threatened by global pressures and one in which he would defend the national interest against such "foreign" threats. If "special concern for the well-being of the country" leads to such policy positions it would be a very suspect sentiment.

These examples raise the question of what might be meant by "the national interest". In capitalist countries it seems to include national prosperity based on successful private enterprise, along with protection of the borders and the state's territorial integrity. National security is often said to be central to the national interest, but this frequently extends from protecting the nation's territory and economic resources at home to enhancing commercial opportunities and securing natural resources abroad, whether by diplomatic or by military means. But the more important question is whether the objects of these interests correspond to what is loved when we speak of "love of country". By and large the national interest corresponds to the interests of the elites that dominate the nation-state. Given that the nation-state is a legally defined jurisdiction over which a government holds responsibility and within which commercial enterprises and individuals engage in their pursuit of prosperity and pay taxes, there can be no doubt that there is a close link between every individual's pursuit of happiness and the success of the national economy and of the government in protecting it. However, is this what we love when we love our country? Is this what we take pride in when we identify with our country? Is this what we are concerned for when we display a "special concern for the well-being of our country"? There may be some instances where we take pride in the achievements of our country's entrepreneurs just as we do of our country's sporting champions, but this will be because they are conspicuous high achievers with whom we can identify rather than because they have contributed to the country's prosperity. Many people admire them even if the profits they have generated go offshore. It is enough that they are our compatriots and that they are successful. Our pride and identification are based on their being successful compatriots rather than on the benefits they may have given our nation-state. It seems, then, that love of country is not coextensive with a special concern for the national interest.

Let us return to the phrase "love of one's country". I have suggested that "love" should not be understood on analogy with romantic or parental love but that it is better understood as a form of identification that ideally leads to pride in one's country and concern for its well-being. But what do we understand by "country"? Do we mean the nation-state of which we are citizens, in whose political and commercial life we participate in one form or another, and whose laws structure our lives? The social psychology account given above seems to suggest a different answer. It suggests that our bonds of loyalty are forged with our historical people, its language, culture and traditions. We may love the ethnicity that has shaped us and our outlook on the world. We may feel an attachment to the land on which we are born and whose very physical features have engrained themselves on our hearts. We may relate to the religion of our forefathers or to the music and iconography we experienced as children. None of this may bear any direct relationship to the national citizenship with which we find ourselves. National borders are notoriously arbitrary. Borders often split peoples who share traditions and languages into different states, not only in countries that were once colonies of European powers, but even in countries with long histories of autonomy and political independence. Consider the Belgians, the Kurds, the Basques or the Tibetans. The most egregious example is Africa, in which hardly any borders correspond to the homeland of a people united by cultural traditions and ethnic identities. So what is the object of patriotism? Is it one's country defined as the nation-state of which one is a citizen? Or is it the ethnic, religious or cultural group with which one identifies?[7]

In his contribution to the Nussbaum debate, Appiah had argued that even though its borders might be historically arbitrary, the state is not a morally arbitrary political structure. It is the basis of the community that constitutes a modern nation. One's nation in this modern sense is a matter of both sentiment and political commitment. Membership of such a nation is voluntary to a greater degree than is membership of a community into which one is born because one can apply for nationality in a country to which one has migrated. Appiah (1996: 28) argues that a nation, understood in this sense, is morally valuable and that it is morally appropriate to feel allegiance to it. People should be allowed to choose their nation if that is their autonomous choice. Many people value their nationality, do not consider their nationality to be arbitrary and consider it morally significant in their lives. If the object of patriotism is the nation in this sense, then it would seem to be a morally appropriate object. However, if only for the sake of terminological clarity, I would suggest that, in talking about the nation in this way, Appiah is actually talking about the modern nation-state.

According to Anthony Giddens:

> The nation-state, which exists in a complex of other nation-states, is a set of institutional forms of governance maintaining an administrative monopoly over a territory with demarcated boundaries (borders), its rule being sanctioned by law and direct control of the means of internal and external violence.
>
> (1985: 121, quoted in Hutchinson & Smith 1994: 34–5)

The notion of one's "country" could refer either to this purely administrative notion of the nation-state or to one's community bound together by history, ethnicity, language or a common social project. Many states contain a number of such communities (and sometimes not as wholes). It seems, then, that the notion of "country" as the object of one's affection or identification is ambiguous. It follows that the notion of patriotism is ambiguous. It can mean identification with one's traditional, ethnic, religious or national community, or it can mean loyalty to the bordered political community or nation-state of which one is a citizen. Nathanson's use of the term "country" obscures this ambiguity and the true nature of the object of one's loyalty or allegiance that he describes as "love of country". But in so far as he places stress on emotions such as affection, it seems to me that the proper object of the patriotism he describes is the cultural community with which one identifies rather than the nation-state of which one is a citizen.

One should not adopt an inflated conception of one's nation-state or of one's nationality. One's nationality is nothing more than one's membership of the nation-state of which one is a citizen. When Appiah talks about nationality, he is actually talking about citizenship. In so far as nationality is a status that can be applied for in law, it is tied to the legal institutions of the state and hence to citizenship of that state. It is simply what is indicated on one's passport. If it is morally valuable it is for the same reasons that one's citizenship is morally valuable. One's nationality understood as citizenship shapes one's moral commitments as a matter of pragmatic convenience and reciprocal justice. All that is needed in even the most multicultural of societies is that all the individuals and communities that constitute it respect the rule of law, contribute to the common good by paying taxes and participate in its political processes in appropriate ways. This is what is meant by a "polity". One's nationality is one's membership of a political community to which one has moral obligations as a citizen. Any deeper form of loyalty such as "love of country" is an optional extra. It seems either artificial or ideological to speak, as Taylor (1996) does, of a common project of seeking a good life or, as Appiah does, of an "imagined community" (1996: 27). The polity of which one is a member is a political reality that has legal and pragmatic effects, while one's community is the object of one's affections and the source of one's identity.

Nationalism

The idea of a nation as an "imagined community" united by a common national project, culture or ancestry contributes to the ideology of nationalism. Nationalism became prominent in Europe during the nineteenth century and was used by rulers of European states in order to foment hatred of other nation-states and to encourage people to enlist in armies to engage in military adventures against each other (Cobban 1969). As an ideology it served the interests of ruling classes in their colonial expansion and in their competition with other nations for wealth and glory. It also served their interests by redirecting social unrest and quests for social justice into hatred of foreign powers. This led to the emergence of the modern European idea of a nation as a territory and a population coextensive with administrative borders and legal jurisdictions reinforced with a mythology that spoke of the destiny of a people as defined by those borders. "Nation building" – at least in its nineteenth-century European forms and also its postcolonial forms in the emerging world – involved the attempt to bind people to the nation-state by bonds that were more than just pragmatic or based on shared interests or reciprocal duties. Even in the absence of a unifying tradition, religion or ethnicity, what such processes seek to create is allegiance and loyalty to the nation that go beyond merely instrumental forms of membership.

Accordingly, the psychological phenomenon of nationalism occurs when one's identity-shaping community and one's nation-state are felt to correspond. For a nationalist, the connection that one has to one's nation-state will not feel arbitrary or merely pragmatic. It will be felt as an inseparable part of one's identity. It is an object of commitment. The nationalist transfers the bonds he feels with his ethnic, linguistic or religious community to the nation-state of which he is a citizen. Cosmopolitans would be highly suspicious of these kinds of allegiance or loyalty and would see them as forms of nationalism that ought to be avoided. Loyalty to one's identity-forming community is a valid form of belonging, but nationalism is a dangerous ideology.[8]

But why is it important to avoid nationalism? Is there anything morally questionable about feeling a high degree of identification with one's nation-state?

Would such a degree of identification lead to morally reprehensible forms of tribalism? To begin to explore this question, let us return to Nathanson. Nathanson speaks of what he calls "extreme forms of patriotism", which involve:

- a belief in the superiority of one's country;
- a desire for dominance over other countries;
- an exclusive concern for one's own country;
- no constraints on the pursuit of one's country's goals; and
- automatic support of one's country's military policies. (1993: 29)

I would suggest that this sketch accurately describes nationalism. If I am right in this, then nationalism would be distinguished from patriotism not only by having a distinctive object – namely, the nation-state – but also by being a different kind of stance towards that object – namely, an irrational commitment bordering on fanaticism. I would suggest that, if love of country or identification with one's country takes this form of nationalism, it is not a morally valuable stance or one that should take priority over the outlook of cosmopolitanism.

The five attitudes above that constitute extreme patriotism or nationalism are irrational. First, if everyone around the world believed that their own country was the best, most of them would have to be wrong, since only one country can be the best. Secondly, the desire that one's country have dominance over others is the same desire for glory and status that has led rulers and kings into battle with each other for centuries. Whether such battles are fought in contemporary business boardrooms or the cabinet rooms of governments, the logic of such competitiveness leads inexorably to war. In a world of finite and diminishing resources, competitiveness can only lead to struggles over access to such resources. Thirdly, to be concerned for one's own country at the expense of others, or even to the exclusion of others, is simply a case of selfishness writ large. Just as selfishness is morally vicious if it is pursued at the expense, or through the exploitation, of others, so national interest, if pursued at the expense, or through the exploitation, of other peoples is ethically reprehensible. It is also irrational in that it will lead to resentment and thence to international instability. Fourthly, anyone who thinks that there are no constraints on the pursuit of one's country's goals is someone who would be prepared to break both civil and international law, and also any moral norms, in order to secure their country's interest and power. Fifthly, the link so often made between patriotism and militarism can often lead to automatic endorsement of a country's military policies. No matter how unjustified a war might be, anyone who questions it will be deemed disloyal or a traitor. Any dissent will be deemed an insult to the sacrifices made by the soldiers brought back in body bags. Any consideration of the humanity or of the interests of "the enemy", or the deaths and injuries suffered by their civilians and soldiers, will be deemed cowardly and treasonous.

It should not be necessary to take much time to show that these attitudes are irrational and unethical. However, if one has conceived of nationalism as an extreme form of patriotism and of patriotism as love of one's country, and hence as an emotion not subject to the scrutiny of reasonable reflection, then it is very difficult to say how this irrational form can be avoided. If nationalism is an extreme form of patriotism and if patriotism is an irrational emotion, then how can reason and common sense be deployed in order to prevent this extreme being reached?

We now have a number of intersecting distinctions. We have Nathanson's distinction between patriotism and extreme patriotism, along with my suggestion that this extreme patriotism should be thought of as nationalism. Nathanson clearly disapproves of extreme patriotism but not of what he calls "moderate patriotism". Then we have my suggestion that patriotism is itself an ambiguous notion referring to both a form of pragmatic and legal citizenship of the nation-state of which one is a member, and to allegiance to the people with whom one identifies and whose traditions one feels oneself belonging to. I have already explicated this form of patriotism through the process of identity formation rather than through the analogy with irrational love. I must now ask what moral judgements should be made about such processes and about the attitudes and allegiances they produce.

In order to do this, let us use a different analogy. Imagine that you are a fan of a football club. Your parents supported the club before you were born and took you to its matches from an early age. You now take a keen interest in the club's activities. You attend all the matches you can, even travelling long distances in order to do so. You dress in the team's colours and give friendly greetings to strangers dressed in the same colours. You enjoy talking with other supporters about past premierships and heroic deeds performed by star players. At the matches you cheer loudly, abuse the umpires, argue with the supporters of the opposing team, sing the club anthem vigorously, regard any free kicks awarded against your team as unjust and any awarded against the opposing team as thoroughly deserved and so on. When the team wins you are elated and when they lose you feel crushed. You have done nothing more than add your voice and enthusiasm to the large crowd of supporters, but when your team wins you bask in its glory. When it loses you feel despondent. When its players cheat you feel real shame and when they display the virtues of sportsmanship you feel pride. You are a law-abiding citizen so you do not become drunk and disorderly during or after the game and you do not engage in any hooliganism or violence against opposing supporters or their property. Nevertheless, you are hearty and boisterous in support of your team. In discussions with others you will claim that yours is the best team, prevented from taking the premiership only because of bad luck or bad umpiring decisions. You give money to the team through club memberships and raffles. You give priority to going to the matches over most other social events, and you read the sporting pages of the press avidly every day for news of your team's players. In short, you love your team, are irrationally committed to it, take great pride in it and identify yourself with it. It is easy to see how this sketch offers a suitable analogy for patriotism and even for nationalism. All the features of those phenomena listed above are present. This allegiance came to you as part of your upbringing and is now part of your social and existential identity. You love your team and are prepared to make sacrifices for its well-being.

The way in which many people passionately follow their sports teams or sporting heroes tells us something about the human condition. Friedrich Nietzsche argued that all of life – and thus human life also – involves struggles for domination. He called this "will-to-power" (Nietzsche [1886] 1966). Animals compete against one another not only for access to food and resources and thus for survival, but also for dominance in their groups and for access to mates. In the context of human life, this competitiveness is sublimated and transformed into a struggle for status, self-affirmation, self-differentiation and dominance over others. We all want to shine. We want to be unique. We avoid merely fitting in with the mass of people. We pursue activities that require high levels of ability and we often create formal competitions to decide who has acquired the greatest skill. Alongside sporting competitions, we have musical talent quests, beauty pageants and business competition. We are restless to succeed and to be better at our chosen calling than anyone else. Of course, these inclinations are tempered somewhat by ethical rules and constraints of etiquette so that the achievements that flow from them are turned to the benefit of others. Without these constraints human life would be a cut-throat struggle. Even if it is not always a matter of acquiring power over others, will-to-power is often a pursuit of recognition and of status. We want to be acknowledged and we want our achievements praised. But we do not only want this for our individual selves. We also want it for the groups we identify with. We want our people or our club to be acknowledged and recognized. Moreover, we bask in the glory that our club or our people might achieve. Being a fan of a sporting club illustrates this well. We identify with the club. The basis of this identification might be historical – our parents and their parents also followed that club; or geographical – we live in the town of which that club is the representative; or arbitrary – we like the colour of their uniforms. But once we have made the commitment and identified ourselves as a fan of that club, the successes of the club become our successes and its failures become our failures. Our enthusiasm for the club is an expression of will-to-power mediated by psychological identification with that club.

My first suggestion is that the emotion of patriotism, both in its moderate and extreme, nationalist forms, should be understood as a form of will-to-power in the same way as being a fan of a football club can be.

But there is a crucial difference. However intense your enthusiasm for a football team or a sports hero and however total your commitment to them, you are always able to say to yourself that it is only a game. If you are a rational person, you will be aware that none of the excitement, ritual, legends, heroes, victories and losses of a football club are of ultimate importance. You might not ever say this to yourself and the rhetoric into which you have immersed yourself may seem to speak of ultimacy, but you would not be prepared to kill anyone to defend the honour or interests of your team. You would not refuse to attend your spouse's funeral if it were held on the afternoon of a match, even if it were a championship decider. Joking with friends over a few drinks, you might swear that nothing is more important to you than your team's fortunes, but you would secretly know that you were acting out a part. You would be able to laugh at yourself. You would enjoy your commitment as a kind of play-acting or a charade. Taking it seriously and avowing its ultimacy is part of that game. You identify yourself as a team supporter and you would play out the role that this gives you, but you would be subliminally aware that it is a role. Your commitment would be ironic.[9]

Such irony is not appropriate in the context of love. You do not love your spouse with the secret thought that it is only a game. You do not love your child with an implicit laugh at the role you are playing as a parent.

According to Harry Frankfurt (1988), human freedom consists in the ability to not only have desires, emotions, motivations and intentions that lead to actions and make them voluntary, but also to reflect on them and to ask ourselves whether we are content to have them. This second-order level of reflection allows us to distance ourselves from our caused emotional states, bracket their motivational power and alter the degree of influence they have over us. If the intensity of our emotional states and commitments overwhelms this capacity to reflect we lose our freedom as human agents. The irony that football fans ought to embrace is not a lessening of commitment, but a retention of this kind of second-order freedom.

My second suggestion is that patriotism should be understood through the analogy not of romantic or parental love, but of being a football fan. If the irony and hidden detachment that marks a sensible commitment to a football team could be applied to one's commitment to one's country or one's people, then patriotism could be seen as an ethically harmless commitment and the excesses of nationalism could be avoided. Nationalism or extreme patriotism arises when the commitment to one's country becomes absolute and inflexible so as to override any moral constraints, any norms of reasonableness, and any capacity for critical reflection. This suggests that a morally acceptable form of allegiance to country – whether in the form of the nation-state or in the form of one's people and its traditions – is a form that is attended by flexibility and an absence of absolutism: that is, by irony. Just as a rational person would judge that a football team has no ultimate importance, so one needs to consider how important the object of one's patriotic allegiance should be. My love for my spouse has an object that is highly significant and demanding, and any degree of irony would be inappropriate. I would say the same in relation to my child. But of my country we can certainly ask how important it is and what the degree and scale of our commitment should be. In so far as nationalism or extreme patriotism is a form of commitment that smacks of fanaticism, any degree of irony will destroy it. And so it should.

But does this mean that the milder emotional form of patriotism that Nathanson has described and which he espouses can be endorsed by a cosmopolitan? While I think such patriotism is as harmless as cheering on a football team, I do not think it should be given much ethical significance or normativity. In and of itself one's country is of little importance. Both patriotism and nationalism become pernicious if the special focus on one's country that they espouse elevates that country into having an importance of its own and militates against the scope and urgency of one's concern for human rights and social justice on a global scale. The ethical commitment of a cosmopolitan is to human rights and global justice. Because the cosmopolitan's own country has a role to play in the pursuit of human rights and global justice both in its internal policies and in its foreign policies, she pursues her global ethical concerns through the political processes of her own country and therefore has a pragmatic commitment to those processes.[10]

Political patriotism

Accordingly, what we need is a political conception of patriotism. I define "political patriotism" as loyalty to the *polis* of which one is a member.[11] It was Socrates in Plato's *Crito* who first articulated this form of social and political loyalty and respect for the rule of law. Offered the chance to escape from prison and from his judicial execution, Socrates refuses on the ground that "the Laws" have been of service to him by establishing the society in which he was able to flourish and have thereby earned his loyalty and commitment. To subvert the rule of law by escaping would be to undermine the political consensus on which Athens had established its social order. Whereas other cities were ruled by power, force and fear, Athens was a polity that depended on the cooperation of its members. This cooperation is an instance of political patriotism: a practical stance towards the political structures of which one is a part based on the extent to which those structures protect human rights and produce social justice.

In the modern European tradition this idea is best expressed by the notion of a social contract through which both the legitimacy of the state and the citizen's obligation to respect the rule of law are established by an implicit acknowledgement of the contract-like practical commitment of both to social justice. Allegiance to the state is secured by the state's adhering to its part of the implicit bargain when it protects citizens from foreign incursions or from domestic criminality and when it secures a just distribution of social goods. And this allegiance to the state is expressed by a willingness to contribute to the common weal by paying taxes, serving in the military, contributing to the economy and participating in political decision-making. This form of patriotism may be most readily elicited in a modern, pluralist and liberal state, but it can also arise in other forms of political organization in which rights are protected and laws applied impartially. Such patriotism defines the political community as an object of one's allegiance. The willingness to participate in political processes in accordance with civic duty is a form of that allegiance. However, the political community is seen not as an object of ultimate importance or of blind loyalty, but as a means for securing the political goals of justice and the protection of human rights. This form of patriotism is not seduced by the romance of the nation or constrained by the sanctity of tradition. Nor does it imagine that the demands of human rights or of justice stop at the borders of the state of which one is a citizen. Political patriotism could even be seen as a practical and localized form of cosmopolitanism.

Nathanson's argument against militaristic forms of patriotism provides an unintended hint of this idea. He argues that it is a mistake to admire as patriotic only soldiers who are prepared to, or actually have had to, give their lives for their country. We should be prepared to praise as patriotic anyone who sacrifices something to promote the country's good: people like firefighters, nurses and teachers. According to Nathanson, businessmen who pay their taxes, judges who administer the law with impartiality and politicians who seek the people's good without fear or favour are all patriots in this sense. I would respond by arguing that the term "patriot" has now become too broad. What these ethically admirable people are doing is pursuing a range of values that are good in themselves. The national identity of these values or of the people who benefit from them is irrelevant. Safety from fire, social justice, impartiality in the rule of law, education and health care are all values that it is good to pursue. But they are not values that depend on any identification with a nation or a country. It is admirable to pursue them and we should praise those that do so, but it adds nothing to expressions of that admiration to call those that one admires in such contexts patriotic. It is commitment to people, to justice and to human rights that motivates such virtue. One's country has nothing to do with it.

And yet it does at a political level. If we interpret "one's country" as the nation-state of which one is a citizen or legal resident, then we can acknowledge the political system of this nation-state as the forum in which we can pursue the moral values of human rights and social justice. The nation-state has a role to play. The administrative concept of a state is a social and historical necessity (Glazer 1996).[12] The territorial boundaries of legal jurisdictions need to be defined. The range and scope of government responsibilities need to have borders. And the capacity of political institutions and participants to effect change is limited and defined by such jurisdictions and boundaries. If the citizens or government of a state wanted to effect a change in another state for humanitarian reasons, they would not have the jurisdiction to do so and would have to act on a government-to-government basis or through international political institutions such as the UN. The issue of humanitarian intervention is a vexed one and I shall discuss it later, but my point for the moment is that any actions taken in the pursuit of social justice or for the protection of human rights around the world need to be taken through governmental and political institutions in one's own state and in the other relevant state. Even cosmopolitans have to acknowledge the practical importance of the state in the pursuit of both cosmopolitan and national goals. It is this necessity that grounds that form of patriotism I have called "political patriotism".

Igor Primoratz has argued that patriotism may consist in pride in one's nation-state based on the moral accomplishments of that state rather than on its successes in international competition, whether in the fields of commerce or war. Primoratz (2008) calls this "ethical patriotism" and describes it as a concern for the ethical status of one's country and of its moral standing in the world community. This position pursues not the political, economic and cultural advantage of one's country, but its moral interests. It asks a country to take a cosmopolitan stance in its foreign policies. What one is committed to when one is an ethical patriot in this sense is the value of global justice and the importance of human rights both within one's own nation-state and beyond it. One's nation-state is a vehicle for pursuing those values. The pride one might feel in one's citizenship of an ethical state will serve to motivate the political engagement that ensures that one's state acts as a good global citizen. But the state is not, of itself, an appropriate object of nationalist or patriotic fervour.

There is one qualification that I need to make to my rejection of nationalism as extreme patriotism of the form expressed in such slogans as "My country, right or wrong!" and of even moderate patriotism understood as "love of country". Nationalism can have politically progressive effects as well as bellicose and competitive effects. As Immanuel Wallerstein (1996) has argued, solidarity can be a weapon of the weak against the strong. When a people united by language, culture or tradition is subjugated or colonized by a more powerful people or state, its sense of itself as a people and the way in which individuals identify themselves with their language, culture or tradition can become a powerful political force. Struggles for national liberation or for self-determination on the part of peoples are seen by many commentators as legitimate and are frequently acknowledged by international law. The UN affirms the right of peoples to self-determination, although it acknowledges that it is neither practicable nor desirable for all peoples united by language, culture or tradition to become sovereign states. Self-determination needs to be given form as political autonomy within federated states or other political structures acceptable to all concerned. Whatever the difficulties that arise from struggles for self-determination, my point is that they are motivated by a form of nationalism that is politically legitimate. Such forms of nationalism are political expressions of linguistic, religious or cultural forms of identity and, as such, are deeply motivational. They are yet another form of Nathanson's "love of country". While I would consider that a dose of irony is morally required with even these kinds of nationalisms so as to avoid the bellicose forms of national pride that might emerge after self-determination has been achieved, I would consider them legitimate bases for political engagement and struggles for human rights and social justice in those cases where a people is unjustly subjugated or oppressed. It is at such points as these that identification with one's people combines with political patriotism to produce a valid form of nationalism.

With the clarification of the concepts of patriotism and nationalism that we have now achieved we can reflect on the examples with which we started this section.

(a) Not only does Australia Day provide a reminder of the foundation story of Australia but, by celebrating it as a holiday each year, Australian citizens are encouraged to take pride in that story and imagine themselves as participants in its continuation. In this way they come to live that story as their own and to identify with the nation that had such a humble beginning.

(b) Anzac Day operates much as Australia Day does in forging the identification of Australians with their history and national pride. But on this occasion it is soldiers rather than convicts and their guards who are memorialized. On this occasion it is war with its power to forge the national identity that is celebrated. It is on such days that the willingness to give up one's life for one's country in battle is offered as a model for civic virtue. It is on such days that the link between patriotism and militarism is forged.

(c) The republican debate in Australia is said by many to be merely symbolic. The British Crown has very little influence on Australian political affairs even though the British queen is Australia's head of state. That the queen's representative in Australia, the governor-general, has the power to dismiss a government – as was done in 1975 – is due to the Australian constitution rather than to any prerogatives held by the British monarchy. Nevertheless, it is felt by others that the issue is important because it represents a growth in national maturity in which ties with the "mother country" can be cut and a public affirmation of independence and self-determination made. It is argued that a more vigorous and committed participation in political life on the part of citizens can develop if citizens feel greater "ownership" of the polity than would be the case if that polity were subject to the Crown. Here symbolism ties in with will-to-power. Self-affirmation – both individually and collectively – is expressed as political autonomy and self-determination. It is also argued that a fully autonomous nation will have greater prestige and influence in Australia's geopolitical region. Status and self-image are not merely symbolic issues because they are deeply motivational and influence the degree to which citizens see themselves as involved in the political life of the nation-state. If republicanism means not having an overlord and if it is expressed in high levels of political participation (Pettit 1997), then becoming a republic is an important and practical issue. What I have called "political patriotism" is encouraged by just such symbolic gestures.

(d) That we are not told who won the gold medal during a news broadcast, even when we are told that an Australian athlete won a silver medal at the Olympic Games, illustrates the insularity that many forms of patriotism produce. On this view, a patriot is interested only in the affairs of compatriots. This example also illustrates how apt the football fan analogy is for understanding patriotism. Just as a fan takes an inordinate amount of interest in the goings on of their team, so a national patriot takes an interest in the successes of those with whom she identifies. Even if she is not all that interested in athletics, the fact that the medal was won by an Australian is enough to make the event interesting.

(e) That events are more interesting if they involve compatriots is also illustrated by the air crash example. But here there is the further element of caring about the victims of a tragedy. We often care more about compatriots even though all those who are killed leave behind grieving relatives and shattered lives. The tragedy is not less for a non-Australian than it is for an Australian. Nationality should be irrelevant to our feelings of sympathy and should also be irrelevant to our willingness to help.

(f) Rowdy behaviour at beer festivals, sporting events and the like is a widespread phenomenon. That it often takes the form of flaunting the national colours and shouting national slogans and songs indicates that what is at stake for the participants is national identity. As uncouth as the behaviour is, it expresses a pride in being Australian and an insistence that others notice one's nationality. It is will-to-power as public display and does not carry much moral value.

(g) For the patriotic citizens of what is now Marree, the name of the South Australian town of Hergott Springs sounded too German when nationalist fervour inspired a hatred for everything associated with the wartime enemy. This illustrates the ideological use of nationalism for fomenting hatred of those who are not on one's side.

(h) The singing of the national anthem before major sporting events is also a display of national pride and a means whereby participants identify themselves with their nation. In cases where the sporting events are international competitions there is the added frisson for the audience of staking one's nation's reputation on the outcome of the competition. Once again, it is an expression of will-to-power but one that has no more importance than the victories of one's local football team.

(i) Kathy Freeman's display of both an Australian and an Aboriginal flag during her lap of honour is a much more interesting event. Had she carried only an Australian flag I would make the same comments as with the previous example. Like all national flags, the Australian flag is a powerful symbol of the nation-state to which many people avow great loyalty. Soldiers are said to have died fighting under this flag and it is said to represent everything that is noble in the nation. It is considered a crime to desecrate the flag in any way. It is not without interest to note the link between flag-waving and militarism. Flags were originally signs for identifying who was on whose side in military formations and which navy a ship belonged to, and they served as banners around which soldiers would rally during battles. They are carried in military parades and given military salutes as they are raised on flagpoles. National flags take on an almost sacred value as symbols of the nation-state. The Aboriginal flag, in contrast, is not the flag of a nation-state and has never been used for military purposes. It was created relatively recently as a rallying point for the many and disparate Aboriginal activist groups seeking social justice for Australia's indigenous peoples and a higher degree of self-determination for Aboriginal communities. As such, the Aboriginal flag also has a highly charged symbolic value, but an oppositional one. Conservative voices in Australian politics would regard the Aboriginal flag as subversive and as threatening to Australian national unity. Whereas Kathy Freeman was expressing pride both in her nation and in her Aboriginality by carrying both flags, her critics saw her as seeking to undermine the pride that mainstream Australians feel in their nation by reminding them of unresolved social problems arising from the treatment of Australia's first inhabitants. They saw her as being unpatriotic.

(j) For "The Australia First Party", being patriotic means showing allegiance to a concept of Australian nationhood in which the traditions of the English masters and Irish convicts are given pride of place. Aborigines and migrants who do not look, speak or behave like the first English and Irish settlers are outsiders or latecomers who do not share the cultures and traditions that define one as a true Australian. Clearly, such a stance is definitive of chauvinism. The party is also suspicious of welfarism, especially to the extent that welfare benefits are given to Australians who do not fall into the acceptable category of cultural conformity. The major target for this political movement is multiculturalism, and it seeks to define patriotism and nationalism in chauvinistic terms so as to exclude any groups that are not of the narrow range of ethnicities that it defines as genuinely Australian. This and the following examples also illustrate the close link between patriotism, nationalism and racism. So long as the nation to which patriots are urged to be loyal is defined as a people with a specific ethnicity or cultural tradition rather than as an administrative nation-state, patriotism will lead to chauvinism, jingoism, racism and xenophobia.

(k) Immigration and refugee policies are a test case for the cosmopolitan outlook. In rejecting refugees and developing punitive policies of detention for asylum seekers, the Australian government saw itself as acting in the national interest and in defence of the national borders. Leaving aside the cruelty and administrative injustices that accompanied the implementation of the policies, the central point is that they exemplify a central dogma of state-based nationalism: the difference in legal status between citizens and non-citizens. Once again there is something inevitable and necessary about this distinction. If a state is defined as an administrative unit with a defined range of legal jurisdiction, then there will be some who fall within this range and some who fall outside it. But we might ask whether a government should not accept the responsibility to exercise hospitality towards strangers, especially when those strangers are in dire need. I shall discuss this issue at greater length in Chapter 3. For the moment it is important to see the political role that the ideas of patriotism and nationalism play in this issue. Policies of exclusion are justified on the basis that the government has responsibility only for Australians and for protecting the national borders. The claim is that it has no responsibility for outsiders. It would be unpatriotic to take any other view. "Australia for Australians" is a slogan that expresses chauvinistic forms of nationalism and patriotism.

(l) The Cronulla riots were a further expression of chauvinistic or extreme forms of patriotism. But a further element is present here also. In the wake of the 9/11 terrorist attacks in the USA and in the wake of a highly publicized gang-rape trial involving Lebanese youths in the area, an anti-Muslim xenophobia was developing in the Australian community. Add some local hooliganism into the mix and the disturbances become layered with a new level of meaning. It becomes a case of Australians defending their way of life against "foreign" attack. Once again, the threat is to multiculturalism. The use of Australian flags and symbols seeks to identify one side of the fight as Australian and the other as foreign. For their part, the youths "of Middle Eastern appearance" also define themselves by their ethnicity and the nationality of their families. What is, at base, criminal behaviour is dressed up as an expression of patriotism. It is, in fact, tribalism at its worst.

(m) The "buy Australian" campaign is a response to economic globalization. The many economic and social effects of globalization include the demise of Australian business, the loss of Australian jobs and the repatriation of profits earned in Australia to multinational business corporations. This is seen as inimical to Australia's national interest if that interest is defined in terms of Australian profits and jobs in the affected industries. The form of patriotism that is being evinced here is a quest for Australian economic self-sufficiency. Globalization involves not only a redistribution of global wealth and opportunity but also a great degree of economic interdependence between nation-states. As independence, self-determination and self-sufficiency are typical goals for traditional nationalism, it is thought to be unpatriotic to open Australia's economic system to global influences (Falk 1996).[13]

(n) Australia's hesitation about entering into agreements to limit carbon emissions or reduce reliance on coal for the sake of slowing global warming is another example of economic patriotism or nationalism. It illustrates how the national interest can become conflated with the economic interests of companies based within the legal jurisdiction of the nation-state. As Pogge (2002a) has argued, it is not legitimate for national leaders to pursue unfair advantages at the cost of others in the international sphere, even if they do so on behalf of their own countries. Moreover, the threat of global warming affects all countries and peoples globally. The problem that this raises is whether national governments have responsibility just for their own national interests or whether they should also have global interests at heart simply because they are global interests. Whereas an internationalist or a political realist might argue that governments should cooperate to prevent environmental degradation because it is in their own national interests to do so, a cosmopolitan would argue that the interests of all the peoples and ecosystems of the world are proper objects of governmental responsibility.

(o) That Australian soldiers serving overseas are praised as heroes and as patriots demonstrates once again the link between patriotism, nationalism and militarism. Militarism involves valuing soldiering as an expression of nationalistic hubris. However, the matter becomes more complicated when it is noted that many of the missions in which Australian soldiers serve are peacekeeping or humanitarian missions endorsed by the UN. In this their service has less to do with making war than with policing the world's trouble spots or providing life-saving assistance. Such actions are laudable. But it is unnecessary and misleading to describe such actions as patriotic. It is sometimes necessary to reinforce the quest for justice, the defence of human rights and the protection of people from criminals in international settings with military force. The aims of such missions can be endorsed by cosmopolitans as being universally valid goals, such as the alleviation of suffering and the protection of human rights. To describe such actions as patriotic is nothing more than an attempt to identify oneself with them and to take pride in them. This has no more moral value than glorying in the achievements of one's nation's international athletes.

(p) That Australian expatriate workers or emigrants feel nostalgia for home illustrates my thesis about the psychological bases of "love of one's country". The land in which we are born or have our most important formative experiences is always going to have a special place in our hearts. Just what follows from this as to the moral duties we have towards our countries or peoples beyond them is not clear. The basis for our obligations to obey the law and contribute to the social and political life of our nation-state is a separate issue from any emotional attachment that we may have to the peoples, lands or traditions of that nation-state.

(q) The claim that artists give expression to an Australian sensibility and way of life through their art relies on there being an Australian sensibility and way of life. There is no denying that there are sensibilities and ways of life that arise and occur in Australia. If they are interesting there is value in presenting them in artistic or narrative forms. But their interest is universal. Any profound human experience or compelling human story is of human interest and would potentially be of interest or edification to anyone anywhere. If Australians take a special interest in Australian art, music, literature and cinema, it is so that they can achieve self-understanding in terms of the traditions, ethnicities and languages through which their identities are shaped.

(r) Australia's being described as having a civilizing and enlightening role in its geopolitical region by virtue of its heritage in British traditions of democracy and the rule of law is a form of neo-colonialism. While there is no doubt that Australia is a beneficiary of inherited traditions of democracy and the rule of law, it is chauvinistic to suppose that they could have arisen only from Britain (although as a matter of historical fact, they did) or that they could not arise in indigenous forms in neighbouring states and communities. This view is a local version of the moralistic universalism that assumes that Western liberal democracy is the only valid form of political organization and that it should be spread to the rest of the world, by force of arms if necessary. This is a matter to which I shall return in Chapter 5.

(s) The lauding of allegedly distinctive Australian egalitarian virtues such as "mateship" and "a fair go" is an example of the kinds of misleading generalization and oversimplification of national characteristics that calls Scotsmen skinflints, Italians cowardly or Irishmen stupid. Such stereotypes deny the variability of the human condition and suggest people's characteristics can be defined by their nationality.[14] There is no empirical evidence to support such sweeping statements and they feed into the chauvinism and racism that so often characterize extreme patriotism. Moreover, the concepts of "mateship" and "a fair go" are notoriously ill defined.

(t) That applicants for Australian citizenship are required to pass a "citizenship test" would be valid if it could assure their political patriotism as defined above. Some knowledge of, and commitment to, Australian political processes and values would be relevant to this, although how these could be measured by a simple quiz is not clear. But to require knowledge of such cultural information as the achievements of Australian cricketing great Don Bradman is to devalue Australia's multiculturalism. Not everyone in Australia cares about cricket or about its champions. There should be no requirement that, to be a genuine Australian, one must be interested in specific sporting, cultural or social phenomena. To lack such interests and the knowledge that goes with them is not unpatriotic.

(u) The epithet "un-Australian" assumes that there is a clear set of ethical and cultural criteria for what it is to be "Australian". This is a false assumption not only because Australia is a multicultural society, but also because, even if it were not, people are still so different from each other in terms of their preferences and ways of being that no single set of characteristics could capture what it is to be Australian or, contrariwise, what it is to be "un-Australian". If this phrase is meant to capture a way of being or of behaving that is to be morally disapproved of, then it should appeal to moral norms that are of general validity rather than being valid only in Australia or for Australians. Is there a distinctive Australian way of being a cheat, a liar, an adulterer or a murderer such that such behaviours could be described as "un-Australian"? Such failures are breaches of moral norms that apply anywhere. Perhaps it is being suggested that Australians are more moral than anyone else, so that to act immorally is to be un-Australian. This may be a patriotic thought, but it is a false one.

(v) The Australian government's formal apology to the Aboriginal people of Australia for past government policies that removed Aboriginal children from their families for racist reasons illustrates the importance of creating a national ethos with which people can identify. If national celebrations such as Australia Day and Anzac Day create myths through which Australians can take pride in their nation and their nationality, past events can also leave them with shame. Moreover, the Aboriginal victims of the government policies in question feel both grief at their loss of family life and anger at the injustice that has been done to them. Reconciliation through an apology comprises two movements. It tells the victims of government policies that the present generation disowns those policies, is ashamed of them and will seek to overcome them, and it allows the members of the present non-Aboriginal community to put aside the shame that their forebears have caused them so that they can, once again, take pride in their nation's history. For both communities this will produce a new commitment to political patriotism.

(w) It is because I am Australian that all the examples offered above matter to me. I feel the need to belong to this community and to participate in its social, cultural and political life. I feel the need to take pride in being Australian and to feel attached to this country even though I was not born here. Events of moral significance that occur in other countries concern me also, but I can engage with them only through the political and social means that are at my disposal in Australia. My motivation to use these means is driven not only by my concern for the global issues that are in question but also by my sense of belonging to this political community. My political patriotism locates my political engagement in Australian political institutions and focuses my loyalty and allegiance on Australian laws and processes. But this does not limit the scope of my moral concerns. My quest for social justice and the protection of human rights knows no borders. I am an Australian cosmopolitan.

Conclusion

We are now in a position to return to the Nussbaum debate and, particularly, to the claim of Barber that cosmopolitanism is a "thin" moral commitment while patriotism is a "thick" allegiance based on heartfelt attachments. My answer is that cosmopolitanism can also be seen as a heartfelt attachment – albeit an attachment to a humanity not confined to any of the specific communities in which all human beings live. I agree with Nussbaum's claim that one's commitment to humanity can be "thick" in the required sense, whether that humanity is embodied in one's family, community, nation or the world as a whole. Moreover, I can accept one idea that Nussbaum's communitarian critics insist on: one does need to be a patriot in order to be a cosmopolitan because one must operate within one's polity. But this is political patriotism rather than nationalism. Nationalism leads too easily to chauvinism, militarism and the prioritizing of one's national interests over global responsibilities. The kind of patriotism that cosmopolitans can endorse includes the kind of irony that understands one's political community in pragmatic and instrumental terms rather than as an object of blind allegiance. There need be no incompatibility between cosmopolitanism and patriotism if patriotism is understood to entail a political commitment to human rights and social justice that is not confined to local loyalties, but that can extend to global responsibilities. It is to an understanding of the objects of such a commitment that we must now turn.

Chapter 2
Human rights

> Today, in general, "human rights" means rights that human subjects mutually grant one another in order to guarantee a life that meets the necessary conditions of "dignity" and respect; the guiding notion here is that a morality of social existence minimally demands that all others are equally able to lead a human life. (Honneth 1997: 168)

Of the many components of the idea of cosmopolitanism listed at the end of the Introduction, I want in this chapter to explore the philosophical foundations of the following:

(4) respect for basic human rights as universally normative;
(5) acknowledging the moral equality of all peoples and individuals;
(6) respect for the peoples of the world as united by reason, sociability and a common humanity; and
(7) belief in a globally acceptable concept of human dignity.

The discourse of rights has very wide currency today and is an inescapable aspect of debates in international relations. As I mentioned in the Introduction, the most important articulation of the idea of human rights is the Universal Declaration of Human Rights (UDHR) proclaimed by the UN in 1948.[1] The UDHR does not have the force of law but it does express an international consensus on the social and political aspirations of the members of the UN after the horrors of the Second World War. Since then, there have been legally binding agreements such as the International Covenant on Civil and Political Rights (1966) and the International Covenant on Economic, Social and Cultural Rights (1966). The concept of human rights also appears in the Convention on the Prevention and Punishment of the Crime of Genocide (1948), the International

Convention on the Elimination of all Forms of Racial Discrimination (1965), the Convention against Torture and Other Cruel, Inhuman or Degrading Treatment or Punishment (1984), the Declaration on the Right to Development (1986), and the Convention on the Rights of the Child (1989). Most recently there has been a UN Declaration on the Rights of Indigenous Peoples (2007).

What are human rights?

Given all this, it will be important to understand the concept of a right. There have been many suggestions as to what rights are, including: one's basic entitlements; reasons for others to act in certain ways towards one; one's moral power to produce obligations in others; one's power to invoke sanctions or force to induce others to do what one requires of them; or socially constructed expectations.[2] Although the concept is most often used in relation to individual people, it can apply to groups or peoples and to nation-states as well. Rather than seek a definition of rights, however, I shall begin by exploring what difference the concept makes in our thinking.

Let us imagine a scenario in which the people of a rich nation – through their government or through NGOs – are offering assistance to the people of a poor nation in the latter's pursuit of economic development. It might be an aid programme that centres on providing health care or other social services, or it might be a programme that forgives national debts accumulated by previous governments of the recipient nation. Whatever the details, we are asked to imagine that the people of the donor country give the assistance through their government or through NGOs without any conditions that serve the interests of the donors, such as tied loans or demands for economic restructuring. There are at least two ways of understanding the relationship between the people of the donor country and those of the recipient country. The first sees donors as acting with generosity or charity. In this understanding, the government and people of the donor country respond to the poverty, morbidity and mortality rates, and economic underdevelopment of the recipient country by deciding to rescue the people of the recipient country from the troubles and premature deaths that their poverty is causing them. This is a fine and noble stance for people in the donor country to take and the world would be a better place if more nations did the same. However, it sees the people of the recipient country as recipients of charity. People in the recipient nation are supplicants. In more everyday language, they are beggars. They must beseech the richer nations for assistance and when they receive such assistance they must show gratitude. The relationship between the two peoples is therefore morally unequal as well as being materially unequal. Not only are the recipients poorer, but they are also of lesser dignity. They are the beggars in the relationship, while the donors are the magnanimous givers of aid. The relationship of charity is one that elevates the status of the donors and diminishes that of the recipients. Of course, this may not be the most significant feature of the relationship. After all, the urgent needs of the population of the poorer nation are being met by the aid programme and this is a good that should not be gainsaid. It is good to be generous and we rightly admire those who are charitable towards those who are in need. In technical terms we describe their actions as "supererogatory": that is, as morally admirable but not strictly required as a moral obligation. To act generously is to act above and beyond the call of duty. This is why the charitable person can feel a high degree of self-esteem. She feels that she is acting in a way that is better than those who act merely to fulfil their obligations. However, a negative side effect of this extra level of self-esteem is that it creates the danger that the generous person might also think of herself as superior to others and, in particular, those others who are the object of her charity. While such an attitude is not inevitable, and while the truly virtuous person will avoid falling into such a way of thinking, the problem is entirely absent when the relationship between donor and recipient is thought of in terms of rights and of justice.

The second way of conceiving of the relationship between the two peoples in my scenario involves the concept of rights. If we say that the recipients have a right to the assistance that they receive from the donor country, the moral quality of their relationship is quite different. In this way of thinking, the recipients are not supplicants but claimants. They claim the assistance they receive as a matter of right and hence of justice. They claim that they are entitled to the aid and that it would be wrong or unjust for them not to receive it. This is a claim that needs to be justified, of course, but what such a justification might be based on is a question I want to leave aside for the moment. The key point is that the moral quality of claiming assistance as a matter of right is different from the moral quality of begging for it. Moreover, the moral quality of the act of giving on the part of the donors is different. Whereas when they gave out of a spirit of charity we could describe them as being generous, we now describe them as being just. The moral quality of the relationship between one who claims assistance as a matter of right and one who gives assistance as a matter of duty is one of equality. The system of relationships that is established between people or nations under the rubric of rights or of justice is a system in which each node is defined as having an equal moral status as defined by the principle of impartiality.

The discourse of rights is part of a moral framework in which justice decrees that the same benefits and privileges are owed to each and every person unless there are morally relevant differences between them. For example, if a rich nation were faced with a natural disaster in two neighbouring poorer states, and if it had the resources to help both of those poorer states, it would be unjust for it to direct its assistance solely to one of those states on the grounds that it, and it alone, shared a cultural history with it. That the rich nation shares a heritage or a religion with one of the stricken countries but not with the other is not a relevant reason for withholding the assistance that it could give to the second nation if it had the resources to do so. To act in that way is not merely to fail to be generous and admirable: it is to fail to do what justice requires. It is unjust to discriminate on such grounds when the needs of the people in both stricken countries are equally grave. The principle of impartiality applies when the action being envisaged is a duty or a moral obligation, or falls under the rubric of justice or of rights. If the donor country were being generous rather than responding to the call of duty, it could reasonably extend its generosity to only one of the disaster-affected countries. A merely generous agent is entitled to extend her largesse in any way she sees fit. We might still think that to do so selectively was somewhat less than admirable, but we would have no grounds for saying that the act of discrimination was wrong or unjust. If you choose to be good over and above what duty requires, you can also choose whom you are going to be good to, and the nation or person who does not receive your assistance has no basis for complaint. However, impartiality is required when one is acting within a framework of justice because, in this context, the moral status of all parties to the relationship is one of formal moral equality.

This point helps us understand the sense of grievance that arises if rights are not honoured. If it were a matter of receiving something out of the charity of the donors, would-be recipients would not be justified in complaining if it were not given to them; whereas, if people have a right to something, they would be justified in feeling aggrieved if they did not receive it. They have a right to claim it as a matter of justice. When such a claim is denied or ignored, a feeling of grievance[3] is justified to the same extent as the system of justice that grounds the claim is justified. This notion of grievance is important in political thinking because it distinguishes the hurt that comes from not getting what one wants from the hurt that comes from not getting what one is entitled to. To not get what one wants may be merely a matter of bad luck. But to not get what one has a right to is a matter of injustice. I shall return to this distinction between rights and wants presently.

There is a formal complementarity between rights and duties. In the conceptual framework of justice, when one person or nation has a right, another person or nation has a duty. As Onora O'Neill puts it: "Once we start talking about *rights*, we assume a framework in which performance of obligations can be *claimed*. Rights have to be allocated to specified bearers of obligations: otherwise, claimants of rights cannot know to which obligation bearer their claims should be addressed" (1998: 96). It is part of the "logical grammar" of the way these terms are used in the discourse of justice that rights and duties go together. If one has a right, then another has a duty to provide, protect or restore what the first has a right to. And if one has a duty to another, then that other has a right to receive what the first has a duty to provide. This point is well illustrated by a commercial contract. As a result of a contract to purchase a bag of potatoes, for example, the vendor has a right to payment for the potatoes and the purchaser has an obligation to pay for them. Again, if the purchaser has paid for them, she has a right to receive the potatoes and the vendor has an obligation to supply them. It would seem from such homely examples that there is indeed a symmetry between rights and obligations and that they emerge together: in this case, from the existence of a contract.

The contract example also serves to illustrate what kind of reality a right is. A right can be said to have a moral reality, and claims to have the right honoured can be said to be justified if there is a contract or agreement in place that establishes the right and that allocates to others relevant and specific duties to provide what holders of the right are empowered by the contract to claim. A right is real only to the extent that the relevant rights claim can be justified and the corresponding duties allocated. But if these points are relatively clear in the case where there is a contract that has been agreed to, and that specifies what parties to the contract are entitled to and what they are obliged to do, can we find such clarity in the case of putatively universal, basic human rights of the kind enunciated in the UDHR? Is there a kind of global contract or agreement on which the validity of human rights claims can be based and duties allocated? Or do we need some other kind of moral or metaphysical grounding for such claims?

The legitimation of human rights

We should distinguish the legitimation of human rights from their justification (Maffettone 2007). The justification of human rights is a philosophical process that makes use of concepts that are deemed to be both fundamental and rational in order to secure belief in the reality of such rights. Such concepts and arguments will derive from the value commitments and traditions of those who propose them and may therefore differ from one culture to another. Accordingly, it may be unreasonable to expect universal agreement on such justifications. The legitimation of human rights, on the other hand, is a political process involving public debate and historical struggle directed towards establishing a list of human rights that will be effective in influencing political decisions both nationally and internationally. Such a process would be exemplified by the formation of the UDHR and subsequent covenants. Given that the UN has propagated those rights by due process, those rights are legitimate whatever justification we might give them. The world's nation-states have agreed to them and have established quasi-legal institutions to monitor and propagate them. There is, at a formal level, global agreement on their validity and all nations have agreed, in formal terms, to abide by their requirements and accept the obligations they imply. Accordingly, respect for human rights is now a legitimate part of the official fabric of international relations and an accepted basis for global ethics.

Cosmopolitanism argues that there is a global framework of international law in which all nations, peoples and individuals participate. While this framework does not have the positive formality of a contract, it is sufficiently well established to count as the kind of agreement appropriate to establishing the normativity of relevant rights and duties. It is the historical fact that nations have signed up to the UDHR and further UN covenants that constitutes the contract-like legal framework on which human rights and the corresponding obligations are based. Every nation, people or individual has rights and duties within this framework. We have yet to explore what moral or human considerations these agreements and declarations are based on and what justifications can be offered for their normativity, but the first claim that I shall explore is that this moral framework is legitimate and has global applicability. Cosmopolitans would argue that no nation, people or individual can opt out of this global framework of justice and exempt themselves from its requirements. Unlike charity, which is optional, the protection of the rights demanded by global justice and the performance of the duties that correspond to those rights is incumbent on all nations, peoples and individuals around the world. Cosmopolitanism would argue that human rights are universal in the sense that every person universally is entitled to claim them and every person universally has the obligation to honour them irrespective of the political and cultural traditions in which such persons find themselves.

But not everyone agrees with this. It has been alleged that the UDHR does not articulate rights that are applicable or understood universally, but rather that they express a distinctly Western conception of rights. They are said to be individualistic and to pay too little regard to the community-based norms with which traditional societies constrain individual freedoms. Moreover, in the context of various international struggles, including the cold war and the struggle for independence and economic self-sufficiency on the part of emerging nations in the third world, it has been claimed that the rights proclaimed in the UDHR aid the processes of capitalist expansion at the cost of the social aspirations of developing and socialist nations (Pollis & Schwab 1979; see also Tharoor 1999/2000). Some have even said that the UDHR is part of an attempt on the part of Western capitalist nations to increase their hegemony over the world and pursue their imperialist aspirations. Even so eminent a statesman as Boutros Boutros-Ghali, a former secretary-general of the United Nations, is reported to have described human rights as "an instrument of intervention to serve the political objectives of the developed world" (quoted in Traub 2006: 73).

If these are empirical claims, they are easily proved wrong by investigating the historical circumstances of the development of the UDHR. The document was drafted by a committee set up by the newly formed UN, chaired by Eleanor Roosevelt, and comprising representatives from Australia, Belgium, Byelorussia, Chile, China, Egypt, India, Iran, Lebanon, Panama, the Philippines, Ukraine, the United Kingdom, the USA, Uruguay, the USSR and Yugoslavia. According to a historical study by Micheline Ishay:

> To help the work of the human rights drafting committee, a questionnaire had been commissioned from a UNESCO philosophers' committee to study various rights traditions, including Chinese, Islamic, Hindu, American, and European worldviews on human rights as well as their customary legal perspectives. (2004: 219)[4]

There were seventy responses to this questionnaire from eminent persons around the world, including Mahatma Gandhi, the Muslim poet and philosopher Humayun Kabir and Chinese philosopher Chung-Shu Lo. The final draft was prepared by Eleanor Roosevelt working with "the Chinese philosopher, diplomat, and commission vice-chairman Pen-Chung Chang, the Lebanese existentialist philosopher and rapporteur Charles Malik, and the French legal scholar and later Nobel Prize laureate René Cassin" (*ibid.*: 220). It would seem, then, that representatives of the major religious and philosophical traditions of the world – Muslim, Hindu, Christian and Chinese – along with contributors from capitalist countries, socialist countries and developing countries, all had opportunities to shape the final document.

It has to be admitted, however, that cold war rivalries had an impact on the drafting of the declaration. Led by the USSR, the socialist countries wanted to stress social values and welfare rights, while the USA and its allies placed greater emphasis on the political rights associated with liberalism. There was a great deal of argument and compromise before the draft was finalized but, on 10 December 1948, the declaration was adopted by the then fifty-eight members of the UN with no votes against. However, eight nations abstained: Byelorussia, Czechoslovakia, Poland, Saudi Arabia, South Africa, Ukraine, the USSR and Yugoslavia. Apart from Saudi Arabia and South Africa, who had internal reasons for opposing the spread of human rights into their own countries, the other abstainers were members of the communist bloc. It is clear, therefore, that voices of dissent were raised against the declaration from the very beginning and that these voices represented a conception of human rights and of human well-being that differed from those current in the capitalist West. That said, the endorsement of the declaration was overwhelming and it continues to represent the highest aspirations for human flourishing expressed by the world community. It should also be noted that, apart from Saudi Arabia, the representatives of the abstaining countries came out of the Western philosophical tradition. Those countries are heir to the traditions of Christianity and of the Enlightenment that have shaped the Western conception of human existence rather than participating in such great religious and cultural traditions as Islam, Hinduism, Buddhism or the various strands of Confucianism. It follows that the dissent that was present at the birth of the declaration cannot be interpreted as supporting the claim that the declaration was a Western cultural imposition on other traditions.

There is a further and more abstract way of refuting this charge. This is to accuse those who make it of committing the "genetic fallacy". Informal logic describes this as the fallacy of charging that a claim is false or invalid if it arises from suspect sources. For example, it might be charged that scientific research that shows that drinking red wine can be good for you by reducing the risk of heart disease would be suspect if it were shown that the research was funded by the wine industry. We might indeed be a little suspicious of such research if it were funded in this way, but it would certainly not follow from the fact that the wine industry funded the research that the results were false. If the research is conducted with sound methodology, it may well yield credible results no matter the source of the research funding. There is no relation of logical implication between the proposition that the research was funded by the wine industry and the proposition that the result of the research is false. Similarly, if it were argued that the UDHR is false – in the sense that it does not express rights that are universally applicable – on the grounds that it was an imperialist imposition, such an argument would be committing the genetic fallacy. Even if it were true that the capitalist nations forced the document through an unwilling General Assembly of the UN, nothing would follow about the validity or otherwise of the rights that are articulated in it. Whether those rights were consistent with the national interests of some nations and not others or whether they were vigorously promoted by some nations and opposed by others is irrelevant to their validity. The historical facts about the diplomatic manoeuvrings surrounding their adoption are not logically relevant to the question of whether those rights are universal in their application.

Given these arguments, a great many international relations theorists and philosophers accept that human rights are legitimate in so far as there are international laws and other legal instruments that affirm those rights. The UDHR and the other conventions mentioned earlier are instruments of this kind, albeit differing as to their legal status. However, the UN often lacks the policing power to enforce even those covenants that have a high legal status. There is now an international court that tries cases involving crimes against humanity such as genocide, but this court and other ad hoc tribunals that have been set up to try cases of this kind are highly dependent for their effectiveness on the policing powers and legal cooperation of various states. Nevertheless, these laws, covenants and declarations have been promulgated and have set up an international normative framework that all peoples are expected to abide by. Even if there is no effective policing power to enforce these norms, there is a sense of expectation and a sense of honour in relation to them such that a nation that flagrantly violates them can have at least the pressure of shame brought to bear on it. Moreover, if sanctions are applied, aid denied or trading privileges suspended in relation to a state that violates human rights, the justification for such responses need not depend on abstract philosophical arguments but can allude to the body of rights declarations to which the whole world has formally acceded. The existence of this quasi-legal international order of acknowledgement of rights is sufficient to establish the legitimacy of global rights norms without the further need for theoretical justifications.

We might call this position "pragmatic positivism".[5] It is positivist in that it grounds the legitimacy of rights in the quasi-legal declarations and covenants of the UN, and it is pragmatic because it recognizes that the purpose of such declarations is to secure global stability. As I noted in the Introduction, it was in response to the horrors of the Second World War and from a determination to avoid such devastating wars ever again that the UN formulated the UDHR. This pragmatic legitimation of human rights does not preclude the possibility that philosophical accounts of human rights that draw on local cultural or theological traditions might not be developed in one part of the world or another. People in the West may wish to refer back to the traditions of liberal thought or of Christianity to enunciate theories of human rights, while thinkers in other parts of the world may want to allude to concepts developed in their own traditions. My claim, however, is that the concept of human rights has been given a universal legitimation that enables fruitful discourse on human rights and global justice in all parts of the world just on the basis of the pragmatic considerations adduced by the framers of the UN declarations.

A further basis for the legitimation of basic human rights is the fact that people have struggled for them throughout history. Jay Drydyk (1997) has developed what he calls a "transformationist" conception of human rights in which human rights are constantly being developed and expanded through a bottom-up struggle for justice rather than any top-down declaration of such rights.[6] People around the world have always struggled for rights and continue to do so. People feel indignation at the harms they suffer that is more than an expression of mere disappointment or frustration, and that motivates them to engage in political struggle. Rather than say that the concept of rights is not applicable in societies that have cultural traditions that are inhospitable to that concept, we should acknowledge that individuals and groups in such societies often struggle for what we would call their rights. Many voices will be raised within those societies to influence political discussions and create democratic processes in order to claim human rights. To cite a contemporary example, a Chinese court condemned Hu Jia, aged thirty-four, to three and a half years in jail in April 2008, for "inciting subversion of state power" following his criticisms of Chinese repression in Tibet and of other Chinese policies (Amnesty International 2008). It is the struggle and sacrifice of such activists that constitute the reality of rights claims much more than any permissions or liberties granted by governments or declarations made by global bodies. Although it is correct in one sense to say that there exists no right to express political dissent in China, it is nevertheless possible to argue that Hu Jia was justified in his actions and in the claim he was making to be allowed to express such dissent. But the reality of his right to dissent is founded on his courageous struggle rather than on any agreement to accord such rights to Chinese citizens that the Chinese government might make in the future, or on any philosophical justification that Hu Jia or his supporters might offer.

Drydyk also does not agree that the rights enunciated in the UDHR are meaningless in traditional societies because they are largely individualistic in tone. He argues that all societies, including highly traditional or authoritarian societies, have concepts that are akin to those of rights. The most obvious of these is the concept of duty. It is the obligations that members of such societies have towards one another that forge the coherence of those societies. Moreover, most normative systems and moral codes – such as the ten commandments that are central to the Judaeo-Christian tradition – are articulated in the form of duties, commands or prohibitions. I have argued that there is a symmetry between duties and rights in the sense that if one person has a duty to another, then that second person has a right to whatever the first person has a duty to do. Accordingly, the concept of a right can emerge in any situation where the concept of a duty or obligation is already current. Those societies to which the concept of human rights is alleged to be meaningless do not lack the concept of duty. It follows that the concept of a right is incipiently or inchoately present already in such societies. Drydyk quotes Kwasi Wiredu, who has made a study of the Akan people of West Africa: "On the face of it, the normative layer in the Akan concept of person brings only obligations to the individual. In fact, however, these obligations are matched by a whole series of rights that accrue to the individual simply because he lives in a society in which everyone has those obligations" (Wiredu 1990: 247; quoted in Drydyk 1997: 164). The basis of the notion of rights here is that of duty. Even though it is duties and obligations that are mostly spoken of, people will feel that they are entitled to receive from others what it is those others' duty to provide.

Drydyk provides a rationale for this symmetrical system of rights and duties: the vulnerability and needs of individuals and groups. We are all vulnerable to various kinds of harm. We can be physically injured in accidents. We can have insufficient resources to provide for our nourishment and shelter. We may lack parental or family support. We may be subjugated and exploited by more powerful individuals or groups. Because these conditions are harmful to us, it is natural to feel that we should be protected from them. Accordingly, among the Akan people that Drydyk is alluding to, people feel themselves under an obligation to provide others with assistance in, and protection from, such harms. Further, given the symmetry between duties and rights, people will feel that they have a right to such protection. Accordingly, Drydyk believes that "calling for a human right to something is calling for social protection against standard threats that exemplify a particular type of danger for humans" (1997: 163).[7] Other theorists, such as Bryan Turner (2006), have also called attention to the link between rights and human vulnerability (see also Nickel 2004). Turner's argument is that we have evolved institutions through our history in order to protect us from the dangers to which we are vulnerable. These institutions are based on a prior sociability, which forms a society or community and which gives expression to values such as caring and sympathy. This inchoate level of social solidarity provides the motivation for establishing more formal institutions, including that of human rights, which give juridical expression to it. But these suggestions take us from the task of legitimating rights to the task of justifying them.

A philosophical justification for human rights

Although it goes a long way towards establishing the reality or validity of human rights in pragmatic and positivist terms, legitimation is not enough. Even if the concept of human rights and the list of which of them are basic has been positively legitimated, we still need to see if they can be justified. We need to understand and justify the existence of the so-called "fundamental human rights" that are the yardstick against which laws and the actions of governments and other agencies are morally evaluated. The UDHR has a preamble that affirms that "the inherent dignity and the equal and inalienable rights of all members of the human family is the foundation of freedom, justice and peace in the world" (United Nations 1948). What justifies this claim that everyone in the human family has rights? We can highlight the problem by formulating two contrasting questions:

- is a permission to do something or an entitlement to a good a right because the law establishes it as a right; or
- does (or should) the law establish that permission or entitlement as a right because people have a right to it?

Positivists would answer the first question in the affirmative, while most philosophical theorists of rights would pursue the second question. And this pursuit entails the need to justify the concept of a right in intrinsically normative terms.

To highlight this need, let us recall an example that occurred in Australia not long ago. There was a shooting of a number of innocent tourists at a historical site in Tasmania called Port Arthur. A deranged gunman had opened fire without any apparent reason. Soon after, the Australian government changed the law that permitted most people to own and carry guns so that having a gun became highly restricted and subject to licence conditions. Many sporting shooters around Australia were outraged and bumper stickers appeared on cars saying, "People have a right to own and use guns", or words to that effect. The sporting shooters were making a rights claim. What was the basis for such a claim? Various arguments were offered about the harmlessness of sports shooting, the need to protect life and property against criminals and the freedom to do whatever would not harm others. In the USA such debates also refer to a historical tradition of standing up against despotic rule, but this argument is less telling in Australia. However, I suspect that these arguments are but covers for what really matters: that shooting things for sport is something that many people are very keen on doing. They strongly want to do this and to be able to own and carry guns in order to do it. They were outraged when the law was changed so as to make it extremely difficult to continue their hobby and very upset that a well-established lifestyle and recreational choice would no longer be available to them. It seems, then, that their claim was based on a strong desire to do the thing being claimed and a very strong disappointment at no longer being able to do it easily. If I am right in this suspicion, then it was the strength of their desire and disappointment that led them to make their claim in terms of a right. In this context, "I have a right to carry guns" means little more than "I very strongly want to carry guns".

John Stuart Mill (1806–1873), who, like most utilitarians, was very suspicious of the concept of rights, analysed it in just this way. People are apt to talk about rights, he said, when they want something very intensely or are extremely upset about something being taken away from them (1987). It was clear to him that very strongly wanting something is not a justification for claiming to have a right to it.[8] The reason for this is simple. When you claim the right to something you are claiming that someone else or some other agency has a duty to provide it to you or to protect you in your possession of it. But does very strongly wanting something give someone else a duty to provide it, to permit you to have it or to protect you in having it? Is the Australian government under an obligation to permit widespread gun ownership just because a number of people, no matter how many, strongly want it? A government has to consider social consequences such as public safety, the risk of guns falling into the hands of criminals and perhaps even the welfare of the animals that would be hunted. It is under no obligation to accede to a request just because what is requested is desired or insisted on very strongly. Strong desire or disappointment, therefore, provides no justification for rights claims. Because Mill thought that we should confine our ethical thinking to what people want and would make them happy – to what he called "utility" – he concluded that rights were spurious.

However, the problem with confining our ethical thinking to what we want – and this is a problem with the concept of "utility" more generally – is that it takes people's preferences at face value and urges us to satisfy as many of them as possible without distinguishing those preferences that are for things necessary to a dignified human life from those that are for superfluous things that we merely desire. Without this distinction the ethical demand to maximize utility is too indiscriminate. It can lead only to injustices where the preferences of the many are given priority over the vital needs of the few (Wiggins 2005). We need to be able to distinguish things we merely want from things we have a right to. And we need to be able to justify any claims that we have such rights.

Cosmopolitans would argue that such justifications need to be offered in terms that would be acceptable to all the peoples of the world irrespective of their cultural traditions and systems of belief. If basic human rights are said to be universal, their justification must be universally acceptable. Accordingly, in justifying human rights I may not appeal to divine commands, a transcendent human nature or any abstract notions that arise from specific cultures, political traditions or religions and that could therefore not be accepted universally. For example, I may not appeal to the theories of the ancient Greeks, who taught that we were invested with an immortal and rational soul that marked us off from the animals. Christianity went on to teach that God created us with a human essence or nature and, indeed, with a destiny or purpose, which was to achieve union with him. Once again, it was through our souls that this destiny could be fulfilled. We have already noted how Christianity acquired from the ancient Greeks a conception of "natural law", which was the embodiment, in nature, of the rational will of God or of the cosmos itself. This law dictated what we should do by declaring that every kind of thing should (or causally would, in the case of animals without free will) fulfil its own inherent and distinctive purpose. Even so recent a thinker as the Catholic philosopher Jacques Maritain

(1882–1973), who had some involvement in the drafting of the UDHR, said that:

> possessed of a nature, being constituted in a given, determinate fashion, man obviously possesses ends which correspond to his natural constitution and which are the same for all – as all pianos, for instance, whatever their particular type and in whatever spot they may be, have as their end the production of certain attuned sounds.
>
> (1986: 140–41, quoted in Mahoney 2007: 128)

The idea here is that either God or biological evolution has given us distinct purposes and goals that it is morally incumbent on us to pursue. However, the advance of modern science, with its rejection of teleological explanations, has led to the abandonment of such views. Accordingly, the concept of a universal human nature has also come to be regarded with suspicion. We need a less metaphysical and more widely accepted basis for human rights.

Gillian Brock (2005) has suggested that the most distinctive, fundamental and universal feature that we have as human beings is that we are agents. This is not a metaphysical feature but one that anyone anywhere could understand in common-sense terms. We do things voluntarily on the basis of deliberation and choice. Accordingly, we have a basic need for anything that is necessary for human agency. In so far as agency involves bodily activity consequent on deliberation or choice, it requires physical and mental health, a degree of security, a sufficient level of understanding of what one is choosing between and a certain amount of freedom to act. Moreover, one will need some social relationships to support one in one's action. These are conditions that we do not merely desire, but also need. Accordingly, it can be argued that we are justified in claiming them as rights.

I would develop this argument one step further by pointing to a feature of human existence that is even more basic than agency. The least metaphysical basis for postulating human rights is that all human beings (or at least all mature human beings with no serious abnormal disabilities) display "subjectivity". Subjectivity is that feature of human existence – manifest in our ability to think, to reflect and to make choices – that is the basis for not only agency, but also for the rational critique of the social conditions in which agency is exercised. I have already alluded to Frankfurt's analysis of human freedom as the ability to reflect on and change our preferences and desires. We can desire to change our desires. Subjectivity contains this capacity for reflection. This is not to be confused with the notion of "autonomy", which many theorists use to ground a theory of human rights.[9] Autonomy might be defined as the ability that many people have to create their own life plans and live by them without unjustified hindrance from others. However, this seems to me to be a Western liberal ideal more directly consistent with individualism than with the communitarianism inherent in many traditional forms of life. I shall discuss this further in Chapter 5. My use of the notion of subjectivity points to something at once more basic, less socially constructed and more universal. For human beings many actions are voluntary rather than instinctual or caused reactions to stimuli. Although we do many things as a result of instinct, reflex or routine, we also deliberate about what we might do or reflect afterwards about how we might have done things differently (Ricoeur 1966). Even in the most traditional societies, everyone is a subject who can reflect on his or her own preferences and make decisions as to how to act and what to do within the framework constituted by the community and its traditions. Subjectivity is a necessary condition for any form of human experience at all. It comes to expression in thought and action. Even thoughts and actions that display a high degree of conformity to community norms will be voluntary rather than caused and will be "owned" by the subject who thinks or performs them on the basis of their ability to reflect on them. From these unexceptional considerations we can deepen Brock's point that to live as a human being requires that we be able to enjoy those conditions that would allow us to act voluntarily and to reflect on our existence. Our subjectivity renders any social conditions that prevent us from reflecting on our circumstances and seeking to improve them on the basis of such reflection unjustifiable. It is in this capacity for reflection and change that our dignity as human beings consists.[10]

Because the view that human beings can act from choice and can own their actions and their choices through reflection is not a view that depends on metaphysical doctrines about human nature or about God and the universe, it is readily and universally understandable. It is an observation available to anyone who can reflect on their existence and on the fact that we make choices and require certain conditions to be enabled to do so. But how does it follow that we have a *right* to these conditions? Why are we entitled to them rather than just urgently desirous of them?

The conditions necessary for choice, voluntary action and reflection are not just desired in order to live our lives as human beings, but are *needed*. The importance of the notion of "need" is that, once we establish what we need in order to live as a human being, we can conclude that we have a right to have these needs fulfilled. We have this right because only in this way can the fundamental features of human existence be established and protected.[11] Accordingly we have to develop a theory of basic human needs and then argue that basic human rights stem from them. What is it about us that could help define some of our needs as fundamental or basic?[12] What needs do human beings have universally by virtue just of being human beings? It would seem that to define which of our needs are basic we need to have some conception of human nature after all.

Let us explore this matter by using an analogy. I had occasion to visit China in 1978 and was taken to a zoo in a regional city. It was a very old-fashioned zoo in which animals were kept in small cages. One such animal was a male tiger, which was being kept in a cage that measured about five metres by four metres. The cage had a concrete floor, bars on three sides, a tin roof and a little hut-like enclosure against the back wall. There was an opening in the back wall big enough for the animal to pass through and which was also used to introduce food into the cage. The tiger, when I saw it, was lying half asleep against the bars. I found the spectacle deeply depressing. It seemed to me that there was something profoundly wrong with the conditions in which this tiger was living. It could be argued that these conditions were morally wrong (see Taylor 1986), but this is not an argument that I will pursue here. It is enough to note my impression that there was something unpleasant or inappropriate in the way in which the animal was being kept.

It is not difficult to understand why I might have had this impression. Like most people in the West (but perhaps not in China), I have seen my fair share of nature documentaries narrated by David Attenborough or other naturalists that portray how tigers and other animals live in the wild. It is clear from such popular programmes, and even more importantly from scientific field studies engaged in by ethologists, that tigers in the wild move about freely in their forest environments, hunt other animals, congregate in packs, fight with other males either in play or for access to females, mate and lie basking on the moist ground in the afternoon sun. These kinds of activities are engaged in by male tigers in the wild. It is natural to them to behave in that way. You might say that it is in their nature to behave in that way. Ethologists will tell us that this is not quite accurate: their behaviour is somewhat shaped by their environment. But if the environment is the one to which natural selection has fitted them, then that is how tigers behave in such environments. It makes sense to capture this idea by saying that it is in the nature of tigers to act this way or that they act this way because of their nature. However, the Chinese caged tiger certainly did not behave in these ways. Because it was in a severely restricted environment, its patterns of behaviour were also severely restricted and it appeared to an observer to be listless and lacking in stimulation. Of course, it might be said that this is behaviour that fits it to its restricted environment and that this reaction to that environment is also natural to the tiger. It is out of its nature that it reacts to these restrictions and to this lack of stimulation by being listless. But my key point is that, because it is a wild animal, the conditions that are optimal for it and in which it can behave in the ways that are fully consistent with its nature are those of the wild forest in which there are spaces in which it can roam, animals on which it can prey and other tigers with whom it can associate and mate.

Given this analysis of what we might call "tiger nature", it will not be difficult to see what is wrong with locking up a tiger in a concrete and iron cage. The caged tiger will not be enabled to fulfil its nature as a tiger by running about freely, hunting in packs, mating and so forth. Its circumstances prevent it from engaging in the kind of activity that is optimal for it, given its nature. Its circumstances frustrate the fulfilment of its tiger nature. And we feel that this is wrong in an important sense.

Notice that this analysis does not depend on it being the case that the tiger is suffering in any obvious way. The caged tiger is not in pain. It is not starving. Indeed, it might be thought that it has an easy life. It is fed regularly. It is sheltered. We can assume that it receives all the veterinary attention necessary to stay healthy. It might even be able to participate in the zoo's controlled mating programme so that the zoo can have tiger cubs to show its visitors. We can assume that it does not pine for life in the wild in anything like the self-conscious ways that we might if we were in similar circumstances. This tiger might have been born in the zoo and have no experience of life in the wild. On the other hand, if it had been captured in the forest, we can assume that it does not have the kind of conscious memory that would now lead it to be depressed because of its being aware that it has lost its freedom. Even if tigers have some kind of mental life, I would assume that they cannot have a desire for life in the wild. This would be true because, on even the most generous assumptions about animal consciousness, a tiger cannot desire something that it has not experienced or that it cannot now remember experiencing. The object of an animal's desire needs to be more immediately present to it than that. What this tiger can desire is only what is available to it in its caged condition. It cannot have the same range of desires that a wild tiger has. In this way we can conclude that the caged tiger is not suffering the frustration of any of its occurrent desires. And yet the animal seemed to be listless and even, if I may be somewhat anthropomorphic, depressed. My claim would be that this is because the life that is possible for it in its cage is a highly reduced life for a tiger. It is a life that does not contain the possibilities that the life of tigers in the wild contains: the life that is in accord with the nature of tigers.

Notice too that this analysis of what is wrong with caging tigers in the way that Chinese zoo keepers did in 1978 does not depend on any metaphysical views about the nature of tigers. There is no argument that suggests, for example, that God has given tigers a certain nature and that it is therefore our responsibility to ensure that tigers can live in accordance with that nature. Nor is there a theory that says that tigers have a certain kind of soul: a soul, let us say, that makes them fit for, or predisposes them towards, roaming, hunting, fighting over mates and mating. These kinds of theory would depend on theoretical postulations of a "nature" that arises from some metaphysical entity or other. These would be speculations that do not depend on observation of the animals but on theological or philosophical constructions that are imposed on the phenomena from a purely theoretical or *a priori* perspective. In contrast, my idea of a tiger nature, or of a natural set of ways for tigers to behave, is based on empirical observations. Ethologists have studied the animals in the wild environments to which the evolutionary processes have fitted them – as opposed to studying them in captivity where their behaviour would be untypical for their species – and have discovered what their natural patterns of behaviour are.

In so far as my story contains an argument to the effect that it is wrong or inappropriate to keep tigers in cages because of their nature as tigers, it might be said to fall foul of the "fact–value" or "is–ought" distinction. This distinction was famously drawn by David Hume, who used it to argue that we cannot validly draw any inferences from factual statements expressed with a verb that operates grammatically like "is" to value statements expressed with a verb that operates grammatically like "ought". How this argument works can be illustrated with reference to my example. I have said that it is in the nature of tigers to roam, hunt, mate and so on. A great deal of factual data from the science of ethology bears this out. A further factual premise in the argument is that small concrete cages do not allow tigers to roam, hunt, mate and so on. And then I have concluded that it is wrong to keep tigers in small concrete cages. We can express this conclusion by saying that one ought not to keep tigers in such cages. But this is a value conclusion drawn from factual premises and is thus, according to Hume, an invalid inference.

However, I maintain that the inference is valid. I argue that to say that it is in the nature of *A* (where *A* is a living thing) to do *X* is already and immediately to say that *A* should be enabled to do *X*. To argue this case it is necessary to explore the word "nature" somewhat more fully. The concept of *A*'s nature involves the concept of what kinds of things *A* wants to do or is disposed to do (call them "*X*") in whatever environment is natural to it. (The word "want" here need not refer to any occurrent desire of which *A* is conscious; it can refer to a disposition or an unconscious inclination.) Accordingly, it implies that *A*'s not being able or permitted to do *X* is a frustration of its wants or dispositions. On the further premise that the frustration of *A*'s natural wants and dispositions is an evil, it can be concluded that such frustrations should not occur and should not be brought about by a morally responsible agent. The key to the argument, therefore, is that the concept of nature, as it is used in the example, is both factual and normative. It expresses both facts about a species of animal, and indicates optimal conditions for the way of life of that species of animal. That such conditions are optimal for animals of that kind is not only a fact, but also a value that, *prima facie*, makes it incumbent on any being that is in a position to take the relevant responsibility to ensure that those conditions obtain to the maximum degree possible given other moral imperatives and values that might also be applicable to the matter at hand. If "nature" were a value-neutral term, then we could say that it is just as much in the nature of a tiger to lie listlessly in a small cage – given the link between behaviour and environment – as it is for the tiger to be running freely in the wild. But we do not say this. We acknowledge that the caged behaviour, while in some sense caused by the interaction between the animal's nature and its environment, is not as "good" for the animal as would be its behaviour in the wild. The latter is "good" because it is consistent with the nature of tigers in the way that the former is not. We can conclude from this story, then, that tigers, as a species, have a "nature" in a non-metaphysical sense, and that this nature can ground norms for how tigers should be treated and what they should be enabled to do.

Notice that, although this argument bears some similarity to "natural law", it is, in fact, somewhat different. What the natural law tradition argues is that, given the nature of a thing, it has an obligation to pursue that nature. To illustrate this we need to refer to human beings since the notion of duty does not apply readily to animals. For example, it is argued that, given that human beings have a natural aversion to death, they are obliged to preserve life and have a duty to maintain their own lives and forbear from taking the lives of others. If you add to this way of thinking the notion that God created human nature, then those moral duties become absolute because they express the will of God. On this theory, human nature gives rise to duties to do what nature indicates we have a tendency or inclination to do. This is the kind of inference from "is" to "ought" that Hume impugned. However, my argument is not that nature gives rise to duties in the being that has that nature. It is that the nature of a being gives rise to duties in others to treat that being in accordance with its nature. In my argument from "is" to "ought" I move from the nature of a being to what it should be enabled to do, rather than to what it has a duty to do. I have developed the tiger analogy at some length because it shows us how to draw the appropriate moral inferences from the claim that human beings also have a universal – albeit non-metaphysical – nature.

Human nature

This claim has been defended by Martha Nussbaum. Inspired by Aristotle, Nussbaum draws on literature, legends and stories from a number of cultural traditions to identify the aspects of human living and concerns of human beings that seem to be present in all cultures (1992; see also Nussbaum 1998). These become the aspects of life that will make that life count as a human life. They are the basic aspects of human existence.[13] Nussbaum is not trying to describe human beings in the way that biologists might when they classify species. Rather, she explores the self-expression of human beings in various cultures in order to highlight the problems of human existence that all of them come to deal with in one way or another. In this way she builds up a conception of human living, with all its challenges and aspirations, that seems to be applicable to all human beings. The features of human living that are most salient include: our sense of mortality; our embodiment, with its attendant needs for food, shelter, sexual expression and mobility; our capacity for feeling pleasure and pain; our ability to perceive the world and to think and imagine; the fact that we are born as helpless infants; our ability, up to a point, to plan our own lives and conceive of our goals; our inclination to form bonds with others and to live peaceably with them; our interrelation with other animals and with nature; our ability to laugh and to play; and our being the subjects of our own experiences. This list is not exhaustive and different people will stress some over others. Moreover, cultures will pursue these concerns and issues in various ways. The differences between cultures and historical epochs are differences in how these aspects of life are formed and structured in specific times and places. But the claim is that, whatever these differences might be, they are the differential formations given to these fundamental aspects of human life. A life that lacks these features in some form will hardly be a human life. It would be a life that lacks human dignity.

The conclusion that Nussbaum draws from this sketch of the universal concerns of human existence echoes the conclusion that I drew from my sketch of the natural life of tigers in the wild: they should be enabled to live in that way. If this list, or something like it, is a description of those aspects of a life that give that life the quality of humanity or of human dignity, then it immediately follows that it would be wrong to deny to any human being the opportunity to live out those concerns. Indeed, Nussbaum draws a stronger conclusion. She argues that not only should human beings be left free to pursue those aspects of life, but they should also be enabled to. This means that others should not only forbear from interfering in their pursuit of these aspects of life, but they should also provide the means in cases where such means are lacking. This point will have considerable implications for public policy on both a national and an international level. I shall explore these later. For the moment, we should note that this enlargement of the scope of what should be done on the basis of a description of what constitutes a dignified human life, and from what human beings should be permitted to do, to what they should be enabled to do leads Nussbaum to speak of "capabilities". Her argument is that whatever social institutions and cultural contexts human beings find themselves in, they should have the capability to pursue the concerns that typify human living.

Nussbaum has developed a number of versions of a list of ten such capabilities. In 1999 she articulated the list in this way:

1. *Life.* Being able to live to the end of a human life of normal length, not dying prematurely or before one's life is so reduced as to be not worth living.
2. *Bodily health and integrity.* Being able to have good health, including reproductive health; being adequately nourished; being able to have adequate shelter.
3. *Bodily integrity.* Being able to move freely from place to place; being able to be secure against violent assault, including sexual assault, marital rape, and domestic violence; having opportunities for sexual satisfaction and for choice in matters of reproduction.
4. *Senses, imagination, thought.* Being able to use the senses; being able to imagine, to think, and to reason – and to do these things in a "truly human" way, a way informed and cultivated by an adequate education, including, but by no means limited to, literacy and basic mathematical and scientific training; being able to use imagination and thought in connection with experiencing and producing expressive works and events of one's own choice (religious, literary, musical, etc.); being able to use one's mind in ways protected by guarantees of freedom of expression with respect to both political and artistic speech and freedom of religious exercise; being able to have pleasurable experiences and to avoid nonbeneficial pain.
5. *Emotions.* Being able to have attachments to things and persons outside ourselves; being able to love those who love and care for us; being able to grieve at their absence; in general, being able to love, to grieve, to experience longing, gratitude, and justified anger; not having one's emotional development blighted by fear or anxiety. (Supporting this capability means supporting forms of human association that can be shown to be crucial in their development.)
6. *Practical reason.* Being able to form a conception of the good and to engage in critical reflection about the planning of one's own life. (This entails protection for the liberty of conscience.)
7. *Affiliation.* (a) Being able to live for and in relation to others, to recognize and show concern for other human beings, to engage in various forms of social interaction; being able to imagine the situation of another and to have compassion for that situation; having the capability for both

justice and friendship. (Protecting this capability means, once again, protecting institutions that constitute such forms of affiliation, and also protecting the freedoms of assembly and political speech.) (b) Having the social bases of self-respect and non-humiliation; being able to be treated as a dignified being whose worth is equal to that of others. (This entails provisions of non-discrimination.)

8. *Other species*. Being able to live with concern for and in relation to animals, plants, and the world of nature.
9. *Play*. Being able to laugh, to play, to enjoy recreational activities.
10. *Control over one's environment*. (a) *Political*: being able to participate effectively in political choices that govern one's life; having the rights of political participation, free speech, and freedom of association. (b) *Material*: being able to hold property (both land and movable goods); having the right to seek employment on an equal basis with others; having the freedom from unwarranted search and seizure. In work, being able to work as a human being, exercising practical reason and entering into meaningful relationships of mutual recognition with other workers. (1999: 41)[14]

Nussbaum insists that her list of capabilities is not contingent on what specific people actually want. She claims that her list is objective in the sense that it does not depend on what people actually seek or desire. The list identifies capabilities the exercise of which constitutes human dignity. Nussbaum insists that all of these capabilities are necessary and none should be sacrificed for the sake of enhancing any of the others. Nor does she specify how these capabilities should be exercised. Item 2, for example speaks of nourishment. Everyone should be able to secure for themselves adequate nourishment and be helped in doing so if they cannot manage it for themselves. But it is still open to any individual to choose what they will eat or even to refuse nourishment. They may have religious reasons for being on a fast, or they may be suicidal. There is no suggestion that anyone should be forced to take nourishment or should be required to eat a particular kind of food. It is required only that they should be free to do so and made capable of doing so.

Further, local cultural traditions should not inhibit these capabilities even when those subject to those traditions seem to be compliant. Any non-exercise of those capabilities should be freely chosen by that agent rather than enforced by the guardians of the tradition. There should be public and unforced reasoning in any given culture about how the capabilities should be exercised in that culture. Nussbaum avoids specifying any particular form of life that people might choose for themselves. Some people may develop an individualistic form of life, while others will conform to the norms of their communities. It is important, however, that all people have the opportunity to influence the communal forms that their societies take.

One capability that is largely absent from Nussbaum's description of a good human life is religion. Despite basing her description on an analysis of the cultural productions and literatures of many peoples, Nussbaum seems to have downplayed an obvious fact: most people in most parts of the world are religious.[15] We in the West may have developed a more secular mode of social existence and separated church from state, but the vast majority of humankind sees religious faith as integral to every aspect of their lives. As an Aristotelian thnker, Nussbaum is well placed to understand this since Aristotle's description of the four aspects of human functioning whose fulfilment constitutes our happiness – the so-called four parts of the soul – includes the activity of contemplation. Contemplation is thinking about the eternal things that we cannot change through our own practical reason or agency. These include the gods, the laws of nature and the truths of mathematics. Although this is a heterogeneous list, I would suggest that this is the level of our existence in which our spiritual concerns find their place, along with our non-instrumental curiosity about the nature of reality. What Aristotle is suggesting is that contemplation and speculation about eternal things is as important a part of human life as exercising our practical intelligence in the pursuit of our worldly goals. Whether our spiritual or contemplative quest is met through belief in a system of religious doctrines and commitment to a god, or whether it is met through a sense of awe and reverence at the wonder of life and the world, we all pursue an overarching conception of reality through which we can give an all-embracing meaning to our lives. Whether that reality is immanent in the world or transcendent to it is immaterial to the reality of the urge that we all have to attach ourselves to it. We do not live by bread alone. Even an atheist has commitments that transcend the givens of everyday life. My claim would be that religious or spiritual commitments, conceived very broadly, should be added to the list of features that give dignity to human life. Nussbaum makes no mention of this in her 1992 list of capabilities (1992: 222) and mentions it in Item 4 of the list above only in so far as it relates to our ability to use our minds and to freely express ourselves. Accordingly, I think we should add an eleventh capability: the ability to conceive of an overarching conception of value that would give significance to human life, and the freedom to engage in any rituals or practices that express a commitment to that conception and that do not harm others. There may be many who think that religious commitments are inherently irrational, but this would be a particular cultural perspective and it denies the apparent importance that religion plays in the lives of most of the world's peoples. However, to say that there might be more capabilities that human beings should exercise in order to live a dignified human life is not to undermine the argument for basic human rights that can be derived from Nussbaum's list.

There is another doubt that might be raised about the list. If it offers a description of what human beings do and the concerns they have so as to posit a human nature, then it might be asked why unpleasant and unfortunate aspects of human life are left out. Aggression and competitiveness seem to be universal features of human life. The recent defeat of communist countries in the cold war might signal the fact that human beings are inherently self-seeking and greedy and cannot adjust to a form of life in which mutual concern and sharing are espoused as communal values (however imperfectly they are realized in history), or it might show that human beings want to exercise control over their own lives rather than live in a totally planned and non-participatory political structure. Either way, it suggests that self-seeking and competitiveness are inescapable features of human existence. In the same way the frequency of war might be thought to suggest the inevitability of aggression. Perhaps any comprehensive list of features of human life should include aggression, competitiveness and self-assertion. However, what I would suggest is that, if such features were to be on the list, they should appear not as capabilities the exercise of which should be protected or enabled by social institutions, but as capabilities the exercise of which others should be protected from. These features of human existence point to the need for social structures that protect people from the predations of others. As Drydyk (1997) and Turner (2006) point out, the concept of human rights that such structures are designed to protect will be central to designing and implementing humane social institutions.

Nussbaum's argument is not only epistemologically universal in the sense that it draws on human self-understandings from around the world, but it is also normatively universal in the sense that its practical conclusions should be applied to all without distinction. It is not a set of capabilities that only men should be enabled to exercise. It is not a list of capabilities that only light-skinned people should be enabled to exercise. It is not a list of capabilities that only Brahmins should be enabled to exercise. It is not a list of capabilities that only Protestants should be enabled to exercise. It is not a list of capabilities that only people who are not disabled should be enabled to exercise. It is not a list of capabilities that only people taller than ninety centimetres should be enabled to exercise. I include that last sentence because to say otherwise would be patently absurd. A person's height is not a relevant factor in deciding how that person should be treated in relation to the eleven capabilities (although it might be in relation to choosing a basketball team). Any non-application of the norm that everyone should be capable of exercising those functions must be justified on relevant grounds and a cosmopolitan would argue that race, ethnicity, caste, religion, nationality, sexual preference and political affiliation are not relevant grounds for making such discriminations. There is not a white nature and a black nature. There is not a European nature and an Asian nature. There is not a Catholic nature and a Buddhist nature. There is only one human nature. The features and concerns that characterize human life are common to all cultural and social formations of that nature. Accordingly the normative requirement on social arrangements and human interactions that people be able to exercise their human capabilities applies equally to all.

It is this last point that forges the link between Nussbaum's thesis and the discourse of rights. The argument has the following structure:

[1] Describe human nature in terms of what would give dignity and worth to a human life by fulfilling that nature.
[2] Note that this description is normative in the way that my description of the tiger's nature was normative.
[3] Conclude from 1 and 2 that all people should be enabled to exercise the human capabilities given in that description.
[4] Assert that people need the resources to exercise those capabilities rather than just wanting them (and need them even when they do not express a want for them).
[5] Conclude from 3 and 4 that social institutions and individuals should not prevent the exercise of the listed human capabilities and should provide whatever assistance or resources that are needed for such exercise. This step derives obligations from needs without specifying who carries those obligations. It is open to different cultures and societies to meet them in differing ways.
[6] Note that obligations and rights are symmetrical.
[7] Conclude from 5 and 6 that all human beings have a right to the freedom and the necessary resources to exercise the capabilities central to human dignity. In so far as there is an obligation – not yet allocated to anyone in particular – to meet the needs of people so that they can exercise the capabilities described above and so live a human life of minimal dignity, so all people have a right to have those needs met.

Nussbaum herself does not highlight the concept of rights and does not move to steps 6 and 7. However, it will be clear that such steps can be taken. To exercise the capabilities on her list and any other capabilities necessary for human dignity requires the provision of resources, freedoms (Sen 1999; see also Alkire 2005) and other social goods. Accordingly, such resources, freedoms and other social goods will be things for which people have a fundamental or basic need. The meeting of basic human needs is a necessary condition for attaining a life of human dignity. But the argument does not move directly from asserting that human beings have basic needs – as opposed to urgent wants – to concluding that they have a right to have those needs met. It moves from the fact that all people have basic needs to asserting that other people or agencies have responsibilities for meeting those needs. By focusing on human needs and human vulnerability, the argument appeals to our sympathy and fellow feeling – contingent and fragile as these might be – in order to ground our obligations towards those who are in need. Global human solidarity and the feelings of humanity described by Hume make it obligatory for those who can do so to meet the vital needs of others. If it is correct that we have responsibilities and obligations to others because those others have needs that only we can meet, and if it is true that our obligations and their rights are symmetrical, then it follows that those others have a right to have us meet their basic needs. It is not the case that we have those obligations because they have those rights. Rather, they have those rights because we have those obligations. In this way, the reality of human rights is founded on the more fundamental concepts of obligation and duty towards others in the way that it is in many cultures around the world, such as the Akan people of West Africa mentioned above.

Conclusion

This argument gives us a universal basis for acknowledging as a basic human obligation our duty to enable people to exercise the capabilities necessary for a life of human dignity, and for claiming as a human right the freedoms and resources needed to exercise those capabilities. There is a universal set of needs that all human beings have for the resources and freedoms that will enable them to exercise those capabilities that are essential for a dignified human life. But how did I move from saying that all people have such needs to saying that all people are *entitled* to have those needs met? I appealed to a non-metaphysical but normative conception of human nature. I argued that all people should be able to exercise their human capabilities because they are the way in which they express their natures as human beings. Given our common humanity, this gives us all an obligation to assist others to exercise those capabilities. This point also involves the principles of impartiality and of equality. In so far as all people have such a nature as is expressed in the exercise of those capabilities, all people equally should be permitted to live a dignified human life by exercising them. All people are equal in having a right to having those needs met. It is our obligation to meet those needs impartially that grounds the human rights of others. These arguments justify the according of human rights to all human beings globally.

But the political reality of basic human rights and of the obligations that go with them resides in the positive, quasi-legal pronouncements of those rights on the part of the UN and its agencies and on the struggles for such rights that individuals and communities have engaged in through history. It is these that legitimate them, while it is philosophical arguments that justify them. It is such activist and positivist legitimations that have established the global respect for basic human rights as universally normative. Moreover, in so far as the UDHR is universal in its reach, it acknowledges the moral equality of all peoples and individuals. And so does my argument justifying the reality of basic human rights. It appeals to needs that all people have. In this way, too, my argument shows respect for the peoples of the world as united by reason, sociability and a common humanity. It identifies those capabilities, including reason and sociability, that constitute the common humanity – or common human nature – which is a premise of my argument. It is because of this common humanity that we accept the responsibility towards others that grounds their right to our assistance and protection. Lastly, in so far as this notion of a common human nature is drawn from empirical and common-sense observations about the human condition, it evinces a belief in a globally acceptable, non-metaphysical concept of human dignity.

The form of most arguments for human rights derives them directly from universal features of the human condition, whether these features are metaphysical, theoretical, *a priori* or empirical. In these arguments the obligation that others have to respect and protect human rights derives from the reality of those rights. My argument takes the opposite course. It derives the reality of human rights from the prior existence of the obligations that people have towards those who are in need. I have argued for the reality of those needs, and I have alluded to the sympathy and compassion that arise from our common humanity as a motivator for responding to those needs, but I have not said enough to establish the reality of those obligations. This will be the task of Chapter 3.

Chapter 3
Global justice

> The metaphysics of the relation with the Other is achieved in service and hospitality. In the measure that the face of someone else truly brings us into relation with the third, the metaphysical relation from me to the Other takes the form of a we, and flows into a state, institutions and law, which form the source of universality. (Levinas 1969: 300)

In this chapter we shall explore the following features of cosmopolitanism from the list I proposed in the Introduction:

(8) benevolence to all others irrespective of race, caste, nationality, religion, ethnicity or location;
(9) willingness to come to the aid of those suffering from natural or man-made disasters, including extreme poverty;
(10) commitment to justice in the distribution of natural resources and wealth on a global scale;
(11) global solidarity with struggles for human rights and social justice; and
(12) commitment to the liberalization of immigration and refugee policies.

I shall argue that a person with a cosmopolitan outlook would respond to the vital needs of others, whether they are near or far and irrespective of their nationality, race, caste, religious commitments, gender or ethnicity. The cosmopolitan outlook refuses to allow the distance, difference or anonymity of those who suffer oppression, poverty or catastrophe to obscure the responsibility we all have to respond to their needs.

Humanitarian aid

Our complacency on this matter was shaken by an article published by Peter Singer in 1972.[1] In that article Singer refers to a famine that was occurring in East Bengal (now Bangladesh) and causing many thousands of deaths through starvation. Singer argued that people in affluent countries have a moral obligation to provide assistance to the victims of such natural disasters. To argue that we have such an obligation, Singer relied on the principle that "If it is in our power to prevent something bad from happening, without thereby sacrificing anything of comparable moral importance, we ought, morally, to do it" (1972: 231). He also proposed a qualified and milder version of this principle, namely: "If it is in our power to prevent something very bad from happening, without thereby sacrificing anything morally significant, we ought, morally, to do it" (*ibid.*). He illustrates how these principles apply by imagining a scenario in which you see a child drowning in a shallow pond. It is envisaged that the pond is so shallow that saving the child involves no danger to yourself, but you would ruin your expensive clothes by wading in and saving it. The only cost to you is the ruin of your clothes. In this case you can indeed prevent something bad from happening without thereby sacrificing anything of comparable moral importance. The moral importance of your clothes is negligible compared to that of the life of the child. Therefore you ought to save it. Using the words of the milder form of the principle, we could add that you could prevent something very bad from happening without thereby sacrificing anything that is morally significant to you. On the assumption that you are a typical person in an affluent society, your clothes and the cost of cleaning them have no moral significance. The point that Singer draws from this analogy is that contributing money to the aid effort for victims of a famine such as was occurring in East Bengal is something that you ought to do. It would save lives and would involve no sacrifice of anything morally significant to you or of anything that is morally comparable to the lives you can save.

One purpose of this argument is to show that giving money for disaster relief is an obligation rather than an act of charity. Just as you are obliged to save the drowning child, so you are obliged to give to famine relief. This point is significant because, as I noted in the previous chapter, an act of charity is thought of as a "supererogatory" act. It is something that it is good to do but that we cannot be blamed for not doing. Such an act is optional from a moral point of view. If you see a busker in the street you are under no obligation to give her any money, but it is a good and admirable thing if you do. In most circumstances this would be an act of generosity that is ethically praiseworthy but not morally required. Many people think that giving money to assist victims of natural disasters is similarly generous and admirable but supererogatory. The burden of Singer's argument is to show that, if his principle is accepted, such a generous act is not just virtuous and admirable but actually obligatory. We have a duty to assist those who are suffering from dire needs such as starvation caused by famine if we can do so without sacrificing anything of comparable moral significance. Following my argument in the previous chapter that rights derive from obligations, we could draw the further conclusion that the victims of famine have a right to our assistance.

Singer goes on to defend his position from a number of possible objections or excuses that people might offer. To people who say that "charity begins at home" and that the needs of people who are close to us should take priority over those who are distant, Singer replies that there is no moral reason why the needs of a child in mortal danger from drowning in a pond that you are standing next to are any different from the needs of a child in mortal danger from starvation half a world away. It takes only a modest sum of money to save the child who is far away just as it costs only a ruined set of clothes to save the nearby child, and their needs are morally equivalent. Singer is here expressing a central tenet of the cosmopolitan worldview. The moral status of a child in need close to me is no different from the moral status of a child far away and my obligation to help in either case is therefore no different either. Nor does it matter that the distant child is Bengali while the nearby child is of my own nationality. If I can help without sacrificing anything that is morally more important, I am under an obligation to do so. Even if we did want to insist that charity begins at home, we need to acknowledge that, in a globalized world, "home" is the whole world. The media bring the sufferings of the world into our living rooms on a daily basis and the facilities provided by global communications and delivery systems make it possible to help even those who live at a great distance from us.

Some people suggest that I have less of an obligation to help if others who can help are not doing so. Since those others are not doing their duty to help the victims of the famine, why should I? Singer shows how preposterous that objection is by altering his example in such a way that there are now other people capable of saving the child standing around the pond but not helping. Would that exonerate a would-be rescuer from the responsibility of saving the child? What would we say to someone who used that argument not to save the child in the pond? Although there is often a very widespread and impressive willingness on the part of many people to help when disasters strike people around the world – the tsunami that devastated many parts of southern Asia in December 2004 is a good example – it is also true that a great many people do nothing to help. Is this fact an excuse not to help? Singer argues that it is not. He goes on to quantify the point. Suppose that starvation resulting from the famine could be avoided if everyone in affluent countries gave $5. This would mean that, given Singer's argument, everyone in affluent countries has an obligation to give $5. Others have made similar suggestions. Tom Campbell (2007: 67) has proposed what he calls a Global Humanitarian Levy. This levy would be imposed and administered by a global body and would be calculated as a function of what is needed to alleviate poverty and what affluent nations and their citizens can afford without major disruption to the lifestyles and economies of those nations. Economists are confident that such a figure could be calculated and would be small enough to be affordable for each individual. Paying such a levy would then not be overly demanding. The problem, of course, is that no such institutional arrangements are in place and, given the reluctance shown by most people in affluent countries to pay their taxes, it is likely that the costs of securing compliance would seriously jeopardize the usefulness of the amounts collected. Moreover, if recent criticisms of the World Bank and of the International Monetary Fund (IMF) are anything to go by, the political problems that would arise from deciding how to distribute the aid would be enormous. Accordingly it is unlikely that everyone would pay the $5 Singer imagines it would take to relieve world poverty if everyone pays it. Does it follow that those who are willing to give have no obligation or have an obligation to give only $5? No, says Singer, they should give an amount that actually saves lives, and if the non-generosity of others means that it requires the willing to give $50 instead of $5, then they have an obligation to give that much. That would still be an amount that, for most, does not involve a cost of comparable moral importance.

Singer's argument asks us to weigh up two things of moral value. In the initial scenario these two things are the life of a young child and a set of clothes. In this instance most people would share Singer's intuition that the life of the child is of greater moral value than the clothes. Accordingly, when we compare the moral importance of the two values at issue we opt for the life of the child. What this comparative structure of the argument asks us to do is to give a moral evaluation of the things or opportunities that we might sacrifice in order to save the lives of others. It assumes that the lives of others are of very high moral value. On the principle of the sanctity of life, we could agree that this is so, and on cosmopolitan principles we can agree that the location, ethnicity or nationality of the would-be famine victim does not detract from that value. The suffering of people who are displaced by famine or who have lost loved ones because of starvation is also of great moral significance and as this is inserted into the comparative structure of the argument it can be agreed that it will require the sacrifice of something of very great moral significance to offset the moral demands that this disvalue generates. Just as the mere ruining of my clothes is too insignificant to offset the negative value of the death of the child, so the mere loss of $5, $50 or even $500 for an affluent person is insignificant in comparison with the lives that can be saved or the suffering that can be averted for the victims of famine. Singer makes several references to the consumer societies in which many of us live in affluent countries and he seems to share the widespread view that much of what we spend our money on is frivolous and unnecessary. Another set of clothes above and beyond what we already have is of no significance. Even the loss of a car or an opportunity to go on a holiday to a luxurious resort are losses whose moral significance is minimal compared to the moral value of the lives we could save or the suffering we could avert by giving the relevant amounts of money to famine relief or other rescue efforts.

It seems then that on the stricter form of Singer's principle, and even on what he thinks of as the milder form, we have obligations to give of our resources that are very demanding. The number of people in dire need around the world is very high and their suffering is very acute. Moreover, the things that I need to spend my money on, compared to all the things I actually spend it on, are but few. Most of my spending is on clothes I do not need, cars whose quality and costs exceed my needs, trips and holidays I do not need to take, concerts, films, computer equipment, mobile phones, various gadgets and compact discs that are useful but not necessary, and so on. Accordingly, Singer argues that, on the stronger form of his principle:

> we ought to give until we reach the level of marginal utility – that is, the level at which, by giving more, I would cause as much suffering to myself or my dependants as I would relieve by my gift. This would mean, of course, that one would reduce oneself to very near the material circumstances of a Bengali refugee. (1972: 241)

This follows from the stronger principle because it calls for a simple comparison between the needful condition of the recipient of assistance and the resourced condition of the donor, and suggests that if there is no moral justification for such a difference then one should give until the difference disappears. The milder form of the principle asks us only to prevent something *very* bad from happening and calls on us to sacrifice only what is of *no* moral significance. On this version of the principle, if my giving would involve my sacrificing anything of moral significance, then I am not obliged to do it. This allows for the material circumstances of the recipient of my assistance to continue to be less than my own. On this version of the principle there could remain a difference in the distribution of benefits and resources between rich and poor since to impoverish myself or my family might indeed be a case of sacrificing something morally significant. Nevertheless, it does follow that, if most consumer spending is of no moral significance, I would not be able to claim my desire for a new

MP3 player as an excuse for not giving to the famine relief effort. Accordingly, even on the milder form of the principle, "we would have to give away enough to ensure that the consumer society, dependent as it is on people spending on trivia rather than giving to famine relief, would slow down and perhaps disappear entirely" (*ibid.*).

Demandingness

Singer's article has generated a great deal of critical philosophical discussion.[2] Many commentators have responded to it by acknowledging its cogency but by suggesting that its conclusion is too demanding. It seems to ask too much of us. It tells us we are obliged to give until we are no better off than a poor Bengali. While the milder form of the principle on which the argument is based, which asks us to give up only trivial consumption in order to help those in need, seems less demanding, this is not the conclusion that Singer embraces. He sees no reason to adopt the milder principle. By endorsing only the stronger principle, even while admitting that it leads to a moral demand that we give of our resources until we hold no benefits or advantages that the poorest recipients of our beneficence do not enjoy, Singer insists on the most demanding conclusion from the argument. Singer's immediate answer to his critics is to say that if the conclusion follows from the premises, then it must be accepted no matter how demanding it is. He challenges us to be suspicious of any response to his argument that seeks to lessen its demandingness. Such responses might be motivated by self-seeking considerations. No one likes to be told that they should give of their wealth until the access to resources and benefits enjoyed by the recipient is no less than that of the donor. No one wants to be told that they have an obligation to impoverish themselves.

Nevertheless, we might question how the argument reaches its demanding conclusion. One assumption that Singer is making is that most of our spending is on trivial consumer goods. But surely we also spend our money on goods that are of moral significance, even if they are goods that would appear to be luxurious from the point of view of a starving Bengali. When we consider our lives and all of the values that inhere in them, it turns out that they contain much more complexity than Singer allows. While we could agree that a great deal of our money is spent on consumer items whose moral value is questionable, we need to see this in the context of the only forms of life that are available to those of us who live in affluent societies. Much of what we spend money on will be felt by us as necessary. Clothes are not necessary only for covering and protecting our bodies. If they were, a simple livery with a replacement set to allow for laundering would be enough. But we need to dress in ways appropriate to many occasions. While the temptations to excessive display and subservience to fashion are real, there is no denying the need to present well in a variety of settings and thus to spend money on clothes beyond the levels that would be typical in East Bengal. Cars have also become necessary in cities in which housing developments are spread widely and public transport infrastructure has not kept pace. While better policy decisions might have been made in the past and will need to be made in the future to reduce carbon emissions, the present situation for many is that they cannot avoid spending money on cars and other forms of private transport. Further, given the responsibilities that parents have for giving their children the economic opportunities that exist in the society in which they live, spending on education cannot be limited by comparisons with the spending on education that are typical in the third world. Thanks to the opportunities that our relative affluence has given us, our cultural lives are richer than for many peoples in poorer societies past or present. We pay for and enjoy popular arts in the cinema and music, along with high arts through concerts, galleries and literature. The lives of many people are deeply enriched by consumption of cultural products or participation in artistic activities. The pursuit of knowledge, understanding and spiritual meaning also involves financial and opportunity costs. We participate in, and contribute financially to, sporting and leisure activities as well. Even eating, which is necessary for life itself, has taken on deeper social and cultural significance. Not only is there the enjoyment and cost of social meals in a variety of contexts, from working lunches to congenial dinner parties, but the art of cooking gives expression to values of both connoisseurship and love.[3]

How are the values inherent in such activities and the monetary costs that they involve to be given a moral weighting so that they can be entered into Singer's comparative schema? Even granted the triviality of much of what we spend money on aside from meeting our basic needs, are we obliged to give up all or any of the culturally and personally valuable activities and forms of consumption until such time as the victims of natural disasters can be saved from their misfortunes? There are people who do so, but perhaps they should be regarded as saints or moral heroes rather than as people who have fulfilled obligations that we all have. It will not help to say that Singer's argument is not too demanding because it asks us only to give what we have a capacity to give or what we can afford. Judgements about what we can afford and what we have a capacity to give are judgements that involve giving monetary value to the many incommensurable values that have a rightful place in our lives, and then comparing these to the lives that can be saved by the gift. But if the values are incommensurable, this cannot be done. Our capacity to give is not measurable in monetary terms. Unless we are so wealthy that a financial surplus can be clearly identified, we cannot be asked to give only what we can afford because we have no way of deciding in a morally satisfactory way what it is we can or cannot afford.

This is a specific case of the more general difficulty that attends many forms of utilitarian thinking. It is difficult to the point of impossibility to measure the utility or benefit of many courses of action and thus to compare the utility or benefit arising from one course of action with that arising from another. It may be that this systemic difficulty lessens the applicability, and thus the demandingness, of Singer's approach.

Cosmopolitanism must also face a form of this difficulty. If cosmopolitanism encourages global impartiality, it needs to compare the moral stringency of our duties to strangers with duties to those who are close to us and to whom we have what are called "particular obligations". In order to save the life of a distant child, should I give away the money that I need in order to provide an excellent education for my children? A cosmopolitan thinker would agree that distance is not relevant to the issue. Whether the child whom I can save is in the pond right in front of me or whether it is thousands of miles away is indeed irrelevant. The principle of impartiality dictates that only differences that are morally relevant should make a difference to our actions. And distance is not a morally relevant consideration because it has no impact on the moral standing of either child. However, the notion of "distance" can also be given a metaphorical meaning. A child who is in danger might be "close" to me in a sense other than a geographical one. It might be a child of which I am the father. On a very strict application of the principle of impartiality it might be suggested that even this should make no difference, but most ethicists accept that one can give greater moral value to one's own child than one gives to a stranger's child.[4] To an impartial observer the two children may be of equal moral standing, but to the father of one of them the judgement might be, and indeed ought to be, different. If the issue then becomes one of spending resources on saving the life of a distant child as opposed to spending it on the education, for example, of my own, how should the comparisons of moral value be made? Can I compare the value of the life of a distant child with the education of my own, given that the life of my own child, barring accidents or fatal illness, is assured? Given my particular obligations to my own child, the spending on my own child that is involved in this case should not be considered trivial as compared to the life of the refugee child.

To defend cosmopolitanism against the charge that it unreasonably insists on the morally equal status of one's own children with distant children, it might be argued that one's moral relationship with one's own children and family members is not of the same kind as one's moral relationship with distant peoples and their children. I spoke in the previous chapter of a global framework of justice in which all people have an equal status and in which the principle of impartiality should apply to them equally. Justice focuses on what we *owe* to others. The concept entails that others have rights or deserts in the light of which they should receive what they are entitled to. In the context of criminal law, convicted felons should receive the punishments that they deserve and that fit the crimes they committed. Moreover, they should receive no punishment if they are not guilty. In the field of distributive justice – a field that is of greater relevance to us here – people should receive what they are entitled to or deserve. If someone contributes a significant amount of good to the community through their work, they should be paid for it. In paid employment, people should be paid amounts that are commensurate with the amount of effort they put in or the level of skill that is required. Social and institutional arrangements should ensure that the distribution of wealth is proportional to what people deserve, and they should be reformed if the rich are getting richer while the poor are getting poorer. This reference to what people are entitled to or deserve also shows the link between the concept of justice and that of rights. A situation or social arrangement can be considered just if it secures the rights of all those involved in it. If a person's rights are violated by an arrangement, that arrangement can be said to be unjust.[5]

But the framework of justice is not the only moral framework that we live in. We also live in a framework of caring in which we are tied to others through bonds of love, affection or concern. In this moral framework the status of another person is defined by their relationship to me, whether it is as my wife, my child, my cousin or my friend. In this framework we do not do things for others because we feel that it is our obligation to do so, but because we care enough about the other to be motivated to do so. If I visit my friend in hospital because it was my impartial obligation to do so, I would be insensitive to the quality of the relationship between us. If my friend came to believe that I had visited him out of a sense of duty, he would not take as much comfort from my visit as he would if he felt I had done so out of my caring about him (Stocker 1976). On the basis of such considerations, many philosophers distinguish the particular obligations that are based on caring relationships and other appropriate loyalties from our obligations to the distant needy that are based on justice, and argue that the kinds of moral value involved in either case are incommensurable.

For example, Appiah (2006: ch. 10) espouses what he calls a "partial cosmopolitanism", which acknowledges particular loyalties as well as accepting global responsibilities. According to Appiah (2005: 228ff.), a cosmopolitan understanding of justice as giving to each what they are entitled to should not confuse us into thinking that cosmopolitanism has to do only with the distribution of goods. Certainly, the framework of justice enjoins us to treat all others equitably. When it comes to the distribution of goods we should give to each person what they deserve or need as judged impartially. But the distribution of goods is a task that does not exhaust our moral obligations to others. We also have to give others what is their due as our friends, or compatriots, or members of other forms of identity groupings. This may involve activities that acknowledge or forge forms of solidarity with, loyalty to and affection for people with whom we have a variety of identity-forming relationships. This kind of activity should not be assimilated to the distribution of goods that is central to the framework of justice. The impartialist and cosmopolitan norms of distribution that apply to the latter do not apply to the former. Indeed, Appiah suggests that the task of distributing goods, especially social goods, falls on the state and other social institutions, while individuals often do good to each other under a different rubric. This rubric is what has been called "the ethic of caring".[6]

The ethic of caring

The ethic of caring embraces all those actions that we perform for the benefit of others out of feelings such as love, affection, concern, sympathy, loyalty or compassion. It is not motivated so much by a sense of duty as by feelings of solidarity and sympathy. These motivations are strongest in relation to people whom I love, and extend to all people with whom I have some kind of personal relationship. Indeed, on Appiah's account, they extend to everyone with whom I have "identity-forming" relationships such as compatriots, co-religionists, people who share my ethnicity, and anyone else with whom or with whose community I identify. In so far as I draw my identity from such groupings I shall care about their members. The key to this ethic is that I am motivated to help others not out of a sense of duty, but out of concern for them.

The problem with this ethic is that it does not seem to be universal. It apparently confines itself to those with whom I have the relevant kind of relationship. Members of my family will be the most obvious such persons, but, even if it extends more widely, my concern will extend only to those with whom I identify in some way.[7] Caring does not seem to have the global scope espoused by cosmopolitanism. Appiah solves this problem by suggesting that concern for others motivated by caring, and grounded in identity-forming relationships, is a different kind of moral motivation from the obligations that arise within the framework of justice. It is of a kind that is not required to be universal. Appiah's argument is that it is not *prima facie* a violation of the norms of justice to give priority to the demands that arise from the identity-forming associations we have with people we care about. But this is not because these demands have a greater weight than our obligations towards strangers or distant others, but because they do not exist in the same domain. It is not that we are permitted by morality to give the needs of those near to us greater priority than those of strangers; it is that the obligations arising from these two categories of needs are of a different kind. The demands that arise from our identity-forming associations are the demands of caring and are demands that we owe to others as individuals, while our obligations towards strangers or distant others belong to the framework of justice and belong to us as human beings and as political agents in a globalized world. Appiah comments: "Equality wasn't what morality demanded of us as individuals; it denotes a regulative ideal for political, not personal, conduct. We go wrong when we conflate personal and political ideals, and, in particular, when we assume that, because there are connections between the two, they are the same" (2005: 230). It would seem that Singer has assumed that they are the same. The value of those we care about and the value of those to whom I have obligations in justice are of different kinds and are therefore incommensurable. Rescuing a distant stranger is but one of the moral values I am rightly motivated to pursue along with values that are incommensurable with it, such as caring about those who share communitarian relationships with me. Of course the difficulty that this leaves me with is that of balancing and adjudicating between the various incommensurable moral demands that are placed on me. I shall return to this difficulty presently.

But first I want to argue that the ethic of caring can itself have a universal scope and needs not be confined to those with whom one has particular identity-forming relationships. We have seen that Nussbaum argued that caring about everyone universally is a form of moral maturity or virtue.[8] On her view, it would be an unjustified limitation of my caring if I confined it to those with whom I had identity-forming relationships. If the domain of caring is defined by my feelings, might it not also embrace the whole world? While the range of my love and affection may be confined to family, friends and close associates, the range of my sympathy and compassion may well extend – and arguably *should* extend – to the starving of the third world.[9] The ethic of caring advocates a willingness to assist others in need simply because they are human beings who have the same needs and vulnerabilities as I have. To live life with a minimum of human dignity is something that I would wish for all other human beings in so far as I care about them as human beings. The motivation for this willingness comes from aspects of my own humanity. My feelings of sympathy and compassion, my caring about the fate of others, and my concern for their well-being are inherent in my nature as a human being. Drawing on the writings of Adam Smith (1723–90) in arguing that human beings have an innate moral sense, James Q. Wilson has argued that "sympathy, defined as the capacity for and inclination to imagine the feelings of others, is a source – to Smith, *the* source – of human moral sentiments" (1993: 32). For her part, Kristen Renwick Monroe has used empirical studies to argue that the heart of altruism is the ability to adopt the perspective of a common humanity rather than confining one's concerns to family, tribe or nation. For her, altruism "consists of a common perception, held by all altruists, that they are strongly linked to others through a shared humanity. This self-perception constitutes such a central core to altruists' identity that it leaves them with no choice in their behaviour towards others" (1996: 216). In my own writing (van Hooft 1995, 2006) I have highlighted caring about others as a fundamental motivational stratum as important to all of us as the self-project on which our identity and feelings of self-worth are based. Accordingly, we can see that it is the ethic of caring that Tom Campbell refers to when he says: "The principle of benevolence or 'humanity' (as in 'humanitarian') is based on the propriety of the elemental response of aiding another human being arising from seeing, imagining, or knowing of the suffering of that being irrespective of who is suffering or why that suffering came about" (2007: 65). The paradigm example of the principle of humanity or the ethic of caring in action is the helpful treatment given to the stranger who knocks on one's door looking for assistance. The villagers of Le Chambon in France who helped Jewish refugees fleeing from Nazi persecution during the Second World War are a striking example of this virtue.[10] They responded to the immediate and direct need of the people who knocked on their doors by hiding and feeding the refugees, often at great danger to themselves. In explaining their actions after the war, they did not make reference to moral principles or obligations but simply to the vital needs of those who had appealed to them for help. As Monroe remarks:

> Our study of altruism, if it teaches us anything, reminds us of the importance of seeing the human face, the person needing help, of moving beyond the anonymity of just another nameless victim, one more faceless Jew shipped off to a concentration camp, another child killed in Bosnia or dying from famine in some distant land. (1996: 236)

In the contemporary world, however, the dire and vital needs of others are not so directly present to those of us in affluent nations who are in a position to help. This remoteness, along with many other circumstances, makes it easy for us to ignore the plight of others or to pretend that we are not in any way called on to help.[11]

These considerations allow us to answer a question that Singer never actually asked in his article: why are we obliged to save the child – who is, after all, a stranger to me – in the pond and, by analogy, the starving children in East Bengal? Singer just assumes that we would all share the intuition that we are obliged to save the child in the pond. On the ethic of caring, the way to understand such an obligation is to see it as a feeling generated within the motivational field of an individual in response to the perceived need of another. What a virtuous person responds to in the world and moves her to act responsibly is not the alleged fact that someone else has a right or that the agent herself has an obligation. Rather, the virtuous person responds to the fact that the other is in need. Whereas the framework of justice asks us to take a rationally structured and abstract view of others so as to see each individual in the world as equal in moral value and thus equally entitled to having their vital needs met, the ethic of caring urges us to care about them. My claim is that the scope of such caring can be global. It can transcend our particular loyalties and community-based attachments to embrace the whole of humanity in compassion.

Having distinguished the framework of justice from the ethic of caring, I now need to discuss how we should adjudicate between them. It remains the case that both those who are "close" to me in the sense of having a bond of caring with me and those who are "distant" from me in the sense of being merely nodes in a system of justice of which I am a part have a right to my attention and to my resources (even if "right" is not the most appropriate term in the context of caring). Should I keep the two domains distinct? Is the cosmopolitan principle of humanity as it applies to everyone globally to be understood as an expression of the ethic of caring or as an obligation in the moral framework of justice? My argument that the needy have rights because the affluent have obligations to the needy would seem to point in the direction of the second option. The human rights of others should not depend on such contingent and uncertain bases as sympathy and concern. In a suffering world we are all subject to "compassion fatigue", but our responsibilities do not dissipate as a result. Cosmopolitanism downplays the importance of identity-forming relationships in the formation of global economic and political policies, especially the relationships that constitute nationalism. To treat everyone as having equal moral status is precisely to insert them into the framework of justice rather than into the framework of caring, where special relationships can trump impartiality. Does the ethic of caring and its endorsement of partiality undermine the framework of justice with its stress on universality and impartiality? Are the ideals of cosmopolitanism undermined by Appiah's acceptance of partial cosmopolitanism?

In order to answer these questions we need to notice that Appiah does not only distinguish the domain of justice from the domain of loyalty and caring in terms of the kinds of motivation that are involved in either. The kind of motivation that is involved in the framework of justice is the feeling of impartial duty to all, where all are understood to have an equal moral status. It sees the other as a generalized bearer of rights. In contrast, the kind of motivation that is involved in the ethic of caring is a feeling of concern and sympathy learnt in the context of relationships with family and with members of one's wider identity-forming groups and extended to all of humanity. It sees the other as a particular person with whom one has a relationship of compassion. It is likely that a mature and virtuous human being would feel both of these kinds of motivation.[12] But Appiah's central point is that the framework of justice does not define one's moral motivations. It defines the responsibilities of political and social institutions that distribute social goods. The framework of justice is relevant to individuals and defines their obligations in so far as those individuals participate in social and political arrangements that distribute social goods to others. While individuals might care about those others in so far as they are fellow human beings or in so far as they are family members, their duties are to distribute those social goods impartially and equitably in accordance with principles that are inherent in those social and political institutions. Caring is a virtuous motivation, but justice is a social duty. These motivations and obligations can coexist in any one individual and they can come into conflict, but when the issue is that of distributing social goods, the principles of justice must guide the motivations of caring. Both justice and caring are universal in scope. But they have differing specific domains. Justice dictates what people are entitled to in the context of political arrangements that distribute social goods, while caring leads us to see why that matters. Caring should lead us to act justly.

The morality of rescue

To see the importance of the justice perspective, let us explore the example that generated Singer's argument – a famine in what is now Bangladesh – and the analogy that he used to illustrate his principle – saving the child in the pond. Both are cases of rescue that appeal directly to our caring. The morality of rescue is marked by a number of distinctive features. The first of these is that there is some sort of disaster unfolding at a specific time that is relatively unusual and extremely dangerous to its potential victims. The most obvious examples are natural disasters such as earthquakes, floods, wildfires and volcanic eruptions. I have already mentioned the tsunami of 2004.[13]

A second feature of rescues is that the situation can be expected to return to normal after the event and following successful rebuilding efforts. While the scale of the 2004 tsunami was such that rebuilding is still going on at the time of writing, in less dramatic examples it can be expected that aid and rescue workers should be able to leave the area in due course so as to allow people to rebuild their lives and continue to live in tolerable conditions for the foreseeable future. In short, rescue workers go into a disaster area, do what is needed and then leave. The effort is relatively short term and ideally has no lasting effects on the lifestyles and infrastructures of the affected areas. Things should return to normal and the presumption is that the normal state of affairs is not such as to require further assistance. Rescue efforts need have no lasting impact on institutional, economic or political arrangements in the recipient countries. From the point of view of donor countries, organizations or individuals, the demand is that there be a one-off donation of necessary resources to provide immediate relief and resources for rebuilding. Once the disaster is over and rebuilding complete, there is no further expectation of donor support. From the donors' perspective this means that the aid provided can be seen to be finite and proportional to the severity of the disaster. It also means that a degree of satisfaction at a job well done can be achieved, which will reinforce a willingness to assist in the event of future disasters. From the recipient's point of view, there need be no systemic dependence built into any relationships with donor countries or organizations. The situation that Singer is commenting on is one where there is an immediate need for rescue and an effective infrastructure for delivering assistance. In these circumstances, monetary contributions from individuals, organizations or governments in affluent countries have a reasonable chance of reaching their goal and doing some good. Moreover, there are no needs beyond the need for immediate rescue.

But much of the suffering, death and poverty in the world to which we in affluent countries are asked to respond is not of this nature and it is therefore questionable how relevant Singer's argument is to them. The problem is that most of the situations in the world that currently call for our assistance are not short-term, immediate and dramatic disasters, but endemic and long-lasting conditions of poverty, ill health, vulnerability, malnutrition, poor sanitation, lack of education, denial of access to economic resources and political instability. Much of the third world suffers from dire poverty, frequent famines, natural disasters, devastation caused by epidemics such as HIV/AIDS, malaria and other diseases, low life expectancy and literacy levels, graft, corruption and political oppression, and an almost endless list of misery and disadvantage. There are more men, women and children dying from poverty-related causes in third world countries every year (an estimated 18 million, or 50,000 a day) than were killed in the 2004 tsunami, but, because they do not die as a result of a single dramatic event, their deaths are barely noticed. "Poverty-related causes" include inadequate nutrition, unsafe drinking water and sewage systems, and lack of cheap rehydration packs for diarrhoea victims and of vaccines, antibiotics and other medicines (Pogge 2007b: 13). Poverty is not just a source of suffering in itself through hunger and starvation. It also leads to not being able to access health and education. In this way it contributes to mortality rates, morbidity and lack of opportunity. It also contributes to political instability. Countries that are too poor to pay their public servants and police adequately are prone to corruption when government employees are tempted to take bribes. Poor countries that have natural resources are prone to political coups as military officers or tribal leaders see the opportunity to seize power and enrich themselves by selling off those resources to developed nations. It follows that affluent people in rich countries are faced with a greater and more consistent set of appeals to their caring and benevolence than arise just from the occasional disaster.

Our understanding of these issues and of how they are interrelated has been greatly advanced by the work of the Nobel Prize-winning economist, Amartya Sen. Commenting on famines, Sen points out that people can starve from famine even when food is in plentiful supply nearby; the problem is that they have no access to it. Indeed, in the very famine that Singer refers to, there was plentiful food available at the time when people began to suffer from starvation. There had been flooding and, as a result, food prices had gone up in expectation of shortages. As a consequence, workers who were displaced by the floods and left out of work were unable to buy the food they needed for themselves and their families. Many died, but it was only later that food actually became scarce. What this shows is that famine is caused not only by lack of food but by lack of access to food. The problem might be that the victims of famine are unable to purchase food or that they are prevented by social and political institutions from having access to it. In many societies women and children are more vulnerable to hunger because there are social norms that give men privileged access to available food. In some societies, government policies, sometimes dictated by international financial institutions such as the World Bank or the IMF, affect food prices so as to prevent poorer people from buying food that is available. Famine relief, therefore, involves more than the short-term distribution of food aid. It can also require long-term improvements in the production and distribution of food, changes to government policy that affect people's entitlement to food and challenges to cultural expectations such as male and female roles, all of which have an impact on the growth and consumption of food products. Even the short-term distribution of food aid has to be handled sensitively since it can undermine the livelihood of local food producers by undercutting their prices (Sen 1999: 164ff.).

Sen's broader thesis is that the goal of economic development in the third world should not be just growth in gross national product (GNP). Nor should it be measured by such growth. Mere growth in GNP measures the gross wealth of a nation but says nothing about how that wealth is distributed or the extent to which it enhances the lives and economic opportunities of its citizens.[14] The GNP of Nigeria is very high because of its oil revenues, but most of that money is being siphoned off by the military kleptocrats who run the country. The ordinary citizens of Nigeria are as poor as they ever were. Sen argues that the goal of development should be the enhancement of freedom of the people in that economy. Being deprived of food, health, economic opportunities or security are just as much forms of unfreedom as literal servitude or slavery. By "freedom" Sen understands five interrelated social conditions: (a) political freedom; (b) economic facilities; (c) social opportunities; (d) transparency guarantees; and (e) protective security (*ibid.*: 10, 38). The first of these refers to the civil rights through which people can prevent exploitation, oppression and the social or economic conditions that amount to enslavement through their political action. The second condition refers to the establishment of institutions that permit participation in trade, production and employment, while the third refers to the ready availability of services that allow individuals to develop and maintain the skills and competencies necessary to participate in economic activity: services such as education and health. The fourth condition refers to institutional arrangements that prevent graft and corruption so that the gains that people make and the income that they earn can be secured to them, and so that there can be public scrutiny to ensure compliance with regulations and laws that protect workers' rights and fair competition. The fifth condition refers to a welfare safety net that ensures that people who lose out in the system or are prevented by disability or bad luck from participating in it are, nevertheless, looked after. Although Sen does not mention it, this might also include policing as a protection from crimes against one's person or property. Economic activity and participation are throttled when the gains that one can achieve cannot be secured to one because property rights are not respected. Such policing would also protect the fourth condition. All of these five conditions of freedom interact causally, and together constitute appropriate goals of economic development. Without them, underdevelopment and vulnerability to natural disasters are inevitable. As evidence for this Sen claims that there have been no famines in democratic societies.

The lesson to be drawn from Sen's argument is that providing aid to the world's poor is a much more complex project than Singer allows in his article. This in no way reduces the urgency and moral stringency of the obligation that we have to render assistance, but it does suggest that the simple giving of money may not be the best means to do so. Many theorists prefer an ethics of development over an ethics of aid (e.g. Crocker 2002). Emergency relief may be necessary but often has no long-term efficacy. Development efforts should be directed to a wide range of measures that enhance people's capabilities, as Nussbaum has described them, and their freedoms, as Sen has stipulated. This has important implications for the practical commitments of cosmopolitans in that it becomes much more difficult to see what one can do. Donating to international relief agencies and to NGOs that pursue development projects remains a viable and important option, but it is becoming increasingly apparent that solutions to the problem of world poverty are very hard to find if one is focused only on the obligation of individuals to give humanitarian aid.[15] Benevolence and compassion are important but local and global economic and political institutions must be interrogated for the role they play in distributing the world's goods. Such institutions must be just.[16]

If we hold the view that Singer seems to prefer – that we are required to give of our resources until our holdings are no greater than that of the poorest in the world – no distribution of goods and opportunities would be just unless it leads to equal outcomes. While Singer draws this conclusion, he does not explicitly endorse this view of justice. It is one that many thinkers find problematic. A more plausible conception of what justice demands arises from Sen's and Nussbaum's ideas. For them, a distribution is just if the poorest in that distribution are nevertheless able, securely and over time, to exercise those capabilities that constitute basic human dignity. On this view there is a limit to what we are obliged to contribute to humanitarian and development aid: we need give no more than would be required for the recipients to reach this standard.

Global justice

Most philosophers think about distributive justice through the framework provided by Rawls in his epochal book, *A Theory of Justice* (1972). The basic principles that Rawls developed there were that any unequal distribution of social goods would be just provided that those who were worse off in the system would still be better off as a result of the wealth of those who are better off, and provided that the opportunities to improve one's position within the system were available to anyone in the system. It would be unjust if the rich were getting richer at the expense of the poor and it would be unjust if anyone, rich or poor, were prevented from improving their position on the grounds of irrelevant factors such as colour, caste, creed, gender, ethnicity or place of birth. Rawls argues that these principles are just because they would be endorsed in an "original position" in which participants who were ignorant of what place they would occupy in a society structured by those principles design the institutions of that society.[17] Rawls focuses on the justice of the distribution of such social goods as economic opportunities, provision of services such as health, education and policing, and wealth outcomes, and it does so in the domestic context of a specific nation-state. Rawls sees a nation-state as an economic and political system in which co-nationals participate by contributing cooperatively to that system and by deriving benefits from it. It is because it is a relatively closed system of cooperation in this way that participants would only agree to the institutional structures of that society if the outcomes that they yielded for poor and rich alike were fair and just.

However, in the context of globalization it is no longer true that a nation-state is a closed economic system. Economic activity that affects the living conditions of the poor and the rich has a global scope and the wealth of those in wealthy countries is won through economic and political activities that create poverty in other countries. Accordingly, thinkers such as Thomas Pogge (1989) have applied Rawls's ideas to the global economic system and its institutions (see also Barry 1982; Beitz 1999a). If the principles of justice demand that the poor should benefit from the increasing wealth of the rich and should have opportunities to acquire social goods equal to those of anyone else, why should these demands be met only within national economies? Why should they not apply to the whole world? Why should we not envisage a global "original position" in which participants agree on global institutions from behind a veil of ignorance that prevents them from knowing what country they will end up living in and what economic position they will hold in a globalized world? Should we not count as just only those global institutions that would be endorsed in such a scenario and that applied Rawls's criteria for justice on a global scale?

Pogge has gone on to argue that we need to approach the problem of global poverty in a radically different way from that exemplified by Singer. Singer was arguing for a "positive obligation": an obligation incumbent on all affluent people to do something positive to help others who are in need. Although he describes it as a duty to prevent harm to those who are vulnerable as a result of famine, it is a positive obligation in that it requires us to do something to alleviate their suffering. But Pogge speaks of a "negative obligation". This is a duty to not harm others through one's own conduct. We could understand the distinction if we ordered our actions on a scale of ascending moral stringency. Least morally stringent are supererogatory acts that are not strictly required of us even if they are morally admirable. More morally stringent are positive duties that require us to do such things as provide assistance where it is needed when we have the opportunity to do so and where there is no resultant loss of anything of greater moral significance. Negative duties are duties that are even more morally stringent. They require us to forbear from doing anything that would harm others. Whereas positive duties urge us to protect others from various harms or to alleviate the sufferings that arise from a variety of causes, negative duties forbid us from actually causing harm to others ourselves. The classic prohibitions such as "Thou shalt not murder" or "Thou shalt not steal" are examples of negative duties in this sense. To fail to fulfil such a negative duty is to commit a serious moral wrong. Even people who neglect the needs of others with hardly a second thought would be appalled at the suggestion that they might kill those others or steal from them. But Pogge's dramatic thesis is that that is precisely what a great many people in affluent countries are doing.

For Pogge the crucial fact is not just that many people in the world are very poor. It is that they are very poor because of what we in affluent countries do to preserve and enhance our luxurious way of life. Accordingly, it is our way of life that is causing the poverty and misery of others. Through this way of life we are failing to fulfil our negative duty of not harming those others. This argument depends on much complex empirical evidence from economics, political analysis and studies of how economic globalization affects economic development in poorer countries of the world. Along with many other commentators, Nobel Prize-winning economist and one-time chief economist at the World Bank Joseph Stiglitz has borne out these claims in a number of books (2002, 2006; see also Falk 1999).

Pogge (1998) argues that poverty in the developing world is due to global political and economic institutions that are designed to benefit those in the first world. These institutions are perpetuating a legacy of colonial exploitation whose effects are still being felt, especially in Africa (see also Pogge 2005; Follesdal & Pogge 2005). Our clothes are relatively cheap for us because they are made by underpaid workers in developing countries.[18] Our coffee comes to us from countries where farmers have had to move from growing food for themselves and their local markets to growing cash crops for export, thereby making themselves vulnerable to fluctuations in global commodity prices. Most recently, the pressures of having to replace petroleum-based products in order to meet our needs for transport and heating have led to the development of biofuels. This in turn has led to the growing of oil-producing crops to such an extent that food crops are being replaced and global prices for food are increasing by as much as 70 per cent. The greatest impact of these price rises falls on the world's poor. Rich nations dominate global financial institutions in such a way that trade arrangements, lending policies, intellectual property rules, farm subsidies in rich countries, labour conditions in poor countries and a myriad of other economic arrangements systematically favour those rich nations and impoverish the poorer ones. Politicians and business leaders in affluent countries are happy to do business with tyrants and putschists and to lend money to them in order to secure access to resources. These tyrants and putschists in their turn use the money to buy arms to oppress their own people and to build palaces to display their ill-gotten wealth.

Secondly, Pogge argues that the poor peoples are exploited because their natural resources are expropriated without compensation or purchased at exploitative prices. Pogge here appeals to a principle first enunciated by the English philosopher John Locke (1632–1704). Writing at a time when natural resources were perceived to be readily available and open to exploitation by anyone with the means to do so, Locke argued that we were entitled only to take as much as we could use and that we should leave "enough, and as good" for others to use (1960, quoted in Pogge 1998: 508). On this principle, if a person finds an apple tree in the forest that is not obviously owned by anyone, she may take as much as she can use (including what she could put away for later without any of it rotting) but must leave enough so that others can also benefit. And she must not chop down the tree. If it turns out that the tree was owned by someone else, she must pay fair compensation for what she has taken. And if everyone in the community agrees, she may take all the apples and fence off the tree in order, for example, to set up a shop and sell apples to others. The community may consider this a pragmatic and acceptable arrangement. In a similar way, if oil is found in a third world country, it may not be taken by those who find it without due recompense paid to the traditional owners of the land and without the agreement of the whole community in the country where the oil is found. This requires that the ruling elite of that country genuinely represents the people and that they spread the wealth generated by the sale equitably and fairly. But poverty and the temptations to corruption that it presents make this unlikely in the developing world.

Thirdly, Pogge reminds us that the histories of the countries that are poorest in today's world are marked by exploitation and colonialism. If the inequalities that exist in the global economic system resulted from differential effort and success after beginning from an equal starting-point, and if the race for wealth began from a position in which no one had an unfair advantage, then the differential outcome might be morally acceptable. But the wealthy Western nations acquired their overwhelming economic superiority by expropriating people as slaves and extracting resources to feed the furnaces of Europe through hundreds of years of colonial expansion. This was theft pure and simple. It was made to look acceptable by racism and morally untenable attitudes of cultural superiority. The moral quality of today's inequitable distribution of the world's wealth cannot be extricated from the moral quality of the colonial oppression on which it is historically based. Accordingly, Pogge concludes that "we, the more affluent, have a negative responsibility and duty to stop collaborating in the coercive maintenance of this inequality" (1998: 510).

While Singer had already argued that alleviating the suffering of the world's poor was a matter not just of charity but of obligation, Pogge heightens the stringency of this obligation by arguing that it is a violation of our negative duty to not harm others. Accordingly, it is a violation of the human rights of those who are victims of global poverty (2007b). Their poverty is an evil not just because of the suffering and reduction of capabilities that it causes, but also because it is an injustice. Pogge's argument is not that the poor have a right to our assistance because their suffering is an evil that we should do something about because we are able to; rather, he argues that, because there is a causal link between the affluent lifestyles of most people in rich countries and the poverty that is endemic in the third world, we are causing this evil and thereby failing in our stringent negative duty to not cause harm to others. We share the same moral status as thieves, cheats and murderers. Of course, we might argue against this conclusion by saying that, unlike thieves, cheats and murderers, we are not aware of the bad effects of our rich lifestyles or that, even if we are, we do not intend these bad consequences. But Pogge will not accept this excuse and argues that our very ignorance is culpable. We participate in, and benefit from, global financial and economic institutions – institutions that systematically deny the basic human rights of poor peoples – and for that reason we are guilty of injustice.

The conception of justice that Pogge is appealing to here is twofold. First, he regards it as unjust of people to obtain goods by lying, stealing or murdering. To do so is to violate important negative obligations. Thus far his argument has been that many of us fail in honouring this negative duty, albeit indirectly and possibly unknowingly. But Pogge also gives thought to distributive justice when he considers what kind of unequal distribution of goods and resources would be just. He formulates a principle very like the one I have attributed to Sen and Nussbaum: "When social institutions work so that each person affected by them has secure access – understood always as reasonably rather than absolutely secure access – to minimally adequate shares of all basic goods then they are, according to my proposed core criterion of basic justice, fully just" (2002a: 38). It also matters to Pogge how such a distribution is assured. If a warlord were to bribe or threaten workers from an aid agency so that they were forced to distribute goods to the tribes loyal to that warlord – even if this resulted in those tribes having reasonably secure access to what they needed for a significant length of time – such an arrangement would not be just. The institutions that provide access to basic goods must also operate justly. Distribution must be fair in the sense that all who are entitled to the goods are able to obtain them and also in the sense that recipients should have an uncoerced opportunity to influence how the distribution takes place. This points to principles of democratic participation that I shall discuss later. Moreover, if it turns out that members of a certain race, caste or gender disproportionately suffer a lack of a good, then the arrangement is unjust to that degree. It is institutions and the way that they operate that ought to be just. As Pogge puts it, "We should conceive human rights primarily as claims on coercive social institutions and secondarily as claims against those who uphold such institutions" (*ibid.*: 45).

This focus on institutions takes some of the moral pressure arising from global poverty off individuals and any non-coercive organizations that they might be members of, including business organizations, and places it on governments of nation-states. It is governments that are the central agents that create the global economic framework that exploits the poor and perpetuates their poverty. Accordingly, it is governments that have the primary responsibility to alleviate world poverty and to create a global economic system that is just and equitable. The injustices and rights violations that the poor suffer are the responsibility of governments, and the justified complaints and rights claims that the poor might issue against affluent nations should be addressed to the governments and international economic institutions that they have set up. The poor have rights to whatever they need to live lives of human dignity as described in Chapter 2 because governments and similar agencies have a responsibility to see that those needs are met. The cosmopolitan position would be that it is not only the governments of the poor nations themselves that are responsible for securing the human rights of their citizens and residents, but all the governments of the world, especially those of the more affluent nations. This does imply that, despite the cosmopolitan suspicion of national sovereignty that I shall discuss in Chapter 4, such sovereignty continues to be important.

Pogge's argument dovetails with that of Appiah. Appiah had distinguished the framework of justice from the ethic of caring by making governments and governmental institutions responsible for justice while individuals and any NGOs that they might set up give expression to the ethic of caring. As motivations, caring and indignation at injustice might overlap, but securing justice remains the responsibility of coercive state institutions. In arguing that global inequality is an example of injustice, therefore, Appiah is attributing the responsibility to do something about it to governments. This does not imply that individuals should not themselves take action. Virtuous individuals will be motivated by caring and by indignation at injustice to donate money to NGOs that serve the global poor and they will take whatever political means are available to influence their governments to act more justly in our globalized world.

As a consequence of this argument, the demandingness of Singer's approach and of any arguments that depend only on the ethic of caring would seem to be reduced. It is not up to individuals to eradicate global poverty. While individuals still have a role to play and while they are still called on to respond to the needs of the poor by the ethic of caring, the eradication of injustice as such is a government responsibility. The ethic of caring is invoked when the suffering to be alleviated is not the result of injustice – as when a tsunami has struck – although even here the suffering is borne disproportionately by the poor and may be the result of pre-existing injustices. In such circumstances people act well and fulfil their positive obligations when they provide resources through aid agencies or other organizations to alleviate the suffering. But the redress and avoidance of injustice is the responsibility of those who cause that injustice: governments, the financial institutions they establish and the business corporations whose interests they serve and whose activities they should regulate.

However, this does not let individuals off the hook. In democratic societies, government policies reflect the will of the people and so every individual has a responsibility to engage in the political processes of their countries in order to ensure that government policies are such as to secure justice for all around the world. Individuals should be motivated to such engagement both by compassion and by the recognition that they are participants in the unjust institutions that cause poverty. According to Pogge:

> A human right to basic necessities, as postulated, for instance, in Article 25 of the UDHR, becomes more plausible when construed along these lines. On my institutional understanding, it involves no duty on everyone to help supply such necessities to those who would otherwise be without them. It rather involves a duty on citizens to ensure that any coercive social order they collectively impose upon each of themselves is one under which, insofar as reasonably possible, each has secure access to these necessities. (2002a: 67)

The political patriotism I described in Chapter 2 suggests that, through the political processes whereby we participate in the policy formation of our governments, we also participate in the guilt that arises from the violations of negative responsibilities that our governments commit. We fail to fulfil our negative duties towards the poor to not harm them, but we do so collectively through the governments that we elect. Our governments owe it to the global poor to correct the injustices that flow from global institutions and we owe it to the global poor to engage in such political activities as are needed to bring this about. People who think of politics in individualist or libertarian terms may claim that their enjoyment of affluence has caused no harm, but the deprived have a claim against anyone who participates in a coercive system that harms them. It follows that we should not participate in such a system without trying to change it.

This argument also suggests that a cosmopolitan commitment to justice involves global solidarity with struggles for human rights and social justice on the part of oppressed and exploited peoples. Such struggles must be political struggles aimed at altering government policy so as to produce the changes needed to secure to everyone in the world the freedom to engage in such economic activities as would enable them to live lives of simple human dignity.

Immigration

Both the principle of justice and the principle of humanity would entail that countries that are able to should receive and succour refugees from political and religious persecution or from theatres of war. This principle has been enshrined through the establishment of a United Nations High Commission for Refugees (UNHCR).[19] The forced movement of people around the world as a result of war, natural catastrophes or persecution is an overwhelming problem requiring huge resources to house people in temporary camps, see to their basic needs and, where possible, return them to their homes. Global warming threatens to increase the number of displaced persons around the world even more. Countries that have the required resources have a responsibility under the principle of humanity to accept such people within their borders and have a responsibility under the principles of justice to do so if the displacement is caused by conditions that the richer countries have, knowingly or unknowingly, helped to bring about (Boswell 2005). However, it is immigration motivated by economic needs that presents the most acute problems for cosmopolitan thinkers. The huge number of Latin Americans moving to the USA and the huge number of Africans moving to Europe are but the tip of an iceberg of huge changes that are occurring in the world's demography. Governments need to develop policies concerning the legal status of aliens, refugees and guest workers and concerning access to citizenship for legal residents. How would a cosmopolitan approach such issues?

Global justice concerns itself with the distribution of social goods and economic opportunities around the world. It must also concern itself with any hindrances to the capabilities that people might have through no fault of their own to participate in the system of cooperation and distribution that marks the sphere of justice. The classic example of such a hindrance would be a physical disability with which one is born. A just society will ensure that such a disability, and any other disadvantage that a person or group might suffer as a result of bad luck, is compensated for in such a way that those persons or groups have a fair chance at participating in, contributing to and benefiting from the society in which they live. But one such hindrance will be the place where one is born. That one person is born in a poor country while another is born in an affluent one is a matter of luck. Should not the norms of global justice be invoked in order to suggest that there should be global institutions that would compensate the poorly born for their misfortune and give them an equitable opportunity to access the social goods that are available in the wider world? Should poor people not be allowed to move to rich countries in order to find their fortunes?[20]

Applying Rawls's and Pogge's conceptions of justice to this matter has some striking implications. Not only would it lead us to question the justice of such global institutions as the World Bank, the IMF and the governments of rich nations, which, as was argued above, systemically disadvantage the global poor, but it would also lead us to question the justice of national borders.

National borders serve to prevent a free movement of people from one country to another. While the UDHR gave people the right to emigrate, there is no corresponding obligation on countries to allow free immigration. However, if this prevents poorer people from pursuing economic opportunities in richer countries, this would seem to offend against Rawls's principles. People would not choose from behind Rawls's "veil of ignorance" to establish or maintain largely closed borders in an original position because they would consider the possibility that they themselves would be being locked into an inescapable situation of poverty in an underdeveloped country. Such a restriction would therefore be unfair.

The idea that people could move freely around the globe, settling in whatever countries they choose in order to pursue economic opportunities, or, indeed, to enjoy whatever amenities are available there, constitutes a radical questioning of the idea of a nation-state. It has been argued that, in so far as a nation-state is a political community based on some kind of nation-based, identity-forming solidarity – whether that solidarity is based on a shared heritage, ethnicity or language, or whether it is a more recent ideological construct – that nation-state has the right to decide who will be members and who will not (Walzer 1981). A national community may feel that its distinctive cultural and traditional identity would come under threat if there were a significant number of immigrants from a different cultural background in its midst. Whether this feeling takes the ugly form of the Cronulla race riots I mentioned in Chapter 1, or of more measured policies for integrating foreign communities into a multicultural society, there is a widespread assumption among national leaders that any state has the right to protect its cultural integrity and the national identity of its people. The debates on this issue are not likely to be resolved any time soon.[21]

However, cosmopolitans could make a radical proposal. Rather than confront the issue as one that is detached from the broader issue of global justice such that a nation's immigration and refugee policy is decided in the light of one set of considerations while its trade and economic policies are decided in the light of another – even when the first set is humanitarian while the second set is motivated by the national interest – it would be better if the problems were seen holistically. If a country adopts trade and economic policies that systemically impoverish other countries and if it is tardy in contributing, for example, to the UN's Millennium Development Goals,[22] then it should not be surprised if it is beset with economic refugees. The best way to slow the movement of people driven to emigrate by economic necessity is to reduce the economic necessity. If a nation-state wants to preserve its ethnic or cultural homogeneity – I leave aside whether this perceived homogeneity might be an ideological construct – by excluding outsiders, then let it contribute to the full extent of its obligations to the alleviation of world poverty. By reducing the need for people to flee starvation and indigence, they will have contributed to a reduction in the flow of immigrants and to a more stable and just world.

Conclusion

Cosmopolitanism endorses a global principle of benevolence based on the shared humanity of all peoples: a benevolence to all others irrespective of race, caste, nationality, religion, ethnicity or location. We have seen that such benevolence can be motivated by caring or by a passion for justice. While caring is an important virtue, it has the disadvantage of encouraging partiality and of often being limited to only those with whom one has a relevant kind of relationship. While it is a mark of virtue to acknowledge that this feeling extends to the whole of humanity, to do so involves having to contend with countervailing inclinations of selfishness and group identification. It is difficult to extend caring to the whole of humanity. Justice, on the other hand, gains its moral validity and motivational strength from a rationally constructed conceptual framework in which everyone is conceived to be of equal moral value and in which one's self or one's identity-forming group is not to be given priority. But the most significant difference between these moral frameworks is that the ethic of caring belongs to the individual as the responsible moral agent, while honouring the framework of justice is the responsibility of coercive state institutions. Accordingly, the cosmopolitan willingness to come to the aid of those suffering from natural or man-made disasters such as extreme poverty can be expressed both by contributions to international aid efforts and by participation in political struggles for global justice. The cosmopolitan individual's commitment to justice in the distribution of natural resources and wealth on a global scale must seek expression in political action. Only in this way, and motivated by a feeling of shared humanity, can a cosmopolitan evince effective global solidarity with struggles for human rights and social justice.

Chapter 4

Lasting peace

> We must resort to force only in case we may not avail ourselves of discussion. The only excuse for going to war is that we may live in peace unharmed; and when the victory is won, we should spare those who have not been blood-thirsty and barbarous in their warfare.
>
> (Cicero, *De Officiis* I.x, in May *et al.* 2006: 5–7)

In this chapter, I propose to discuss the following features of cosmopolitanism outlined at the end of the Introduction:

(13) acknowledging the sovereignty of nation-states while insisting on limitations to that sovereignty in order to secure human rights and global justice;
(14) quest for lasting world peace;
(15) respect for the right to self-determination of peoples;
(16) preparedness to prosecute crimes against humanity internationally.

These features alter the focus of our considerations. Whereas the previous three chapters discussed the personal ethical stances that a cosmopolitan adopts towards others as individuals, this and the next chapter will discuss cosmopolitan ideals and attitudes towards states, international relations and global institutions. These ideals and attitudes require individuals – especially those who exercise political, economic and social power – to adopt and pursue responsible positions towards the relations between states and other transnational actors on the world stage. How should states behave towards each other? Are they permitted to seek their advantage by force of arms or by dishonouring international agreements? In order to set the stage for considering these issues, we should first understand what nation-states are and what their "sovereignty" consists in.

Sovereignty

The origin of the modern idea of the nation-state was the Treaty of Westphalia of 1648. The Thirty Years War had been fought from 1618 in northern Europe between a number of kingdoms and principalities. The ostensible cause was religion, with Protestant rulers seeking to impose their specific forms of Christianity and Catholic rulers trying to do the same. It could, however, be argued that the religious motivations of these struggles were a continuation of previous and more deep-seated struggles over territory. Since time immemorial the territorial boundaries of European principalities – and this was true for most lands around the world – were defined by the ability of the relevant ruler to seize and defend such territory. If he had an army stronger than that of his neighbouring rulers, he could seize more of their lands and extend his territory. If he was weaker, his lands would contract because of incursions from his neighbours. Clearly, the more lands he controlled the more wealth and population would be at his disposal so as to enable him to create larger armies and pay for more mercenary soldiers. Natural boundaries such as deep rivers, mountain ranges or seas would help to defend one's land and thereby became natural borders, but where no such impediment to armed incursions was available the only way to define and defend one's territory was by force of arms. The only means of defence available to smaller kingdoms was the formation of alliances with stronger powers. As a consequence, the boundaries of principalities, dukedoms and the like were constantly shifting. The Thirty Years War only added religious hatred to this already unstable form of territorial definition.

Moreover, Catholic Christianity had bequeathed to Europe a divided system of political authority. Following the biblical injunction to give to Caesar what is Caesar's and to God what is God's, European peoples owed a temporal or political allegiance to their king, prince or emperor, but also owed a religious allegiance to their priest, bishop or pope. Issues of land tenure, taxation and military readiness were the province of the king or the prince, while issues of morals, religious observance and tithes were the responsibility of the Church. While this division seems simple enough in principle, it laid the foundations for many conflicts of authority. Many princes sought to overturn the authority of the Catholic Church and to set themselves up as the arbiters of the religious observance of their subjects.

Accordingly, the Treaty of Westphalia needed to establish new bases for territorial boundaries and new definitions of the rights and responsibilities of temporal rulers in relation to other powers. It was agreed to define firm boundaries for states and to give a defined range of authority to the relevant ruler over the lands so bounded. This gave rise to the all-important concept of the "sovereignty of states", giving to each state or kingdom the fundamental right of political self-determination. No prince or bishop had the right to impose his religious convictions on the prince or people of another state or to invade another state for any but a clearly defined set of reasons. Any non-military form of interference in the internal affairs of other states was also forbidden. From a legal point of view, all states were to be of equal standing to each other even if their actual military strength might differ. But if the power of temporal rulers to interfere in the affairs of other states was radically reduced, their powers over their own territories were greatly enhanced. People were now clearly defined as subjects of their princes with no overlapping or extraneous allegiance to any other power, be it an emperor or a bishop.

Even though the Treaty of Westphalia established the system of nation-states that we recognize today, it did nothing to overcome the rivalry and competitiveness between states that had been the norm before its institution. It certainly did not introduce a new era of moral relations between states. It was the product of the exhaustion brought on by thirty years of destructive war in which the population of northwest Europe was thought to have been reduced by over a third. It was the product of a pragmatic wish to bring the destruction to an end. It sought to do this by ensuring a balance of power between states that could, either by force of arms or by alliances with better-armed states, stave off the predations of more powerful neighbours. It did not usher in a new era of harmony based on moral or religious consensus, but a new form of peace that was more like a truce between armed camps. The animosities did not die away but were merely contained by the division of Europe into nation-states with standing armies that kept their neighbours at bay.

In the Westphalian system a state was not just a legal entity but also a power-based entity, so that a "real" state was one that could defend or expand its borders and be part of the balance of power that maintained stability in the international order. A would-be state that did not have such power (such as colonies or countries from which trade concessions could be forced without the traders being subject to local law) was regarded as fair game. The system of states was therefore unequal, with only the powerful effectively having full state rights. This is the situation described by theorists of international relations as "realism". Such theorists argue that the situation between states today is not essentially different from that developed in the seventeenth century.

As an account of the nature of international relations, political realism often appeals to the thought of Thomas Hobbes (1588–1679), who had suggested that the natural condition of human beings was one of conflict and rivalry. In order to argue that we need strong and absolute political authority within nation-states in order to keep the peace among individuals, Hobbes suggested that in the "state of nature" – a condition in which there is no civil or political authority – men and women would struggle to the death for what they need and what they want without any regard for public order or the well-being of others. People would be aggressive even if only to protect themselves against the deadly aggression of others. The only way to keep property in a context marked by scarcity would be to acquire it by work or theft and then defend it against the predations of others by using whatever force one had at one's disposal. In such a world, human life would be "solitary, poor, nasty, brutish and short" (Hobbes 1651: §xiii). While in such a world individuals possess a natural right to preserve their lives and to take possession of whatever they need in order to do so, there is no morality restraining how people behave towards one another. People simply act out of self-interest without any moral constraints on their wills. Accordingly, such a world is one where, as Hobbes put it, there is a "war of all against all". Hobbes went on to argue that in order to establish an orderly society, individuals would have to give up their natural right and invest it in an all-powerful ruler, or "Leviathan", who would secure the peace by force. While this argument was developed with reference to the internal politics of nation-states, its logic can be applied to the international sphere by suggesting that, just as a powerful sovereign rather than a moral consensus was needed to maintain the rule of law in specific countries, so, if there were to be lasting peace and an end to the constant state of war between nation-states, a single sovereign would have to rule the world. In this way states and principalities would all disappear and there would be a single world government. In the absence of such a global authority states would exist in something like an amoral "state of nature" and the only basis for stable relations between them would be the mutual threat of force. In such a world, might is right.

While the world order introduced by the League of Nations and by the UN does not constitute a world government, it did introduce a moral, and therefore non-realist, consideration: that all states were to be considered equal – to have "sovereign equality" (Chandler 2003). They are all equally states, no matter how weak they are, in so far as they are recognized as such by other states. The UN in its charter is committed to respecting and defending the sovereignty of states, and it is through its institutions that the existence and legitimacy of states can be formally recognized. If there has been a violent regime change, or if there has been a successful secessionist struggle, it is other nation-states that accord recognition to the new state and it is the UN that extends the rights of membership in the world community of nations to the new government. This recognition is accorded provided that the state possesses a permanent population, a defined territory and an effective government over that territory and its population. The governments of states that are duly recognized have the authority to enter into political and commercial arrangements with other states, with multinational corporations and with any other bodies that can assist it with its governmental responsibilities, such as the World Bank, the IMF or relevant NGOs.

Immanuel Kant

To see how the cosmopolitan ideal of peaceful, moral and uncoerced relations between states evolved, we need to explore the writings of one of its leading progenitors. Immanuel Kant published his famous pamphlet "Perpetual Peace: A Philosophical Sketch" in 1795 with a second enlarged edition in 1796 (see Kant 1991). The essay begins with a numbered set of moral or political principles that Kant thinks would eventually be agreed on by peoples in their dealings with each other, whether because the natural evolution of society would have brought them to this point or because all rational peoples would see them as prerequisites for a state of peace.

(i) "No conclusion of peace shall be considered valid as such if it was made with a secret reservation of the material for a future war" (Kant 1991: 93). Here Kant distinguishes a state of peace from an armed truce. Any nation that builds up its armaments and armies, even if not engaged in actual conflict, cannot be considered to be at peace with its neighbours. This sets a high standard for what is to be regarded as a state of peace. It is not just an absence of armed conflict but a harmonious and trusting, unarmed coexistence between states.

(ii) "No independently existing state, whether it be large or small, may be acquired by another state by inheritance, exchange, purchase or gift" (*ibid.*: 94). This thought expresses a fundamentally "republican" conception of what a state is. It is not a piece of property to be turned into an exchangeable commodity by absolute monarchs, but a national community with roots in the life and loyalty of its people. This principle would also rule out colonialism, since this consists in the possession of a state as a piece of property by another. The main point seems to be, however, that if states were to be conceived of as possessions, they would be more likely to be fought over and forcibly acquired by princes.

(iii) "Standing armies (*miles perpetuus*) will gradually be abolished altogether" (*ibid.*). This principle reaffirms that an armed state is not in a genuine state of peace with its neighbours.

(iv) "No national debt shall be contracted in connection with the external affairs of the state" (*ibid.*: 95). The text seems to be saying here that a state should not borrow money to pay for its army or to buy armaments. There is a suggestion also that for one state to be in debt to another is contrary to the ideal of peaceful relations between them. Indebtedness involves a form of power over the debtor that is inconsistent with a genuine state of peace. Whether this principle is applicable in the contemporary world of globalized commerce and international monetary institutions is a matter that I shall leave to economists to ponder. However, it certainly does raise the question as to whether economic competition and dependence between states is antithetical to a genuine state of peace between them.

(v) "No state shall forcibly interfere in the constitution and government of another state" (*ibid*.: 96). This would seem to be the principle of sovereignty and the policy of non-intervention that it implies. Even in the event of civil war or a war of secession, it would not be appropriate for a third-party state to intervene. A people must be allowed to decide its own destiny, according to Kant.

(vi) "No state at war with another shall permit such acts of hostility as would make mutual confidence impossible during a future time of peace. Such acts would include the employment of assassins (*percussores*) or poisoners (*venefici*), breach of agreements, the instigation of treason (*perduellio*) within the enemy state, etc." (*ibid*.). While the list of examples that Kant offers are acts of treachery, it can be supposed that Kant also intends to rule out any means of waging war that would flout international conventions such as relate to the treatment of prisoners, exempting non-combatants from attack, and outlawing rape and pillage. This reading is supported by the fact that Kant goes on to point out that his principle also rules out wars that would utterly destroy another state or its people. The importance of this principle is that unless it is adhered to – unless states deal with each other honourably even while at war – no subsequent peace will be lasting and stable because of the lingering mistrust and hatred that will have been engendered.

The second section, "*Which Contains the Definitive Articles of a Perpetual Peace Between States*" (*ibid*.: 98), articulates the social, moral and political conditions that would be necessary and sufficient to establish peace between states. It begins with the claim that a state of peace must be formally constituted through some political and diplomatic instrument such as a treaty or international institution, since a mere peaceful coexistence without guarantees does not rule out the possibility of mutual aggression. It is not enough for states to be at peace because circumstances happen to be such that they are not in conflict. States that are not even aware of each other could be at peace with each other in this sense. A genuine peace is a peace agreed to and declared between states.

Kant goes on to propose several conditions for peaceful relations between states. The first of these is an idea that has come down to us in the form of a theory that democratic states do not wage war on each other.[1] He says that it is a necessary condition for peace to exist between them that states be constitutional republics. Kant understands a republican state in terms that we would recognize as liberal-democratic:

> A *republican constitution* is founded upon three principles: firstly, the principle of *freedom* for all members of a society (as men); secondly, the principle of the *dependence* of everyone upon a single common legislation (as subjects); and thirdly, the principle of legal *equality* for everyone (as citizens). (*Ibid*.: 99)

For Kant, a republican state is one that does not enslave its citizens, respects the rule of law, and does not accord hereditary or any other form of unequal privilege to any of its citizens. Kant himself does not prefer the term "democracy" since he sees that as a form of tyranny by the majority. Yet a republican state is democratic in a recognizable sense since a key element of a republican state is the separation of powers between legislature and executive so that both can be held accountable by the people. The reason that republicanism would lead to peace is that in a republican state citizens would need to either make or endorse any decision to go to war. But such citizens would not be likely to approve going to war since they are well aware of the cost to them of doing so. It is absolute monarchs who readily go to war since they do not personally suffer the hardships of fighting.

The second condition for lasting peace that Kant identifies is that states should form themselves into a global federation. Kant envisages a global lawful order founded on principles that a rational person can conceive being endorsed by everyone who is affected. Such an international lawful order is one that, even if it is not formally instituted in international law, exists *a priori* as an idea that should be so realized. The claim is that if there were a federation of republics or of peoples living within republics, then there would be no cause for war. Matters of dispute between states would be settled on the basis of principles that everyone concerned could endorse. Such a federation would not be a world state since there would not be a central government. A single world government is likely to become despotic and to centralize too much power within itself to be acceptable. Kant criticizes states for wanting to maintain a form of sovereignty premised on belligerent independence and self-aggrandizement: what we would today call "nationalism". Unless states agree to place themselves under the sway of "Right" – that is, of international law – they will always act as individuals do in the Hobbesian state of nature: aggressively. Accordingly, states need to voluntarily form "a *pacific federation*" (*ibid*.: 104), which is more than just a peace treaty forced on the weaker by the more powerful: it is a voluntary eschewing of recourse to arms to resolve conflicts on the part of all participating states. So long as they are republics, states will be disposed to do this for reasons we saw in Kant's previous point. The principles of international law would simply flow from the rational self-interest of citizens in republican states.

Unfortunately, even though Kant says that this free federation of states would serve as a guarantor for the rights of individual states, he does not make clear how this would work: whether an international police force would be needed, for example. Such a force would be an armed instrument of violence and it would have to be under the command of some super-state agency. But the principles of international law could not be based on war or the threat of violence. If they were, it would be a case of "might is right". Accordingly, they must be based on an unforced international agreement between states. This is an argument to show that no genuine international law could be engendered by the overarching power of a world government. Accordingly, the best that can be hoped for in an agreement between states is a world federation in which the use of arms between states is voluntarily surrendered.

After a discussion of the duty of "hospitality", which is the duty of protecting and helping strangers that I discussed in Chapter 3, Kant returns to his central themes in a set of appendices that add considerable philosophical depth to the cosmopolitan principles for international relations that he has been advocating. He suggests that international agreements between states should be based on a universal morality grounded in reason.

The first appendix begins by discussing the apparent conflict between morality and politics and the claim often made by realists in international relations that politics requires politicians and state leaders to be at least amoral if not positively immoral on the grounds that reasons of state override the demands of morality. Kant asks whether it is possible to be a "*moral politician*, i.e. someone who conceives of the principles of political expediency in such a way that they can co-exist with morality" (*ibid.*: 118). But Kant's attention is not focused on the crises of conscience that politicians and national leaders may suffer from time to time as they balance the interests of their countries against the rules of honourable international behaviour. Rather, it is still on the question of what conditions are necessary to secure lasting peace in the world. He suggests that it is only when peoples are united globally in holding to a single and universal morality that peace can be secured. He is suggesting not that all peoples should have the same marriage customs, dietary rules or other domestic precepts, but that there is a core set of moral principles that they must all share as rational human beings.

To defend the role of morality in politics, Kant distinguishes between taking one's material interests as primary, and taking *a priori* principles that can be endorsed as universalizable by pure reason as primary. When a politician or a people is acting under the influence of their patriotic passions, or their desire for their state's gain and glory, they are acting on reasons that have only local purchase rather than on reasons that anyone anywhere could endorse. Therefore they are not acting on universalizable reasons. They are pursuing their specific interests and, without the constraint of universalizable principles, will do anything that would advance their ends. In contrast, when a politician or a people is acting on the basis of policies that they could imagine any rational person anywhere endorsing, they cannot fail to take the dignity and rights of all others into account. Accordingly, this way of thinking leads to acting morally. In so far as acting morally here consists in adopting the view of anyone who might be affected by one's action no matter what country or culture that person belongs to, it cannot but lead to international peace and harmony. For politicians, therefore, acting morally – being constrained by considerations of the dignity and rights of all others – is necessary and sufficient for the attainment of perpetual peace. Kant reinforces the point when he says that "the general will" or the basic values and interests of all human beings, based on a universal, purely rational morality abstracted from people's particular interests, is the only thing that can unite people across borders. Accordingly, states must not pursue their ends as if they were more important than the general will, but must pursue them within the constraints of the moral law. In this way there would be no conflict between morality and politics. Accordingly, to secure lasting peace, "the rights of man must be held sacred, however great a sacrifice the ruling power may have to make" (*ibid.*: 125).

Kant goes on to argue in his second appendix that no political decision or policy would be moral or valid unless it were able to be made public. If making a policy public were somehow to make it impracticable or inapplicable, or if the effectiveness of a policy were to depend on its being kept secret, then it could not be a morally permissible policy. The reason for this is that if I cannot publicize my policy, then it cannot be endorsed by the general will and it will fail the test of rightness expressed in Kant's argument that only a policy that is known to respect the rights of all those affected can be morally justified. As an example we might consider the Nazis' "final solution to the Jewish problem". If the Nazis had announced their policy ahead of time, most Jews would have tried to escape and so the policy would have failed. Success depended on secrecy. And this is a *prima facie* indication that the policy was immoral. While its wrongness did not consist in its being secret but rather in its being an attack on the lives of the Jews, this wrongness was indicated by its having to be kept secret in order for it to be implemented effectively. As an example in international relations, Kant suggests that if a state were secretly to have a policy to renege on its agreements with other states, then international diplomacy would become impossible. The very suspicion that such a policy was in place would destroy any trust between the relevant states. Moreover, the state that was suspected of having such a policy would not be able to enter into agreements with other states. In this way the policy would also be self-defeating. Hence such a policy would be irrational, non-universalizable and therefore immoral. Moreover, public disclosure would also be a condition necessary for an effective federation of states, and as this is the only basis for perpetual peace, it will be necessary for such peace that states adhere to the requirements of publicity and enter into frank and open relations with each other. Secret treaties and hidden intentions can lead only to the breakdown of peace. In politics everything should be out in the open. Publicity is a necessary though not sufficient condition for a policy's being moral.

This condition applies to domestic politics just as much as to international politics. It applies because if the condition for a policy's being moral is that it acknowledge and respect the rights of all those affected, then the best way of ensuring that such acknowledgement occurs is to have the policy-making process take place in the open where all those who are affected can contribute to the debate and voice their opinions. There can be no correspondence between a political policy and the "general will" unless there has been an opportunity for all those affected by the policy to participate in debating it. The arbitrary will of an absolute ruler is effective because of the fear it inspires in his people, whereas the will of a democratic body is effective because of the agreement with the general will that public debate will have secured for it. Through these arguments, Kant forges a close link between cosmopolitanism, republicanism and democratic political processes.[2]

Kant concludes his essay by expressing confidence that, if international politics gradually becomes more moral, lasting peace can be attained. The sections below will show that, in this essay, Kant has set the terms for philosophical debates about international relations and global institutions that are still relevant today.

World government

State sovereignty is less complete today than it was in the recent past. Given the complexity of international arrangements and agreements, given the greater power that some states have to influence others, and given the capacity of multinational business corporations to pressure national governments, the actual power that many states have to order their internal affairs and to secure their safety and advantage in the international sphere is dramatically less than it used to be. The investment decisions of major corporations can have an even greater impact on smaller nation-states than the hegemonic ambitions of more powerful neighbouring states (Held 1995: chs 5, 6). Moreover, in a world of sovereign states pursuing their own interests, international institutions need to coordinate responses to global problems. Many such organizations exist, ranging from the UN, NGOs, financial institutions such as the IMF and courts of international law. Whether such bodies reduce the sovereignty and autonomy of nation-states is both an empirical and a conceptual question (Shue 1999; see also Parekh 2003).[3] Are they agencies through which nation-states can exercise their governmental responsibilities on the world stage but which remain subject to the sovereign will of those states, or are they supranational entities that impose conditions and rules which constrain the sovereignty of the states that are subject to them? But there is also a normative question. Would the world be a more just and peaceful place if it comprised sovereign states or would the world be better off if state sovereignty were reduced or even extinguished?

Given the commitment of cosmopolitan thinkers to human rights and global justice and given their focus on individuals, they have a tendency towards downgrading the importance of the sovereignty of nation-states. As it is frequently national governments that oppress their peoples, engage in exploitation of their country's resources for the benefit of their officials and assume national debts that later governments are unable to repay, it is argued that national governments should be bypassed and human rights and global justice secured by transnational institutions or by global forms of democracy (Pogge 2002a: 169; see also Beitz 1999a: 287; Held 1997; McGrew 1997). As it is frequently states that go to war with each other for the sake of their national interests, it is thought by some cosmopolitans that peace could be secured only if there were a world government that would extinguish the sovereign rights of states and inaugurate a global rule of law effective enough to hold all nations in check. Many realist international relations theorists, drawing on Hobbes, see this issue as involving only two options. The first is a world in which force exercised or threatened by autonomous, sovereign states is the only basis for stability, while the second is the notion of an all-powerful world government capable of maintaining peace through its exclusive right to exercise force over non-sovereign states. I shall argue that cosmopolitans should advocate a third, Kantian option in which global and lasting peace is based on open and public international agreements entered into by states acting rationally.

Advocacy of a global government with the power to enforce international law depends on a Hobbesian theory of political realism that claims that only an overarching force can quell the conflicts that arise from irreconcilable national interests. On this view, the world needs a "Leviathan" to keep the peace. However, as Kant had seen, this theory would also suggest that, in the absence of any power to curtail its reach or hold it to account, such a global government would become an oppressive hegemonic power acting in the interests of whatever political or commercial interest groups could influence its policies. It would seem then that global governance centred on institutions with global jurisdiction would be politically dangerous. The basic liberal principle that the rights of individuals are best protected when governments are marked by a division of powers is realized in the current world order to a higher degree than it would be under a single world government. Accordingly, most cosmopolitans continue to accept the necessity of the state as a form of governance of peoples (Sassen 2003, 2006).

A further reason for this position is the necessity of the nation-state as an administrative unit. Just as a local municipal council is responsible for the maintenance of a defined set of services in a city, and a state or provincial legislature is responsible for a defined set of functions in a larger territory, so the nation-state is responsible for the administration of a still larger territory and for the maintenance of appropriate relations with other states. As you cross a national border, you enter into a different legal jurisdiction. Whereas on this side of the border the laws of state A apply to you, when you cross the border, the laws of state B apply to you. While it is conceivable for a world body to legislate and administer a global set of laws that would cover the many issues that laws have to deal with, it is impracticable for it to do so. The nation-state delegates the maintenance of city parks to municipal councils and the maintenance of schools and hospitals to provincial governments. Different countries might arrange these matters differently but it is unusual for a central government to take responsibility for all of the many matters that governments at lower levels have to deal with. Nevertheless, legal or constitutional responsibility resides with the nation-state since it is its constitution and legal system that spell out what level of government is responsible for what functions. This responsibility is not given to the nation-state by a higher or global level of government; it is a function of its own sovereignty. It is because the state has this sovereignty and the responsibilities that go with it that it can rule its own territory and make laws that apply to it and only to it. Moreover, it is because the state has this sovereignty and the responsibilities that go with it that it can enter into arrangements, treaties and contracts with other bodies in order to fulfil those responsibilities and pursue the interests of its citizens.[4]

The fundamental reason for the necessity of the state is that some entity has to have jurisdiction over a specific population living in a specific territory. This jurisdiction has to be acknowledged by other bodies, be they other states or business corporations that wish to have dealings with anyone or any organization based in that territory. It is states whose laws allow the flows of money, people and goods that constitute globalization. Moreover, decisions that affect the wider world have to be made in the context of domestic political struggles and debates. Even if a foreign power or a multinational corporation is able to influence the government of a poor and weak state, it is obliged to do so through the laws, regulations and officials that operate in that state. It may be able to influence the formation or application of those laws, but if it were to disregard them, its actions would be illegal and it would be regarded as an invader.

Accordingly, if it became the desire of the majority of citizens of states throughout the world that there be a new form of global governance, it would have to be states that entered into the necessary arrangements and handed over the relevant powers to such a global body. In that event states would still not wither away. They would become another tier of government just as municipal councils or provincial governments are. These new states would give up some of the prerogatives of sovereignty but they would retain relevant forms of legal jurisdiction over their territories. This might have the advantage of giving their citizens less reason to attach themselves to their states with the kind of mindless fervour that marks nationalism, but the administrative necessity for having territorially defined legal jurisdictions would not disappear. Indeed, what we would then have is the kind of federation of states that Kant had advocated. Any federation of states, whether it is ruled by an armed authority or whether it is held together only by cooperative agreements, will involve some reduction in the number and scope of sovereign rights that a nation-state enjoys. A state with such a reduced form of sovereignty would also be less likely to see its national interests in ways that would encourage it to relate to other states and territories in competitive and aggressive ways. Such a state would be united ideologically not by an insular nationalism, but by a feeling of global citizenship that would be in accord with the cosmopolitan ideal.

Given that the nation-state would continue with some form of reduced sovereignty even in a globalized world, a more cosmopolitan form of patriotism would also survive. People need to feel some kind of belonging to their communities. Just as people take pride in the town, city, province or local state in which they live, so they will attach themselves to the nation-state that holds constitutional and legal jurisdiction over the institutional arrangement of their lives. This produces a political and civic solidarity among citizens that they do not share with citizens of other nation-states. But this is to be distinguished from the nationalism that cosmopolitans decry. It would be what I described in Chapter 1 as "political patriotism".

World peace

As we have seen in our discussion of Kant, cosmopolitans are committed to lasting world peace. Given the death, destruction and mayhem war causes, it cannot but involve violations of human rights, acts of injustice and the kinds of harm that cosmopolitans decry. The fact that war today might involve the use of nuclear armaments, with the unimaginable devastation that would bring, merely intensifies the disapproval of war that all cosmopolitans feel. Of course, this stance is not unique to cosmopolitanism. Many theorists in many cultural and political traditions share it.

Nevertheless, it should not be thought that the rejection of war is a universally endorsed stance. In times past there were very notable European philosophers and writers who applauded war, and this view can be found in other traditions also. War has been seen as a way for a nation to show its mettle and for men to show what they are made of. It has been suggested that a nation or a people that avoids war would become soft and degenerate. It would enjoy the kind of luxurious life conditions that prevent it from developing the many virtues that allow a people to achieve greatness. Even Kant expressed this sentiment when he said:

> War itself, provided it is conducted with order and a sacred respect for the rights of civilians, has something sublime about it, and gives nations that carry it on in such a manner a stamp of mind only the more sublime the more numerous the dangers to which they are exposed, and which they are able to meet with fortitude. On the other hand, a prolonged peace favours the predominance of a mere commercial spirit, and with it a debasing self-interest, cowardice, and effeminacy, and tends to degrade the character of the nation. (1928: bk 11, 112–13, quoted in Coady 2008: 46)

The rhetoric inherent in these sentences draws on a competitive form of nationalism in which a people feels it to be important that it be seen as superior to, and more powerful than, another people. Talk of "the character of the nation" indicates a perspective that sees a nation as a unitary body with a single character. What this ignores, of course, is that, quite apart from the possibility that the nation might comprise different ethnic, racial or religious groups, it also comprises different socioeconomic classes. In war it is the high-ranking officers – most of whom will be from the richer and more dominant classes – who send lower-ranking officers and soldiers – most of whom will be from the working classes – to their deaths. It is all very well for the ruling classes to applaud the cultural effects of war and celebrate the way it enhances the fortitude of the nation, but it is not they who normally bear the brunt of the destruction and suffering. This rhetoric also expresses a masculinist outlook in which manly virtues and masculine prowess are valued. War is seen as a test of both manhood and of nationhood. It will be clear that these attitudes are fundamentally immature, and that they have links with the militaristic nationalism that I discussed in Chapter 1. No modern political thinker should be influenced by them.

Some have thought that war is an inevitable part of the human condition because it is a natural and unavoidable expression of an innate human aggressiveness.[5] Evidence for this view might be found in comments made by front-line soldiers. As an example, here are the words of an Australian soldier writing from the trenches of Gallipoli in the First World War: "Oh! The bloody gorgeousness of feeling your bayonet go into soft yielding flesh ..." (quoted in Sparrow 2008: 14). It is also true, however, that many soldiers at the front line refuse to fire their weapons at the enemy and that extensive training is needed to turn recruits into killers.

Thinkers who believe that natural aggressiveness plays a role in war point to ethological studies of animals in the wild that describe aggressive behaviour, especially among males. However, the context of such behaviours differs from that of war among human beings. Male wild animals will fight each other over access to females and most will do so individually rather than in organized groups. Animals also prey on each other and on other species, but they do so when they are hungry. Warfare among human beings is not of this kind. It is not driven by the instinct to mate or by hunger. Nor is it the result of such emotional states as anger or hatred. Even if it is sometimes the case that troops going into battle are driven to a frenzy of aggression in the heat of combat, it is not the case that the architects of war – the politicians who declare war, or the generals who plan it – are driven by anger or heightened states of emotion. For them, the war is a matter of cold calculation and strategic thinking. And for many soldiers who engage in war operations far from the face of the enemy – soldiers such as airmen who drop bombs from great heights or sailors who patrol the oceans – war is not an expression of aggressive emotions. If it is true that war is a phenomenon peculiar to the human species of animal, it does not seem to be true that it arises from any genetic or instinctual aspect of what it is to be human. War is a human institutionalized activity that is pragmatically designed to serve sophisticated human purposes, rather than an expression of natural instincts.

If hatred is a cause of war, it is so not in the form of aggressive emotion, but in the form of cultural xenophobia or racism in which one people hates another because of its perceived otherness. This otherness may consist in differences in religion, skin colour, political ideology or moral practices and, as such, should be overcome by the cosmopolitan acceptance of global cultural differences. Moreover, the more difficult historical question is whether hatred of the other is a cause of war or a symptom of it. It may be not that people go to war because they hate the enemy, but that they hate the enemy because they have gone to war with them. It may be that the cause of war has been greed for territory and the resources they contain, and that the hatred of the other is fomented and used by bellicose leaders in order to create a willingness in their citizenry to attack the perceived enemy. Did the Spanish conquistadors attack and slaughter the native peoples of Central and South America because they decried their pagan practices, or were they motivated by a lust for the gold, land and wealth possessed by those peoples while using their Christian disapproval of human sacrifice as an excuse? While I cannot answer such complex historical questions here, I do think they should give us pause before we accept that hatred can be, by itself, a cause of war.

A cursory glance at history, which would seem to be a litany of wars from the very earliest recorded chronicles to the present day, might, nevertheless, encourage the idea that war is inevitable. It would seem to be the case that human beings have not yet developed ways of resolving conflict that stop short of violence. In so far as many aspects of human interaction involve clashes of wills – situations where one person or group is trying to force another person or group to do something that they do not want to do – it might seem inevitable that organized violence will ensue. It seems that our powers of persuasion are too rudimentary and that our rational capacities for understanding one another and for coming to agreement over matters of dispute are too limited for us to be able to say that violence used for political ends can be expurgated from the human condition. While we may hope for a day when human beings will have developed enough intelligence, tolerance and restraint to avoid going to war with each other, we may have to accept that, for the time being, war is as inevitable an aspect of international relations as crime is of civil society.

War has been described as politics by other means. As Carl von Clausewitz puts it: "War is the resort by an organized group to a relatively large-scale act of violence for political purposes to compel an enemy to do the group's will" (1976: 75). What this suggests is that war is an instrument of global politics in which the constant threat of war makes weaker states compliant with the will of the more powerful. Accordingly, the morality of waging war is a subdivision of the morality of global politics. It is when global political relationships between states or peoples fail to respect human rights, global justice and the legitimate claims of state and non-state actors that recourse is had to war. Given this, it will be difficult to articulate a position on war that is uniquely cosmopolitan. Given that cosmopolitanism rejects militaristic forms of nationalism and stresses respect for human rights and for global justice, and given that most cosmopolitans acknowledge the fallibility of the human condition, which leads to the need, on occasion, to resolve disputes by force, most cosmopolitans will regretfully accept that the use of arms may be necessary to defend human rights and establish global justice.

For this reason not all cosmopolitans espouse pacifism. Pacifism is the view that war and political violence are always wrong.[6] No matter what the provocation, a pacifist will always seek some non-violent solution to the problem and will accept the option of capitulation to the more powerful if all other peaceful means have failed. While the example of Mahatma Gandhi and others encourages the idea that pacifist and non-violent means can overcome violent oppression and injustice, history also shows many examples of individuals and peoples who have been overcome by invaders or political bullies despite their principled stances of resistance. It would seem, then, that the best way to resist armed aggression is with armed defence. In the quest for human rights and global justice, moral victories claimed over the bodies of willing martyrs are empty victories. The tyrants and oppressors may not enjoy moral praise, but they will enjoy the spoils of their aggression.

The cosmopolitan stance towards political violence – involving a regretful acceptance of its being sometimes necessary – is well illustrated by the life of Dietrich Bonhoeffer (1906–45). Bonhoeffer was a German pastor whose preaching stressed the Sermon on the Mount in which Jesus urges his followers to turn the other cheek and to love their enemies. On the basis of this teaching, Bonhoeffer rejected war as a legitimate means of resolving international disputes. Nevertheless, he joined in the plot initiated by officers in the German army to assassinate Hitler in 1943. Along with these officers, Bonhoeffer had come to believe that the only way to stop the war in Europe that Hitler was pursuing was to assassinate him. The assassination attempt failed and the officers and their fellow plotters were hunted down and executed by the Gestapo. It seems, then, that while he was opposed to war, Bonhoeffer was not opposed to political violence. If violence were required to avoid a great evil, then it could be justified.

What is rejected by cosmopolitans and pacifists alike is the idea that war is a normal and acceptable way of resolving international disagreements and that the nation-state is defined in terms of its ability and readiness to wage war. What is rejected is that permanent state of war-readiness among nation-states that turns the world into a series of armed camps held in uneasy truce by fear of the more powerful. The cold war was only the most recent example of this form of international relations. Even today, nuclear armaments continue to raise the stakes between states. The traditional stance of a truce between armed camps continues with the unimaginable horror of nuclear Armageddon as a constant shadow hanging over human civilization. Although this shadow is said to be justified on the grounds that it deters nuclear armed states from going to war with each other, such states, along with other states, continue to resort to violence to defend their economic interests as well as to pursue their national glory or defend their allies.

But the nature of war has changed since the end of the cold war. The quintessential example of war used to be the staged battle on a defined battlefield in which soldiers in bright coloured uniforms stood at one end while soldiers in bright but differently coloured uniforms stood at the other waiting for the command to engage. When that command was given, all hell broke loose but certain rules were followed. Officers were not targeted and ambushes were outlawed. At the failing of the light of day hostilities would be called off and victory given to one side or the other. Soldiers were clearly agents of the state – even if they were mercenaries – and were seen as expendable. Officers saw it as their duty to further the cause of their countries and maintain order in the lower ranks. This form of warfare is inextricably bound to the notion of the nation-state or, in earlier times, to the right of kings to wage war on other kings. Reasons for initiating war have ranged from territorial expansion and national glory to the propagation of one's religion. It is this kind of war that Kant sought to overcome with his proposals in "Perpetual Peace" and for which, it appears, he nevertheless harboured a hidden nostalgia. Today, however, there are many instances of armed conflict in which it is not states as such that are the central protagonists. There are wars within states caused by ethnic or religious rivalries and hatreds, wars of secession, wars of liberation or revolution, and struggles against imperialist hegemony. Guerrilla groups, terrorist cells, resistance fighters and defenders of ethnic purity take up arms against perceived oppressors. State authorities, for their part, use their armies to quell internal dissent, whether it is peaceful or violent.

One feature shared by many of these so-called "new wars" is that they are fought over the alleged rights that peoples have to self-determination. Even before the creation of the UN, American president Woodrow Wilson had spoken of the right to self-determination of peoples, a statement that had encouraged movements against colonialism after the First World War. The central idea here is that a people should not be oppressed politically or exploited economically by states or powers that do not share its culture, religion, ethnicity or conception of what would constitute a good life. The notion of a "people" as it appears in this discourse is inescapably vague but is meant to suggest a community held together by a common tradition, cultural heritage, ethnicity or religion. When Wilson first made his statement he had in mind peoples who were colonized by European powers, but historical events since that time have made clear that almost all sovereign states include peoples in the relevant sense. Most nation-states include within their borders definable groups who do not share the cultural outlooks of their rulers, whether because of differing traditions or ethnicities. They might be the indigenous people of that place or they might be peoples who have migrated there in recent or more distant times, but they will mark themselves off by speaking a different language, having different customs or worshipping different gods. Some will have integrated themselves into the economic or political systems of their masters, but others will not. Most, but not all, such peoples have close ties to the lands on which they live.

As we saw in Chapter 1, the word "nation" is often used to designate a people understood in these terms. In so far as people feel that their identity is bound up with their attachment to place, race or tradition, they will feel the need to affirm and maintain that identity. Unfortunately, if all such peoples – whether they be Kurds, Basques or the Cham Muslim people of Cambodia – were to be given sovereignty over their territories, the number of nation-states in the world would multiply to thousands, and global governance as well as national governance would be well-nigh impossible. Nevertheless, many such peoples have struggled successfully for their independence and many others continue to do so. And many of these struggles involve political violence.

While it seems impossible to grant statehood to all of the world's peoples, it should not be impossible to grant them a degree of autonomy that would allow them to continue to live their preferred cultural lives in conditions free from political or economic domination.[7] President Wilson's call for "self-determination" was ambiguous as to whether it meant that all peoples should be allowed to govern themselves and form nation-states of their own, or whether, within the nation-states in which they live, they should be permitted such a degree of control over their social and political conditions as would allow them to maintain their cultures. It seems that, in the contemporary world, even this second more modest aim is being denied in many countries. The issues here are complex. No one wants to see indigenous or ethnic minorities shut off in their own countries from the economic and cultural opportunities afforded by the wider community, whether by their own choice or by the policies of their governments. This would be an apartheid system. But neither does one want to see the loss of language, culture or religious practice that assimilation into the wider community would bring, if such assimilation were not desired by the community in question.[8] Whether groups or peoples have collective rights to their language, religion, tradition or culture, and whether national governments have an obligation to protect the identity-forming conditions of cultural groups are questions debated by philosophers who ask whether rights are the sorts of moral entity that can be held by a group or whether it is only individuals that have such rights (Appiah 2005).[9] In such debates cosmopolitans will favour the concept of individual rights. If every individual has the right to those cultural conditions that would allow him or her to live a life consistent with their worldview and their cultural tradition, and if governments have an obligation to protect those individual rights, then the best policies for meeting that obligation will be policies that support and protect the cultural practices and identities of the peoples living in their territories. In this way, governments can have duties to protect and maintain the group identities of the peoples living within their borders even if it is the individual rights of members of those peoples that constitute the rights that correspond to those duties.

Just war

But let us now return to the topic of political violence. In order to bring some order into a warring world, philosophers have thought about what moral rules should apply to war and have developed what is now called "the just war doctrine". This phrase refers to a body of thought, developed in the West since the time of Augustine (354–430), that established criteria for engaging in war ethically. These criteria come under two headings. The first set related to when going to war is justified (in Latin this is called *jus ad bellum*, which could be translated as "right reasons for going to war"). The second set related to how war should be conducted (in Latin this is called *jus in bello*, which could be translated as "right ways of conducting war"). The criteria that were devised for justifying going to war included:

- Just cause. The most obvious just cause is to repel an invasion or to support an ally who has been invaded. It used to be thought that one state could attack another in order to punish it for breaking treaties or invading other states. This view is less widely accepted today. There is debate also as to whether it is acceptable to attack a state in order to prevent it from developing or deploying nuclear weapons. Most agree that it is not permissible to go to war in order to secure access to natural resources such as oil. Further, whether one state is permitted to invade another in order to protect the human rights of the citizens of that state – so-called "humanitarian intervention" – is a question I shall discuss presently.
- Right intention. War must not be waged merely to enhance the glory of the national leader, for example.
- Last resort. All other means such as diplomacy and economic sanctions must have been exhausted.
- Reasonable chance of success. It would be irresponsible to declare war on an overwhelmingly more powerful enemy.
- Having the right authority to declare war. War must be declared by the legitimate leader of the relevant nation-state. If a warlord or the head of a group of gangsters or of a terrorist group "declares" war on a state or on another group, the conflict that follows is technically not a war, and will not be recognized as such in international law. Such conflicts should be dealt with through the criminal law of the affected states.

Among the principles relating to *jus in bello* are:

- Proportionality. It would be wrong to respond to a minor border incursion with an all-out invasion or with a nuclear attack.

- Exempting non-combatants. Blanket bombing of cities causing civilian deaths would be ruled out.
- Treating captured soldiers humanely.
- Forbidding rape and plunder.
- Creating conditions for a lasting peace after hostilities cease.
- Forbidding the use of child soldiers. This is a more recent development endorsed by the UN.
- Forbidding the use of certain weapons such as chemical weapons or flame-throwers. Negotiations on the banning of nuclear weapons, land mines, cluster bombs, and ordnance using depleted uranium are continuing.

While much has been written about how these rules apply to modern conflicts (e.g. Etzioni & Wenglinsky 1970; McKeogh 2002; Christopher 2004; Atack 2005; Fotion 2007; Young 2007a; Coady 2008), our question is whether there is a uniquely cosmopolitan perspective on them. I have already said that cosmopolitanism is not alone in being concerned about war and in wanting to see it engaged in in an ethical manner and only as a last resort. But cosmopolitanism does introduce a new questioning of the role of the nation-state in thinking about contemporary armed conflicts.

Michael Walzer's definitive study of the ethics of war focuses on wars that are fought between states and argues that the first and most obvious "just cause" for going to war is to defend the state against outside attacks. Indeed, he argues that in the case of a "supreme emergency", as when the very existence of the state is under threat, it may be permissible for the threatened state to suspend its adherence to the norms of *jus in bello* and, for example, use torture to extract vital information from captured soldiers or bomb cities with the foreseen consequence of many civilian deaths. A state may also pre-emptively attack another if it sees that other state as an immediate threat to it (Walzer 1992: ch. 16). Simon Caney (2005: ch. 7) has criticized Walzer's position on the cosmopolitan grounds that he assumes that the state is an entity that has a right to defend itself no matter what its legitimacy. On this argument, an aggressive state such as Nazi Germany would have had the right to defend itself against attack from forces seeking to end its rule even after it had begun to murder its own citizens and those of the lands it had conquered. Moreover, it would have been justified in using means forbidden by the rules of war in order to do so. Walzer's concept of supreme emergency, which justifies abrogating the rules of *jus in bello*, makes light of the human rights of combatants and civilians in favour of defending the integrity of the political community, but it does so without questioning whether the state or the political community encapsulate values that warrant setting aside such individual rights. Walzer uses the standard "statist" or nationalist arguments to the effect that states embody the common life of their people along with their cultural traditions, and therefore constitute an intrinsic and supreme value. Accordingly, the modern international order of sovereign states must be preserved. But a cosmopolitan would ask what value a state has if it does not protect the human rights of the individuals that make it up or respect the human rights of foreigners or the sovereignty of other states. Can such a state have just cause in defending itself against other states, especially if those other states are in conflict with it because of its violations of human rights? The cosmopolitan perspective would put the stress on the rights of individuals and accord rights to states to engage in war only if those states have the kind of legitimacy that comes from respecting individual human rights.

Principles of *jus in bello* already have the kind of focus on individuals that cosmopolitans would applaud. They seek to protect non-combatants and soldiers alike because they are human beings with rights. But the norms of *jus ad bellum* seem to admit only of a statist or nationalist reading. Cosmopolitans like Caney would seek to make the two sets of norms consistent by arguing that political communities have value only in so far as they protect the rights of individuals, and that they therefore have the right to go to war only to protect the rights of individuals. While it is illegitimate for a state to go to war in order to seize the territory or enslave the population of another, this is not primarily because doing so would destroy that state or disturb the international order, but because doing so would violate the rights of the citizens of the state being attacked. In this way a defensive war would be justified not in terms of defending the sovereignty of the state, but of defending the human rights of that state's citizens. Not every state that defends itself from external attack could genuinely claim that rationale. It is not acceptable to say that one can kill innocent people in order to protect one's despotic rule or even one's traditional way of life. From the cosmopolitan perspective the principles of *jus ad bellum* focus on defending the rights of citizens rather than on those of the state. Just causes will include the defence of a state only if that state respects human rights and enjoys the consent of the people. Similarly, third-party states may defend attacked states only if more justice will result. On the cosmopolitan conception, the right intention for fighting a war will be the defence of human rights.

Moreover, while not all theorists in the past agreed that punishing a state for international criminal acts, such as invading another state, was a just cause for going to war, a cosmopolitan would argue that it is not justified for one state to punish another because only superstate bodies such as the UN should have that kind of authority. If one state took it upon itself to punish another, it would be claiming hegemonic rights over that state. Cosmopolitans would only acknowledge as legitimate the authority of superstate organizations such as the UN or of any collective security organizations that are accountable to democratically constituted bodies to authorize war in the defence of human rights. Again, if having the right authority to declare war used to rest in kings and more recently in presidents or prime ministers, cosmopolitan proper authority will be democratic authority. This idea fulfils the promise of Kant's suggestion that democratic states will be less inclined to go to war by suggesting that if they do, and if the democratic process has not been compromised by nationalist propaganda, it will only be to defend human rights either at home or abroad.

However, in so far as wars are no longer fought just between states, the just war tradition needs to be expanded. The rules of war cannot readily be upheld by state authorities in the new kinds of contemporary war that involve the breakdown of civil order. The way in which terrorists target civilians is only the most obvious example of this. In such contexts it becomes important to acknowledge that it is individuals and groups of individuals who perpetrate acts of war, whether new wars or conventional wars. Individuals cannot abrogate their responsibility by claiming to act on behalf of a state or a national, ideological or religious cause. Wars should be fought under the aegis of what Kant called cosmopolitan law: laws that apply to individuals rather than collectivities. As Mary Kaldor puts it, "a cosmopolitan approach requires respect for cosmopolitan law. This is international law that applies to individuals and not to states. The two main components of cosmopolitan law are the Laws of War and Human Rights Law" (2002: 277). As an example of what she means, Kaldor mentions the Nuremberg trials, which made individuals liable for the war crimes they committed even when they were obeying the authorities of their states. Just as statesmen have used "reasons of state" to justify acts of global injustice, so soldiers and generals frequently use "military necessity" to justify acts that violate the rules of war. However, no individual is immune from liability for crimes they commit on behalf of the state, whether during war or in times of peace. Cosmopolitanism insists that, just as individual rights should be protected, so individuals should be held accountable.

Humanitarian intervention

I have discussed the cosmopolitan norm of accepting limitations on the sovereignty of nation-states to secure human rights and global justice by asking the question of how, and to what extent, sovereign states are still a necessary component of a globalized world. My conclusion has been that while sovereignty is not as absolute as it once was, it continues to have legal, commercial and diplomatic reality. However, many of the debates around the issue of sovereignty in recent times have been about whether states have the right to intervene in the domestic, social and political affairs of another state.

States have been seeking to influence one another since time immemorial. At once the most obvious and most brutal means for exercising such influence is military force. A more powerful state can force a less powerful one to do its bidding by threatening to invade it or to steal its territory. Under such pressure a less powerful state may agree to unfair trade arrangements, cede some of its territory or change its policies so as to allow foreign takeovers of its resources. The cold war was not a war in the sense that armies invaded each other's territories, but in the sense that two superpowers, the USA and the USSR, sought to influence less powerful states so as to create two opposed "blocs" of nations in the world with a third group of non-aligned nation-states standing off to one side. Any government that showed signs of currying favour with an opposing superpower found itself under diplomatic pressure, infiltrated by secret agents who would encourage and fund anti-government activities, denied trading opportunities or even invaded by the armed forces of the relevant superpower. Economic sanctions, trade embargoes and naval blockades were also used. The moral justifications for such actions were very weak since the fundamental issues were ideological. Although the conflict between capitalism and communism was often portrayed as a conflict between freedom and godless tyranny, it is arguable that it was commercial interests and the expansion of markets that played the most operative role in fomenting the conflict (Koshy 1999).

Now that the cold war is officially over, the most morally justifiable reason for any foreign intervention is said to be the securing of human rights and global justice. In the event that the government of a particular state oppresses its people, exploits them economically and denies them their human rights, do other states have the right to intervene? Does a body like the UN, even when it can secure the agreement of member states to do so, have the right to invade a nation-state in order to restore the rights of its citizens? The term used for such interventions is "humanitarian intervention" because it involves intervening in the internal affairs of a nation-state, whether with military force or other forms of pressure, in order to provide humanitarian aid or to secure human rights. If this intention were not present, the intervention would be rightly seen as an invasion and would be resisted as such.

The UN was initially set up to maintain peace between nations and its charter sets up a series of criteria by which the UN can authorize armed intervention to preserve peace. But all of its rules and guidelines are premised on the sovereignty of nation-states. It is states that go to war with each other and it is states that must be policed so as to preserve peace. War is seen as conflict between states and the UN sees itself as the umpire or arbiter between states. The members of the UN and of its Security Council are states. In this conception sovereignty is never called into question and the right of states to not be interfered with except if they threaten other states is sacrosanct. However, the UDHR introduces a deep tension into the mission of the UN. It focuses on individual human beings. It declares the rights that each individual has irrespective of nationality, race, ethnicity, gender or religion. These rights are to be honoured and protected by the states in which the relevant individuals live and, in the event that they are not so protected, the UN declares that the international community has the duty to protect them. The UN Security Council can authorize foreign interventions to protect human rights and it does so most notably when it provides humanitarian aid in war-torn areas, provides soldiers to protect the delivery of such aid or installs peacekeeping forces in troubled areas. But the goal of protecting human rights puts the UN at loggerheads with its own commitment to state sovereignty. In the event that tyrants attack their own peoples through genocide or through levels of mismanagement that lead to starvation, there is a conflict between protecting the victims of such actions and respecting the sovereign rights of that state.

Henry Shue (1999) has offered an argument for the legitimacy of foreign intervention based on the premise that talk of human rights is empty unless we are prepared to police their observance. His argument rests on a distinction between wrongs that, as he puts it, we have a right to commit (such as being rude or disloyal), and wrongs we have no right to commit (such as stealing or wantonly killing other human beings). If it seems a bit odd to speak of a wrong that we have a right to commit, we might consider that being rude or disloyal are failures of virtue but may not be an offence against strict moral norms. Even if being rude is socially offensive, no one has the right or the duty to stop us from being rude if we want to be. In contrast, we have no right to commit wrong acts such as stealing or murder because of the kind of harm they cause to their victims. People have a right to defend themselves against the kinds of wrongs that would harm them and to use the instruments of the state to do so. Accordingly, we are prepared to enforce those prohibitions with police action. It is because we institute such policing that we can genuinely say that people have a right to property or a right to life. To claim that people have such rights and yet not to institute policing to enforce their observance would make talk of such rights empty rhetoric. Accordingly, to say that we have no right to commit such wrongs is to say that others have a duty to prevent us from committing them or to punish us if we do. Given that rights and duties go together, it would be vacuous to say that there was a right without there also being a duty to protect it and to punish those who violate it.

The reason that Shue approaches this issue in the rather unusual form of asking whether there are wrongs that we have a right to commit is that the doctrine of state sovereignty might seem to imply that sovereign leaders have a right to commit any wrongs within their own borders that they like. Provided they are recognized as the legitimate authority, their right to rule is said to be absolute and they are answerable to no one. The implication of this doctrine is that foreign intervention to protect the human rights of individuals within tyrannical states would never be justified. However, if we apply Shue's distinction to the international sphere, we could say that sovereigns have a right to commit some wrongs but not others. We might look the other way if corrupt leaders use illegitimate means to influence election outcomes, take bribes or engage in economic mismanagement, provided that the lives or fundamental rights of the population are not threatened. But they have no right to destroy their own populations through genocide, for example. The kind of harm that such wrong acts cause is such that we could not tolerate them. They would be wrongs that tyrannical leaders have no right to commit. Human rights constitute a boundary beyond which such leaders may not go. Accordingly, the basic human rights of populations anywhere should be policed by the international community lest such rights become mere rhetoric. If a state will not police them, they will need to be policed by a super-state body. It follows from this argument that the international community has a duty to protect populations even in other countries.

The argument then proceeds to talk of two kinds of duties that attach to rights: the duty to respect the right and the duty to police its observance. Because of the right to bodily integrity, we all have the duty not to assault others. This is a negative duty. But in case an assault does occur, there is also a positive duty to prevent, deter or punish offenders. Shue (1999) calls such positive duties "default duties". Within most states, such duties are borne by the police and the system of criminal justice. When we speak of fundamental or basic human rights, we refer to rights that attract both these kinds of duties. Fundamental human rights concern interests that are so important that positive or default duties must be specifiable. The lesson to be drawn from this point is that a gross violation of human rights, even on the part of the sovereign leaders of the victims, must be responded to with police action to rescue the victims and to bring the perpetrators to justice. This principle applies even when the perpetrators are leaders of sovereign nation-states. To fail to do so would be to not take seriously the claim that the victims had the relevant rights in the first place.

Shue demonstrates the relevance of this argument to cosmopolitanism when he says:

> The fundamental point is: if all the rest of us actually do nothing to define and assign default duties for the case in which a state does not protect its own people against genocide – even for the most common case in which the state is the orchestrator of the genocide – then we genuinely are assigning the vital interests and basic rights of non-compatriots zero

> weight in our calculations about how to organize the planet, specifically how to understand sovereignty – most specially, what a sovereign may allow. (*Ibid.*: 4)

Cosmopolitans should be in favour of armed humanitarian intervention so long as it is authorized by the UN, and also of a global system of criminal justice to bring perpetrators of crimes against humanity to justice. The police powers of the state in which the genocide occurs would seem to be powerless to stop it, and so to assign the default duty of preventing the crime to such state-based powers is not to be serious about protecting the human right in question.

Nevertheless, other cosmopolitans see considerable danger in the alleged rights of states to engage in humanitarian interventions. They argue that, if states assumed that they had a right to intervene in the affairs of other states whenever those states abused their citizens, global anarchy would result. According to David Chandler, "In the Middle East, in Africa and the Balkans, the exercise of 'international justice' signifies a return to the Westphalian system of open great-power domination over states which are too weak to prevent external claims against them" (2003: 37). Chandler is opposed to humanitarian intervention because he sees it as a reassertion of their hegemony on the part of the more powerful states. He sees this as a thwarting of legality and thus as the negation of the international justice that it is meant to protect. The problem arises when interventions are justified by humanitarian ideals rather than by law. International law establishes the formal equality of states and their equal rights to sovereignty. If such law were to be overruled by the pursuit of humanitarian ideals, it would result in the hegemony of the more powerful states. Only weak states would be subject to such policing action and so their status of legal equality in the international system would be compromised. Even if it were for the best of humanitarian reasons, force would once again be the major influence on the relations between states.[10]

The solution to this problem is to enshrine the "duty to protect" as a principle within international law. Whereas traditional justifications for war centred on self-defence on the part of states, a recent report issued by the UN acknowledges a right to respond militarily not only to clear and serious threats to a state but also to threats to its population. The report asserts that whenever the Security Council authorizes the use of force it should apply "five basic criteria of legitimacy" (United Nations 2004: para. 207). These criteria turn out to be similar to the principles of *jus ad bello* (Lango 2008). Such criteria include defending populations against violations of humanitarian law such as genocide or ethnic cleansing. At the 2005 UN World Summit, the General Assembly adopted a resolution in which it endorses armed humanitarian intervention (United Nations 2005). Also relevant to the question of whether military force might be used for humanitarian interventions or to enforce and protect humanitarian aid efforts is the Report of the International Commission on Intervention and State Sovereignty set up by the Canadian Government in 2000 in Ottawa. This report, entitled *The Responsibility to Protect* (ICISS 2001), argues that humanitarian intervention is justified by criteria that resemble those of the just war doctrine, including "right authority", by which it refers to the UN Security Council. As for "just cause", according to Singer's summary of this report:

> The commission cut down the criteria for justifiable military action to just two:
> (a) *Large-scale loss of life*, actual or apprehended, with genocidal intent or not, which is the product either of deliberate state action, or state neglect or inability to act, or a failed state situation; or,
> (b) *Large-scale "ethnic cleansing"*, actual or apprehended, whether carried out by killing, forced expulsion, act of terror or rape.
>
> (Singer 2002: 140–41)

Singer endorses these principles on the grounds that states have a responsibility to protect their own citizens. Accordingly, when a state fails to do so, or actively violates the rights of its own citizens, the international community is entitled to take up this responsibility. But even then, the UN must still consider the consequences and not authorize intervention if more harm would result (including anarchy resulting from the failure of the intervening power to establish law and order). The *jus ad bello* principle of reasonable chance of success would rule out any foolhardy military adventure or any premature withdrawal.

Singer notes that the Canadian report has made a significant contribution to international thinking on humanitarian intervention. Moving from talk of "the right to intervene" to talk of "the responsibility to protect" gives a more constrained and humanitarian flavour to this thinking. The concept of a responsibility to protect the rights of individuals in other states is more onerous and more focused. Only the UN should accept this responsibility, since if it were open to powerful states to do so unilaterally there would be considerable danger of imperialistic abuses of their power. Such states might be tempted to use humanitarian justifications for interventions whose real purpose was the enhancement of their hegemony. If humanitarian intervention were engaged in with the endorsement of the UN, the imperialistic abuses that Chandler and others have warned us of could, in principle, be avoided. Cosmopolitans could endorse the principle of the responsibility to protect the human rights of all, even though the UN is not itself a body that can escape the pressures of its more powerful members. As a matter of logic, it does not count against the validity of a moral principle that it might be abused by unscrupulous agents. That the principle of humanitarian intervention might be abused by powerful nations does not count against the validity of the principle. It does, however, require of decision-makers that they apply the principle with honesty and integrity and that the processes through which such decisions are made be transparent and open to as much democratic scrutiny as is feasible.

It might also help to reconceptualize the notion of "humanitarian intervention" somewhat. By discussing the issue under the rubric of the just war doctrine, it is framed by the question of when war is justified and conceptualized as an international issue centred on conflicts between states. However, if we discuss the issue under the rubric of defending the rights of individuals from the predations of criminal tyrants, we can see it as an issue of policing. Policing consists in upholding the law so as to protect individuals from criminals. In civil society every individual has the right to be protected from theft, murder and other crimes. For this purpose police forces are instituted and given powers within the law to enforce the law, prevent crime and apprehend criminals. If we translated this model to the international sphere, we could conceptualize humanitarian interventions and peacekeeping missions as police actions rather than as acts of war. Forces that engage in such actions would then be seen as international police rather than as invading soldiers. The world will always contain recalcitrant people or criminals. Some of these might be the leaders of nations. They are criminals if they flout international law, including those laws that ensure compliance with international treaties and secure the human rights of their subjects. Such criminals, like criminals in the domestic sphere, need to be made answerable for their crimes. They should be subject to international law and police action should be taken to ensure their compliance with such law. If they do not comply, they should be apprehended and brought to justice through duly recognized international courts.

The use of coercion by police would have to be strictly controlled within justifiable guidelines. Conceptually there is no difference between the domestic justifications for police action and an international justification for police action. Admittedly, there are inescapable difficulties in the international sphere that do not exist in the domestic sphere. The policing powers of the UN and other global agencies are not so clearly defined and institutionalized as are domestic police forces and their use is subject to sometimes arbitrary restrictions resulting from the veto powers of the permanent members of the UN Security Council. Nevertheless, the ethical difficulties of conceiving of humanitarian intervention as morally justifiable are reduced if we conceive of such interventions as police actions that support and uphold international law rather than circumventing it, as Chandler fears. Of course, the results of police action must not produce a worse condition than that which it is designed to prevent, the action must be proportional and it must have justification from legitimate authority. As in the domestic sphere, police brutality can occur when these guidelines are ignored (Young 2007b). But in so far as it is designed to uphold international law, police power can be seen as legitimate much more readily than can military invasions in the name of human rights. While what actually happens in either case may be very similar, the conceptual and justificatory framework for understanding what is happening differs. Police primarily have the responsibility to protect the rights of individuals rather than pursuing the international objectives of nation-states by means of force.

Conclusion

Although it seems that conflict and criminality are ineradicable from the human condition, the incidence of war can be reduced to the extent that nationalism can be. It is the pursuit of the national interest on the part of nation-states and the pursuit of self-determination on the part of peoples who aspire to be nation-states that are the main causes of war. Most developed nation-states devote considerable time to adopting strategic policies to meet the challenges posed by the pursuit of power and influence on the part of other nation-states. The emergence of new powers in the international arena, such as China and India, leads other states to explore opportunities for economic advantage, threats to national security, risks to supplies of natural resources, changes to diplomatic relationships and new military alliances. Seldom do these policy discussions raise the issues of global justice, democratic governance and human rights, except in so far as their denial might lead to global instability and hence to the undermining of national sovereignty. The mindset of the think tanks and policy experts who advise governments on such matters is inescapably strategic and centred on the national interest. While many say that it is unrealistic to expect otherwise, I would say that it is unrealistic to expect lasting world peace if the cosmopolitan concerns for global justice, democratic governance and human rights are not addressed as a first priority. The sovereignty of nation-states must be seen not as sacrosanct, but as a pragmatic, administrative arrangement. There will be less reason to go to war to protect national interests or honour if the focus of world leaders is on individual human rights and global economic justice. If there were a need to protect such rights or the self-determinations of peoples, it should be done by way of UN authorized police actions rather than by wars waged between states.

Chapter 5

Towards a global community

> Cosmopolitanism refers to a form of moral and political community characterised by laws which are universal. The central proposition of cosmopolitanism as a moral and political doctrine is that humans can and should form a universal (that is global) moral community. (Shapcott 2001: 7)

The final set of features of cosmopolitanism that we need to explore is:

(17) acknowledging the rule of international law;
(18) commitment to open and participatory political processes globally;
(19) religious and cultural tolerance and an acceptance of global pluralism;
(20) dialogue and communication across cultural and national boundaries;
(21) seeing the world as a single polity and community.

The suggestion that the whole world might be seen as a global community could express an ideal or describe a reality. It may be an ideal that cosmopolitans advocate as a hoped-for utopia or it may be an apt description of the way the human world actually is. I shall suggest it could be both. A global community may already exist, but in a form that requires further enhancement in order to realize the hopes and aspirations of human beings everywhere.

Community

Before we can begin our discussion of whether the world constitutes a global community, we need to specify what we understand by a "community". A group of people who are together in some sense but only by chance does not constitute a community. A group of people waiting for a train at a railway station are together in the sense that they are in proximity to each other in a specific place, but they have little in common that would constitute them as a community. That they share the purpose of catching a train is not usually enough to bind them in this way. Nor does a prison yard occupied by mutually antagonistic criminals among whom peace is maintained by mutual fear, by bullies within the yard or by armed guards at its perimeters constitute a community. A large number of people gathered together at a football ground to support their favourite team, however, could be thought of as a community, even though it will be a very temporary one. They share a substantial goal and purpose, and enjoy some conviviality and solidarity because of that. Shared interests such as a desire for wealth and social goods may also ground a feeling of community, although they could also give rise to competitiveness and class struggle. We have noted in Chapter 3 how Rawls sees a national economy as a system of cooperation in which participants can demand fair institutions for the distribution of social goods. A community becomes even less ephemeral when it shares an outlook on life or a conception of how life should be lived. This might arise because of a shared social and political tradition, shared ethnicity, shared religion, shared nationality or shared class identification.

What is distinctive of community is some feeling of solidarity. Members of a community share some aspect of identity and purpose, and recognize each other as sharing that identity and purpose. This leads them to be concerned for each other and to set up institutions or arrangements through which they can share aspects of their lives and fulfil obligations towards each other. It should also be noted that one can be a member of a number of communities in this sense and have a number of loyalties and affiliations based on group identity. A most dramatic example of this would be a village that has a national border running through it. The villagers would share a proximity to each other and would share a life based on the village, and yet some would be of a different nationality than the others and be subject to a different legal jurisdiction. These villagers would identify with several overlapping communities. In modern pluralistic societies most people are members of overlapping communities in this way and have overlapping identities as a result.[1]

I have discussed patriotism as a form of identification with, and loyalty to, one's political community in Chapter 1, and I argued there that cosmopolitans try to overcome the tendencies to chauvinism that such feelings of loyalty give rise to by being somewhat ironic about their identification with their own group. In Chapter 3 I argued that our concern for the well-being of others and for justice in the distribution of social goods should not be confined by national borders or group memberships. As we have seen when we discussed the Nussbaum debate on patriotism, many commentators see the modern nation-state as the broadest community of which we are a part, whereas cosmopolitans would see worldwide humanity as the community with which we should feel a degree of solidarity. Similarly, Rawls considers a nation-state to be the broadest context in which institutions can be asked to operate justly, while cosmopolitans demand that the whole world be a context in which institutions operate so as to secure justice for all. The pursuit of global justice and the feeling of global solidarity are inextricable. It is our shared humanity that provides the motivation and ethical basis for such concerns. The question is, however, whether a shared humanity is a sufficiently "thick" form of solidarity to provide the basis for what we might call a global community.

Identity has a horizon: difference. If a group of people share an identity and recognize each other as holders of that identity, they will also define themselves as different from people who do not share that identity. Being a Catholic is in part defined by not being a Protestant and being a Muslim is in part defined by not being a Jew or a Christian. Of course the positive features of what it is to belong to such communities will be more important and more prominent, but the feeling that one is different from members of other communities will also be strong. One could conclude from this point that the human world as a whole cannot be a community because there is no "other" to which members can contrast themselves and from which they can see themselves as different. It has been suggested that the world would only come together as one if it were attacked by extra-terrestrials. However, cosmopolitans would urge that people should overcome the tendency to define themselves by contrast to others and embrace difference as an intrinsic feature of a world community.

I would suggest that a world community exists – despite all the different groupings, nations, ethnicities, religions and traditions that structure and differentiate the global human family – when people acknowledge a global obligation to help each other when times are hard, accord each other cultural respect and political equality across ethnic differences and state borders, pursue global justice on the assumption that in a globalized economic system everyone has a right to a fair distribution of social goods, and see themselves as global citizens engaged with each other through a variety of global political institutions. In a global community individuals and peoples accord everyone equal moral status, protect each other's rights and enter into dialogue with each other with mutual respect. This is a very idealistic conception and the conflict-ridden world of today does not encourage hope that this ideal is close to being realized. However, I shall argue that it is an ideal that, despite all the enmity in the world, is already some way towards realization, and that it is one to which we should be committed. Moreover, I shall argue that cosmopolitanism is the outlook that we need in order to contribute to its realization.

International relations

In the discourse of international relations, the focus is on nation-states and their relations to each other, and the norm would be that they would treat each other with respect – albeit that, in a Westphalian world, this respect is won through the exercise of power. Accordingly, if cosmopolitans acknowledge the sovereignty of states even as they see the need to place limitations on that sovereignty so as to protect human rights and secure global justice, they must also give consideration to the nature of the relations between states. They will consider it important that all states honour the treaties and undertakings that they enter into with each other. Only in this way can the international legal order that protects the rights of individuals be protected. If the UN secures agreement to international covenants that recognize and enshrine human rights, then states that are signatories to those covenants are under an obligation to abide by them. Political realists would argue that the national interest can trump such obligations and that states have the right to repudiate them if their own interests are under sufficiently serious threat. Accordingly, cosmopolitans need to argue why treaty obligations and other international covenants are binding on states.

Such an argument has been offered by Rawls in his book *The Law of Peoples*, a book that displays the influence of Kant's "Perpetual Peace". Rawls envisages a hypothetical situation not unlike the one he had created in his earlier book *A Theory of Justice*. Whereas in the earlier book he had imagined the kinds of social and political institutions that individuals would agree to at the level of a nation-state if they decided on them without knowing where they would come to stand in those arrangements, in the later book he envisages representatives of peoples meeting together to shape the international order without their knowing what positions their peoples would hold in that order. Under such conditions, Rawls suggests that, through their representatives, peoples would endorse the following principles:

1. Peoples are free and independent, and their freedom and independence are to be respected by other peoples.
2. Peoples are to observe treaties and undertakings.
3. Peoples are equal and are parties to the agreements that bind them.
4. Peoples are to observe a duty of non-intervention.
5. Peoples have the right to self-defense but no right to instigate war for reasons other than self-defense.
6. Peoples are to honor human rights.
7. Peoples are to observe certain specified restrictions in the conduct of war.

8. Peoples have a duty to assist other peoples living under unfavorable conditions that prevent their having a just or decent political and social regime. (Rawls 1999: 37)

Although we are familiar with these principles from texts on international law and from our description of cosmopolitanism, Rawls's argument is that a meeting of reasonable representatives of peoples, deciding from behind a "veil of ignorance", would agree to them because in doing so they would secure the kind of global order in which those peoples could pursue their ways of life and other legitimate goals. Accordingly, these principles become fair, reasonable and normative.

In using the term "peoples" Rawls seeks to avoid the theoretical constructs associated with the term "nation-states". He wants to distinguish a people from a state because he thinks that the concept of a state is tied to a utilitarian and realist conception of international relations. According to the Westphalian conception I described in Chapter 4, a state exists in so far as it aggressively defends its borders and hegemony either by its own strength or by alignments with other states. It seeks its own advantage – it is "rational" in that utilitarian sense – and is not bound by the criterion of reasonableness that binds peoples through the kind of global social contract that Rawls envisages. A people that is "reasonable" will be more likely to accommodate itself to others through compromise than a nation-state that is "rational" in the pursuit of its national interests. In this way basic human rights are secured not by a central global authority or by a stable balance of power between states, but by peoples agreeing to exist within, and be subject to, a cooperative scheme of mutual respect and non-intervention.

However, if it is a social contract that is being envisaged, it is a second-level social contract that differs from the first-level contract described in *A Theory of Justice*. Participants at that first level are individuals who decide on principles for fair political association and the distribution of social goods on behalf of themselves and their own kith and kin in the domestic context of a particular nation-state, while the participants at the second level are representatives who act on behalf of peoples. Moreover, the scope of their deliberation is how to interpret the above principles rather than whether to establish them. Rawls thinks that they already have such *a priori* plausibility that they do not need grounding, perhaps because the very definition of a "people" is that such principles are enacted by them. A people is a people in so far as it adheres to principles 1, 3 and 4, for example, and also holds other peoples to doing so. Another reason why Rawls thinks that the second level differs from the first is that, at the second level, the control of territories by peoples cannot be questioned, despite the historical arbitrariness of borders. The reason for this is that unless a state-like body has control and ownership of territory, that territory or resource will deteriorate. A legal jurisdiction is required to maintain property rights and develop the legal instruments and infrastructure needed for economic activity.

The picture of international relations that Rawls is drawing could represent a global community because it leads to social or international stability for the right reasons. "Stability for the right reasons means stability brought about by citizens acting correctly according to the appropriate principles of their sense of justice, which they have acquired by growing up under and participating in just institutions" (*ibid*.: 13 n.2). Rawls is contrasting his conception of international cooperation with that of political realists who argue that the world of nation-states is an anarchy in which brute force is required to maintain peace, whether that force is exercised by one or several powerful states or whether it is exercised by a super-state agency with a monopoly on power. The realist conception of international relations is like that of the prison yard above. Coercion to enforce cooperation or compliance does not create stability for the right reasons.[2]

This point had already been made by the English jurist and philosopher H. L. A. Hart in 1961 in the last chapter of his book *The Concept of Law*. In an attempt to understand how international law can have the status and normativity of law, Hart compares it to domestic law or the law that applies within states. Legal theorists called "positivists" argue that municipal law is binding on citizens – that is, has the status and normativity of law – because it is backed by sanctions. Their model of how the law works is that of a powerful Leviathan or ruler who issues commands and has the power to punish disobedience severely. On this view, it is only because they fear punishment that citizens within nation-states feel themselves obliged to obey the law. If this is the basis of the normativity of domestic law, is international law binding on states for similar reasons? Do states respect international law only out of fear of sanctions? Kant had suggested that there is no international agency to enforce international law in the way that a Leviathan enforces domestic law, and that there ought not to be. For his part, Hart points out that, even if the UN charter provides for sanctions, recent history has shown that this power is severely limited by the use of the veto on the part of the most powerful UN members except when it has suited those members to use the legitimacy accorded by the UN to pursue their own national interests under the UN banner.

But rather than concluding that international law is a sham, Hart argues that the positivist's account of the normativity of domestic law is incorrect. He likens it to a scenario where a gunman has held you up and demanded your money. It makes sense in this context to say that you are obliged to hand over your money. But it is not the case that you "have an obligation" to hand over your money. Having an obligation is not the same as being obliged (Hart 1961: 80). Having an obligation is a moral condition whereas being obliged is the state of feeling motivated by the likelihood of suffering the sanction or punishment threatened for disobedience. Even where there are sanctions, as in domestic law where the criminal code is backed by policing, one must not equate the external predictive statement "I shall suffer sanctions" with the internal normative statement "I have an obligation to act thus". To be under an obligation is simply a different phenomenon from being afraid to transgress. It is a moral condition. According to Hart, domestic law places citizens under a legal obligation rather than forcing them to obey through fear. It may be that the fear of sanctions is needed at the domestic level to stop the criminally minded from committing crimes, since it is often easy to perform criminal acts and even to escape detection in a society where everyone is equally vulnerable, but for most people the sense of being under an obligation will be enough to ensure that they conform to the law and will provide sufficient motivation to overcome the temptations to criminality that might arise in the context of fallible policing. On the basis of this analogy, Hart concludes that, despite the absence of the Hobbesian solution to the problem of international order – the solution that posits a global Leviathan to enforce the peace – international law truly is law in the sense that it secures global order through there being a genuine obligation on the part of states to conform to it. The only question that remains is where this genuine obligation comes from.

This question is answered by Rawls's account in that the second-level social contract that he describes shows how representatives of peoples can place themselves and their peoples under an obligation to adhere to international law; they do so because, as reasonable peoples, they acknowledge that it is fair to do so. It is a system of law that representatives of peoples would agree to if they did not know what standing their peoples would end up having in the world system. In this way stability is attained for the right reasons rather than through fear of punishment or of anarchy. Just as in the domestic case, if a society is a system of cooperation – as opposed to a command system – then it must have the cooperation of its people. People must see it as fair. When they do so they will be under an obligation to cooperate with that society. In the global context, a people will be under an obligation to meet its obligations within the global community to the extent that it sees the principles under which that community operates to be fair.

However, just as in the domestic case there are individuals with differing moral relationships to the state – citizens in good standing, criminals and individuals in need of welfare, for example – so in the international community there are peoples with differing moral relationships to the global community. There are liberal societies, hierarchical but decent societies, outlaw states that refuse to adhere to international law and in which internal governance is ineffective, "burdened" societies that stand in need of international assistance, and what Rawls calls "benevolent dictatorships".

Liberal societies are those that give full political rights to their people – rights such as liberty of conscience, individual equality before the law, and rights to dissent, to democratic participation and to association – as well as providing whatever social goods such as education and health services their members need in order to pursue whatever they consider to be the human good in ways that do not harm others. In contrast, a decent, hierarchical people is non-liberal because it does not give full political rights to its members but has political institutions that allow for consultation on matters of policy. Moreover, decent peoples respect such basic human rights as the right to life, security and subsistence, property, and formal equality before the law. Theocratic societies in which non-elected clergy rule, but do so in accordance with the conception of a good life shared by the whole community, would be examples of such decent peoples. Both liberal and decent societies are participants in good standing in the social contract between peoples that establishes the global community.

An outlaw state, on the other hand, is a people that refuses to enter the global contract and that seeks to secure its advantages by force of arms or dishonest diplomacy. It also refuses to secure the human rights of its members. Like a criminal in the domestic context, such a society may be legitimately subjected to police action or humanitarian intervention on the part of the global community. The global community is also entitled to intervene in the political arrangements of a failed state in so far as the absence of effective governance in such states can lead to their becoming outlaw states. Given the existence of such states, the idealized picture of a global community that the eight principles enunciate needs to be modified so as to acknowledge the need for forms of political violence that go beyond mere self-defence. A burdened society is one that suffers such a degree of poverty, both in resources and in individual wealth, as to not be able to govern itself effectively. In relation to such societies, Rawls's eighth principle suggests that the global community and richer societies have an obligation to assist through the provision of aid to the point where such societies can govern themselves effectively and enter into the global community in accordance with the eight principles. Rawls does not offer much comment on benevolent dictatorships.

The foreign-policy implications for liberal societies in relation to other liberal societies are, as Kant had argued, that they will live in peace. The foreign-policy implications for liberal societies in relation to decent societies are that decent peoples should be accepted into the world community and, perhaps, encouraged to become liberal by non-coercive means such as example and admonition. However, liberal peoples must not show them contempt lest they become aggrieved and create international tensions. The foreign-policy implications for liberal societies in relation to outlaw societies are that they will have to be contained and pacified, and, if necessary, intervened in so as to secure the human rights of their citizens. Moreover, liberal and decent societies have the right to protect themselves from the aggression of such states, even pre-emptively. The foreign-policy implications for liberal societies in relation to burdened societies and failed states are that they will need to be assisted to the point where they have enough economic stability to permit either liberal or decent governments to emerge. Unlike in the domestic context, to which the notion of justice as fairness as developed in *A Theory of Justice* applies, there is no obligation to ensure global justice in the global distribution of social goods or to create any mechanisms that would ensure that the increasing wealth of the world's rich contribute to improving the living conditions of the global poor.

Rawls's thesis has been subjected to scrutiny and many cosmopolitans reject it. The first reason for such a rejection is that, despite Rawls's mention of "peoples", his conception of international relations is still "statist" in form. Critics have pointed out that the notion of a "people" is vague and that, given the kinds of arrangements that are being agreed to, it is clear that states are the relevant parties to the agreement (Nussbaum 2006: chs 4, 5). The eight principles that would be agreed to by reasonable peoples bear a remarkable resemblance to the international laws that secure the prerogatives of states in a post-Westphalian world. But if Rawls is envisaging a utopia, why could he not envisage a world without state boundaries? Why would a "people" define itself as a nation-state distinct from others? What would be the meaning of borders for peoples rather than for states? Cultural, linguistic and religious differences may exist between peoples but there is no necessary link between these forms of solidarity and identity and the existence of nation-states. Accordingly, peoples could decide to create a borderless world in which the issue of intervention and war becomes moot, leaving only a policing function to deal with crime. Such a world could be ordered by political and economic institutions that secure global justice in accordance with the principle set out in Rawls's earlier work (Pogge 2006). The only force that would prevent this ideal from becoming a reality would be nationalism or chauvinism, attitudes to which cosmopolitans are opposed.

Cosmopolitans are also concerned about Rawls's limited conception of global justice. In arguing that rich societies only have an obligation to assist burdened peoples to the extent that they can come to govern themselves effectively, Rawls seems to be assuming that every people has the natural and human resources to lift itself out of poverty, and that it is only because of conditions internal to the social and political lives of those people that this might not happen. Such conditions might include bad governance or a lack of willingness to engage in economic activity or to participate in the global economy. But this ignores the influence on that burdened people of the international economic system, which systematically exploits poorer countries so as to extract natural resources and labour power from them at the lowest possible price. As noted in Chapter 3, poor governance is often caused by bribery and corruption condoned by multinational corporations and the governments of richer countries.

Moreover, many cosmopolitan commentators find it hard to understand why Rawls would not apply the criteria for justice that he developed in *A Theory of Justice* to the international sphere (Pettit 2006). Why not imagine individuals from around the world coming together behind a veil of ignorance in order to establish the political and economic institutions that would govern the world as a whole? Why do these decisions have to be limited to national jurisdictions? If parties to the original position were not to know where in the world they would end up and what nationality they would hold, they would certainly insist on global conditions that would prevent severe and systemic poverty from arising in any part of that world. But Rawls circumvents such theorizing by assuming that "peoples" already exist and bear a striking resemblance to nation-states acting rationally in their own interests. First, individuals contract to form a state, and then states, acting analogously to individuals, contract to form an international order. But this assumes that state delegations to the original position are truly representative of their peoples, that the internal arrangements of those states are just, that people in those states are not seeking redress against their ruling elites through international pressure and NGOs, and that such states are economic and political closed systems. None of these assumptions can be guaranteed. As Nussbaum puts it: "The assumption of the fixity and finality of states makes the second-stage contract assume a very thin and restricted form, precluding any serious consideration of economic redistribution, or even substantial aid, from richer to poorer nations" (2006: 235).

A third source of concern for cosmopolitan thinkers is that Rawls is prepared to accept decent but non-liberal societies as members of the world community. Most cosmopolitans would argue that the denial of liberal political rights should not be made acceptable in the world community. But Rawls does not claim to be a cosmopolitan.[3] His thinking is statist in form. Even as he creates an ideal theory of the global community, he is realistic enough to accept that there can be no such community if only liberal societies were acceptable in it. Moreover, he urges that the normative standard that should apply to such a community be that of "reasonableness". Rawls (1993) developed the norm of reasonableness in his discussions of domestic politics. Most nation-states today are multicultural and contain communities and individuals that have conceptions of the good life that differ from others within that same nation-state. Many of these views are based on metaphysical or religious views not shared by everyone in that larger political community. In such conditions of "value pluralism" a political community must avoid basing policy or law on the comprehensive moral doctrines of any one segment of society, even if that segment were the majority. Rather than insisting on one's own conception of the good, one must be "reasonable" and be tolerant of conceptions that one might disagree with. Public policy must be based on considerations that all reasonable people in that society can accept. Rawls calls this position "political liberalism".

Applied at the international level, this standard of reasonableness implies that parties to the second-order social contract that Rawls envisages should not be driven by an ideal conception of social and political life, human rights or social justice that people in other parts of the world might not be able to accept. The fact is that a great many nations of the world do not accept the liberal ideals of political life and the individualist conception of humanity that goes with it. While there might be room for debate about the rightness or wrongness of this position, such debates are not likely to be resolved any time soon. In the meantime it is important for people to be reasonable. What this means in positive terms is that we should espouse a discursive political culture in which comprehensive doctrines – religious or moral doctrines relating to what constitutes a good human life – are set aside in favour of a pragmatic consensus about basic human rights, justice as fairness, and a minimal set of principles that should guide a political community in conditions of value pluralism. Even peoples who base their lives on a set of comprehensive doctrines can, if they are reasonable, suspend these commitments in relation to other peoples in order to adhere to an overlapping global consensus on basic and minimal political values. As Catriona McKinnon puts it:

> The thought at the heart of this approach is that features of the political context give reasonable persons justifying reasons to tolerate other reasonable persons to whom they are opposed: insofar as we are required to find principles to govern our shared political problems, to that extent we are also required to practice toleration. (2006: 68; see also Walzer 1997)

Just as a modern pluralistic and multicultural domestic society might have to tolerate practices that it disapproves of within its constituent communities, so the global community might have to tolerate peoples whose political arrangements fall short of the liberal ideal. Just as a modern society needs to tolerate unusual but harmless sexual practices, for example, in order not to destroy the cohesion of the political community, so the global community needs to tolerate theocratic or patriarchal societies provided they do not harm their neighbours or destabilize world peace.

However, a cosmopolitan like Nussbaum argues against Rawls's use of the analogy with domestic societies in which there are different traditions of which political discourse should be tolerant. As she puts it:

> In the domestic case, Rawls's principle of toleration is a person-centred principle: it involves respecting persons and their conceptions of the good. In the transnational case, although Rawls depicts himself as applying the same principle, the principle is fundamentally different: it respects groups rather than persons, and shows deficient respect for persons, allowing their entitlements to be dictated by the dominant group in their vicinity, whether they like that group or not. (2006: 253)

The point that Nussbaum is making is that there are societies, for example, in which the clergy dictate and administer the law on the basis of theological tradition and where there is no opportunity for individuals who object to such laws to register their dissent without danger to themselves. While outside observers such as Rawls might want to acknowledge a right for that society to set the norms of behaviour to be followed within it, to do so would ignore the plight of any individuals within those societies who disagreed with those norms on reasonable grounds. The standard liberal position in such cases is that any dissident has the right to have their voice heard without danger to themselves and has the right to leave the society if their position becomes untenable. There are many autocratic and theocratic societies in which these conditions do not obtain. Nussbaum is especially concerned for women whose social and economic opportunities are systemically denied in many societies in which patriarchal conditions are sanctioned by tradition. Her point is that Rawls's tolerance is for the social and political conditions of a society as a whole, and for its traditions and norms, without giving due consideration to the plight of those individuals whose rights are denied by those conditions.

Other commentators have also noticed that claims in defence of a given non-liberal political institution, whether it be theocratic, Confucian or based on any other ancient tradition, are often made by the leaders of the relevant community rather than by the members who live under their rule. But such leaders have an interest in retaining their own power. Accordingly, we cannot be confident that they can genuinely represent the interests of all their constituents. As Kok-Chor Tan puts it, "We cannot with confidence accept that a set of 'values' in force in a society are truly assented to cultural values when there is no avenue for persons to voice their assent to or dissent from these values" (2000: 143). If there are no political institutions that allow for dissent, or if individuals who espouse different values are silenced and prevented from leaving the relevant community, we cannot be assured that there is a genuine consensus around the dominant values of that community.

Toleration

These critics of Rawls insist that there should be no toleration of non-liberal societies. Such societies should not be accepted as members of good standing in the global community. Accordingly, the question we now need to address is whether, in order to create a world community, it is reasonable to insist on liberalism as the content of a global overlapping consensus on basic political values or whether we should rest content with a convergence on such minimal values as the protection of only basic human rights even in consultative but autocratic political regimes. While it is clear that cosmopolitans need not tolerate outlaw and failed states that clearly violate human rights, should they tolerate non-liberal but decent societies? Rawls would say that if cosmopolitanism is a comprehensive political doctrine that insists that liberal and democratic political conditions should obtain in the whole world, then it is not reasonable because it is not tolerant of social and political conditions that fall short of the ideals of liberalism but which are nevertheless "decent". If liberal peoples insisted that the full range of democratic political rights should be available everywhere, then they would have too many reasons to engage in humanitarian interventions and would destabilize the world order (Hinsch & Stepanians 2006). They would be rightly accused of cultural imperialism and of seeking to impose their own vision of the good life on the whole world.

Although most cosmopolitans would deny that liberal states have the right to impose liberal political norms on non-liberal societies by force of arms except in such extreme cases as would involve the duty to protect the lives of people facing genocide or ethnic cleansing, they would insist that in a sketch of an ideal world community no allowance should be made for societies that deny their members democratic political rights. This would not imply that cosmopolitanism was a vehicle for global hegemony on the part of Western liberal states because, while espousing liberal ideals, cosmopolitans do not condone imposing them by force. There is a distinction to be drawn between making an evaluative judgement about another society and deciding to act on that judgement. Not imposing liberal political conditions may be a realistic compromise that has to be made for the sake of world peace, but cosmopolitans do not have to accept as ideal a situation in which ordinary members of a society have no right to democratic participation in the decision-making that affects them.

Tan has explored what toleration means in this context by seeing toleration as an institutional virtue. While individual cosmopolitans can adopt intolerant attitudes and disapprove of illiberal practices around the world, institutions should act in accordance with international law, and do so without forming any specific attitude. In this way an individual who disapproves of political arrangements in non-liberal societies can still be tolerant in the required sense by supporting international institutions that accept such societies for the sake of preserving international stability. As Tan puts it, "We might say that the virtue of toleration is expressed when individuals endorse and support institutional arrangements that protect reasonable ways of life or practices or attitudes that they also find objectionable according to their particular idea of the good" (2006: 82). The preservation of a global community might require institutional tolerance even of practices that offend against one's convictions. In this way, Rawls might be understood to be attributing toleration to the international order and its institutions rather than to the outlook of individuals or their representatives in the original position. If the parties to the second-order original position are representatives of peoples, they should be taking an institutional view rather than a personal one. We might call this "political toleration". Political toleration is a pragmatic and reasonable acceptance of decent but non-liberal peoples into the world community. It is toleration exercised by peoples towards other peoples. The demands of political toleration fall on individuals only in their official capacities when acting on behalf of their peoples. In their private capacity, such officials, like individuals anywhere, can adopt disapproving attitudes and advocate change in accordance with liberal ideals. Within the context of a global institutional framework of toleration, private individuals could still criticize the practices of others and advocate change by persuasion, education and even non-violent pressure.

It might be possible to map the distinction between political toleration and personal toleration onto the distinction between a framework of justice and the ethics of caring. Rawls and Pogge had suggested that justice was a norm for institutions while Appiah had seen it as a political norm for the distribution of social goods rather than a demand made on the personal relationships we have with others. In contrast, caring for others is a virtuous motivation for individuals. Accordingly, we might suggest that caring could motivate us to disapprove of illiberal practices in other societies and to work for their abolition by non-coercive means, while we also acknowledge the institutional or political need to avoid imposing the will of one people on to another even in the name of liberal values. In this way the political sphere of justice might call for political toleration while the personal sphere of caring urges us not to adopt tolerant attitudes to departures from the norms encapsulated in the UDHR. If Rawls's critics are right to suggest that his thinking is "statist" rather than cosmopolitan, it will come as no surprise that he sees tolerance as a normative requirement placed on institutional arrangements between peoples rather than as a personal stance.

But I have argued that cosmopolitanism is a normative stance not only for governments and their policies but also for individuals and their attitudes.

Accordingly, I shall now argue that, at both levels, cosmopolitans should advocate and pursue a full range of human rights for all.

Is political toleration consistent with justice? Does it involve too great a compromise of cosmopolitan values? Is it merely a second-best *modus vivendi* for the sake of avoiding conflict? Like Nussbaum, Tan recognizes that "the problem of tolerating decent peoples is that it lets down dissenting individual members in these nonliberal societies" (2006: 85). Should the fate of dissenters be ignored for the sake of global peace? As an example, should liberal states turn a blind eye to political repression in other countries in order to secure favourable trading relationships with those countries? The cosmopolitan focus on the rights of individuals would imply that no such compromise is acceptable. Cosmopolitans give as much weight to political and democratic rights as they do to subsistence and economic rights. When it is alleged that economic development can take place only if political freedoms are curtailed, it might be argued that we should be tolerant of political repression. However, it is at this point that we should remind ourselves of the connection that Amartya Sen makes between development and freedom. The point of economic development is to enhance freedom. To trade freedom for subsistence is to embrace slavery. There are vanishingly few instances in which the benefits of economic development have flown to non-unionized workers in sweatshops, for example, rather than to the ruling elites in the poor countries in which their factories are located (Drydyk 1997). Political rights are needed in order to ensure that economic rights are honoured.

Tan has discussed these matters at greater length in a book that seeks to resolve a dispute between Rawls's conception of political liberalism and what Tan calls "comprehensive liberalism". For Tan, the central and comprehensive doctrine that all liberals should embrace is that human beings should enjoy "autonomy", understood as the capacity of all individuals to define for themselves what the good life is, and to pursue this conception in a manner that can ensure peaceful coexistence with others. Comprehensive liberalism stresses the rights of individuals harmlessly to pursue such conceptions as they see fit. Political liberalism is a more strictly *political* conception and relegates individual conceptions of the good to the private realm. Politics should be based on such minimal shared values as would allow social life to be free of conflict or repression and should not be founded on a substantive conception of the good, such as autonomy, which only some people embrace. It acknowledges that there may be societies in which autonomy is not a central value. It is only political autonomy that is important to it. It is only departures from political freedom that it will not tolerate while repressions in the private sphere can be tolerated. As Tan puts it, "The political liberal will be willing to tolerate nonliberal group ways of life as long as these do not reject liberalism understood strictly as a political ideal" (2000: 6). As Tan goes on to explain:

> The crucial difference between comprehensive liberalism and political liberalism is that comprehensive liberalism nonetheless remains fully committed to *supporting* individuals who *wish* to live fully autonomous lives, even if this involves questioning and criticizing the customs and traditions of their own societies. That is, comprehensive liberalism's commitment to individual liberty overrides its toleration for diverse ways of life when a way of life conflicts with individual liberal aspirations.
>
> (*Ibid.*: 81; see also Mendus 1989)

Comprehensive liberalism asserts that non-liberal ways of life should not be tolerated because they deny to the individuals who participate in those ways of life the autonomy to choose their own values. Patriarchal ways of life should not be tolerated because they deny to women the right to act autonomously. Theocratic ways of life should not be tolerated because they punish apostasy with death. The denial of freedom of speech and of political dissent should not be tolerated even when there is said to be an ancient cultural tradition to which such freedoms are anathema.

But there are some problems with this position. If liberals support group rights in the sense that they would want to protect groups from oppressive regimes that would deny them the practices that are precious in their cultures, should they also support those groups whose practices involve oppressing their own members? Should liberals tolerate ways of life that deny autonomy to their adherents even when, by virtue of those traditions, autonomy is not sought or valued in those ways of life? Or should autonomy be sought equally for all even if that means that traditional practices that are central to a group's identity would be threatened? Should cosmopolitans value autonomy to such an extent that they would reject Rawls's tolerance of non-liberal but decent societies?

These questions raise issues that have been debated recently under the rubric of "communitarianism" (see Etzioni 1995). This concept suggests that any individual person has an identity that arises from the group or groups of which he or she is a member (Appiah 2005: ch. 3). In traditional societies, for example, a person may live in a farming village and think of themselves as primarily a farmer owing allegiance to the village and its collective farming efforts. It would not occur to such a person to consider what career they might adopt and what place they might want to live in. They will see themselves as belonging to the village and as destined to be a farmer. They will consider that their happiness and fulfilment will arise just from how well they fit into village life and how much they can contribute to the farming activities of the village. It might also be the case that the woman or man that they marry will have been decided for them by their parents or the village elders. It will not occur to them that any other way of choosing a spouse could be meaningful or attractive. They will not have the Western notion of romantic love as a basis for marriage, although they might, as a matter of good luck, experience the joys of affection and bonding with their partner. The children will be nurtured within a larger group than the Western nuclear family, with aunts, uncles, cousins and other village members providing a nurturing function that not only sustains the life of the infants but ensures that their outlook is shaped in such a way that the values and expectations of the village are internalized and passed on to the next generation. The authority of the elders of the village will be accepted without dissent, and obedience to that authority, established in any of the many ways described above, will be complete. Religion, too, will be assimilated along with the shaping of one's worldview within village life. The religious authorities and traditions will be passed on and adopted without question. The idea that one might investigate the truth-claims of one's faith will be unimaginable and if one were ever to be confronted by such an idea it would be felt as an abomination and as heresy. Whatever the religious tradition deems anathema, whether it be the eating of certain foods or certain sexual preferences and practices, will be viewed with abhorrence and vehement action will be taken to eradicate it from the community. One's political choices, too, will reflect traditional structures of authority or village loyalties. In these and many other ways, a member of a traditional community will see their identity as bound up with the lore and customs of that community. They will find the meaning of their existence in that context and will regard any departure from that context, whether in thought or in actuality, as a threat to their very identity.

Communitarian thinkers not only applaud this mode of human existence, but regret its passing from the way of life of Western societies. They see the Western notion of individualism as an "atomistic" conception of human existence. In this conception, a mature adult individual of normal capacities lives their own life. They choose their own career or mode of employment. They choose their own marriage partner or, indeed, have their own sexual preferences. They choose their own friends and other social relationships. While they cannot choose their parents or siblings, they can reject them by choosing to live elsewhere and by adopting a new set of friends or companions. They are even empowered or permitted to reject or accept any religious faith with which their spiritual ruminations might bring them into contact. Moreover, they choose their own political affiliation in the light of rational self-interest or a chosen ideology. In short, an "individualist" person is seen as "unencumbered" by any bonds, affiliations or loyalties that might arise from their upbringing or from their social context and as possessed of an almost limitless capacity for choice.

Many criticize this view because it seems to assume that a mature adult individual of normal capacities becomes, at the moment of their maturity, a clean slate on which they can themselves write the story of their subsequent lives, as if that slate had not already had the products of their upbringing written on it. Such products will include not only the family relationships and friendships through which they have been brought up, but also the attitudes, political outlooks and affiliations that arise from religious, ethnic, gendered and national loyalties.

But the individualist position does not depend on denying what every social psychologist knows well: that we are not clean slates at any time of our lives. We are indeed inducted into social and cultural formations that structure the way we live and that both limit and create the possibilities that lie before us as we travel on life's road. Rather, the individualist position depends on the thought, which I developed in Chapter 2, that we have a capacity for critical reason. We have the capacity to stand back from all the attitudes and affiliations into which we are formed in order to subject them to rational scrutiny. I might indeed be born into a traditional village life, but I can stop and ask myself whether I want to continue to live this way or whether I want to move to the city where I have heard there are jobs and opportunities denied me in the village. I might indeed be brought up in a modern Western society in a deeply religious family and I might indeed have observed that religion's rituals devoutly for all of my young life; nevertheless, I can entertain the question whether the metaphysical beliefs of that religion are true or its rituals meaningful, and I can reject that faith if I find it rationally or spiritually wanting. These are capacities that I have because I am a rational being, able to bracket my beliefs so as to think critically about them.

A communitarian would say that the community, whether in the form of a village or in the form of a state, has the right to insist on obedience and loyalty from its citizens because the formation, nurturing and identity of those individuals come from the state and its traditions.[4] Rather than a stress on rights as permissions or liberties to do what one likes, the stress is on the duties and responsibilities that arise from one's membership of the community. The community represents a consensus on a set of values that constitutes a shared conception of a good life (Sandel 2005). Accordingly, the first expression of one's identity within the community is to conform to its ways and fulfil its requirements. The community represents the most overarching and totalizing framework for the formation of the identity and will of its people. On this view, the people cannot but remain loyal and obedient to that community and cannot but align their own hopes and aspirations with those of the community without being misfits and criminals. In the political form of this doctrine, the community in question is the state. The state articulates the best selves of the people and gives expression to the general will. It would therefore be a denial of self and a form of insanity to repudiate the goals of the state. Dissent is a repudiation of the people's own hopes and can be justifiably repressed. It threatens the economic well-being of the people as well as their cultural progress towards forms of life marked by freedom and fulfilment. As Rousseau (1968) put it, we can be forced to be free.

The individualist, by contrast, stresses the rationality and autonomy of the individual. Every individual, on this view, has the capacity to plan their own life and make their own choices. The state exists in order to facilitate and protect these capacities by providing economic and cultural opportunities and by protecting basic freedoms through the rule of law. Given the inherent tendencies of states to acquire and abuse their power, individuals have the right to band together to engage in political actions to protect their liberties and to protest against illiberal policies. The power of reason defends us each individually from being totally absorbed into the worldview of our societies and is the basis on which our right to political and social independence is based. Autonomy is a basic value in this outlook, while the basic value in the communitarian outlook is loyalty. An individualist may applaud solidarity, but she will see it as the coming together of autonomous and rational individuals in a common cause rather than as a form of absorption of the individual into a collective identity.

Rather than this debate being seen in black and white terms, however, it is better seen as marking the poles on a spectrum of possibilities (Taylor 1989; see also Appiah 2005: ch. 2). Rather than claiming that there exist two kinds of human being in this world – an unencumbered autonomous social atom who is the subject of the Western, capitalist and individualist lifestyle, and an embedded member of a community whose identity and worldview depend entirely on her social relationships – we might suppose that there is a wide variety of forms of human life, which may be arranged on a spectrum of variations. At one end of this spectrum will be the individualist and on the other end of it will be the communitarian. But the figure that appears at either end of this range is an "ideal type": a theoretical construct that presents certain possibilities of social existence in their most extreme form. The radical individualist epitomizes features of the individualist way of life in an extreme form. It is hardly possible for any real person to live in a fully autonomous manner as if there were no social affiliations to which she had to be loyal and as if there were no social or family relationships through which she attained her independence. As Habermas puts it:

> From the standpoint of the theory of intersubjectivity, autonomy does not signify the discretionary power of a subject who disposes of himself as his own property but the independence of a person made possible by

> relations of reciprocal recognition that can exist only in conjunction with the correlative independence of the other. (1993: 43)

As well, the notion of a totally communitarian person could only be exemplified by an individual who had no thoughts expressed with the first-person pronoun, "I". Such a person would see himself only as a member of a family or community and have no ideas or plans that he could claim as uniquely his own. Neither of these extremes is a realizable or desirable form of human existence.

It would seem, therefore, that actual people should be described as standing somewhere along the range of possibilities between these two extremes. Everyone enjoys some of the features of individualism and also some of the features of communitarianism. Some people live lives in which choice and self-sufficiency are more marked and for whom social links and responsibilities are felt as less important. Other people live lives in which conformity to social norms and traditional ways is a more prominent feature but in which they are not prevented from making up their own minds on a variety of issues. Societies in their turn can be described in terms of the kinds of social existence they foster. Some societies will be more individualistic and provide incentives for creativity and entrepreneurship motivated by self-interest, while other societies will be more communitarian and will reward people for their contribution to the common goals and projects of that society. So long as societies and their peoples differ in these ways, we can expect disagreement and contestation about their goals and aspirations and about the rights that they consider to be important.

Tan, in privileging autonomy, is adopting the more individualist position typical of liberalism, while Rawls is more tolerant of political forms of communitarianism. For Tan, autonomy is a substantive value espoused by comprehensive liberalism, while Rawls's political liberalism implies tolerance of non-liberal forms of life. Political liberalism avoids reliance on any substantive conception of the good such as might be taught by religion, tradition or even secular modernity. It sees the ideal of autonomy as a substantive conception and will therefore be more tolerant of departures from that ideal. Peoples that have political structures that are merely consultative rather than fully democratic – that look after their members but do not give them political rights – will be acceptable from that perspective. The only social actions or institutions that political liberalism will not be tolerant of are actions or institutions that deny a limited set of human rights centred on the rights to life, property and economic participation. Comprehensive liberalism, in contrast, includes autonomy in all aspects of life as its grounding ideal. Accordingly, it is less tolerant of non-liberal practices in the allegedly private sphere. Such liberals will insist that, within a given state, all citizens should be able to exercise autonomy no matter what identity-forming group they belong to, and that, in the international sphere, the full range of human rights, including those that guarantee political freedoms, should be protected in all nation-states.

With which of these two positions should cosmopolitanism align itself? It would seem that Tan's position, with its stress on autonomy, is too far towards the individualist end of the spectrum I have described, while Rawls is too accepting of the communitarian norms that typify the other end of the spectrum. Cosmopolitans should endorse a form of liberalism that might not go as far as that comprehensive form that values individualist conceptions of autonomy, but one that is more substantive than a purely political form that will tolerate denials of political rights for the sake of cultural coherence, international stability or economic advantage. The key to this form of liberalism will be the espousal of free and uncoerced public discourse (Habermas 1973).[5] If the communitarian way of life of a people contained non-liberal values that everyone in that community was willing to live by, then those values should be able to be discussed, critiqued and endorsed publicly. It will not be for anyone outside the community to critique or endorse them, but it must be possible for observers to certify that everyone in the community is free to engage in such discourse. If it is open to anyone in the community to discuss the values and norms of that community without fear of repression, then outsiders can be tolerant of those values and norms no matter how illiberal they may seem to those outsiders. In this way, outsiders may acknowledge that the way of life of that community does not encourage autonomy, but still tolerate that way of life for the fact that it permits internal critique. The only basis for intolerance will be the presence in that community of structures or forces that prevent open discussion of that community's way of life in both the public and private spheres. Once again, it is Kant with his insistence on the openness of public discourse who has anticipated this idea.

Lest the insistence that no departure from such a cosmopolitan form of liberalism should be tolerated sounds too hegemonic or imperialistic, Tan reminds us that there are many means short of force to try to influence foreign regimes towards liberalizing their states. One could propagate liberal ideas through international conferences, diplomatic meetings, propaganda, the work of NGOs, or granting favoured trading partner status to states that improve their record on human rights. Many liberals argue that the spread of liberalism is an inevitable historical process that accompanies education, secularization and cultural enlightenment. The recent growth in power and importance of autocratic regimes in Russia and China, however, make this confidence seem somewhat utopian. Freedom remains the object of struggle and cosmopolitans should exercise solidarity with that struggle. It should also be remembered that there is no necessary connection between liberal political rights and the actual democratic institutions that exist in the world. Many of the world's leading democracies fall far short of the liberal ideal through corruptions and distortions of their political institutions. Cosmopolitans need not champion the political systems of any specific nation-state in order to champion democratic political rights. To champion such systems might be imperialistic but to champion such rights is legitimate advocacy.

The cosmopolitan form of liberalism I am advocating will not be tolerant of illiberal political arrangements for the sake of global stability. Even Rawls does not take stability to be the sole goal of political liberalism. There are political values other than stability. It is not only because they lead to stability that justice and human rights are valuable. If the world is to be seen as a community it must converge on more values than stability. If there is to be genuine peace there must be agreement on a range of fundamental values. This is not merely something that cosmopolitans hope for. Global justice and respect for human rights, including political rights, have been agreed to, through the UN, as the basis on which a global community exists. While there are frequent and egregious departures from this ideal, the UDHR continues to be the agreed basis for a world community. There is no need for anyone to resile from it in order to make compromises with states that refuse to live up to that ideal. It would make no sense for cosmopolitans to speak of moral rights, moral obligations or the moral status of individuals unless there were a community that accepted these moral concepts and realized them in its way of life. Through the UN, the world has become such a community.

Global democracy

Some cosmopolitans insist that liberal and democratic political values should be institutionalized not only within all nation-states but also in whatever forms of governance the global community creates for itself internationally. Even global institutions would only be legitimate if they were democratic. In the face of the downgrading of the importance of the sovereignty and autonomy of nation-states, such theorists advocate forms of global democracy in which international bodies such as the UN would be forums made up not only of nation-states, but also of individual world citizens or their representatives. As Daniele Archibugi puts it:

> What distinguishes cosmopolitical democracy from other such projects is its attempt to create institutions which enable the voice of individuals to be heard in global affairs irrespective of their resonance at home. Democracy as a form of global governance thus needs to be realized on

> three different, interconnected levels: within states, between states and at a world level. (2003: 8)[6]

The second level he refers to is the UN and other international bodies. However, members of these bodies are spokespersons and ambassadors for the sovereign states they represent and are constrained by the policies of those states. As a result, these forums become highly constricted and provide opportunities for states to pursue their national interests through verbal posturing and bluster. Admittedly this is an improvement on their doing so by force of arms, but it hardly allows for a genuine exchange of views and the growth of mutual understanding. Especially in the Security Council, where the major powers hold the right to veto any proposal with which they disagree, the chances of genuine dialogue are very slim. However, through many of its other bodies, through international conferences and by recognizing the right to participate of NGOs, representatives of peoples and of religions, gender advocates and other non-state actors, the UN has created international forums through which not only states, but also global citizens, can make their voices heard. This creates what James Bohman (1997) has called a "cosmopolitan public sphere".

Unlike international civic society, in which membership is still based on having the status of a nation, this would be a public sphere in which cosmopolitan ideas such as that of human rights are used to hold governments to account. Such a public sphere would influence states and political institutions through democratic processes at national levels but also through international public opinion. In the face of difficulties arising from the private ownership of most of the media of communication, the new public sphere makes increasing use of the internet and stages dramatic events that the media cannot ignore. All this gives the public sphere an effective role within political institutions and not just the marginal role that those within mainstream political national institutions would prefer to see. Just as the public sphere is an important quasi-institution in national polities, so it needs to become one in the cosmopolitan sphere. Such a cosmopolitan public sphere must be relatively free from mainstream institutions in order to maintain its power to innovate and to critique the existing order (Held 1992). There must always be ways to renew the agenda of existing institutions, including the UN, the World Bank, the IMF and all of the many international bodies that regulate so much of the world's affairs from outside those institutions.

The third level that Archibugi refers to suggests that individuals should be able to participate in international bodies directly rather than as representatives of their peoples or states. A practical form of this idea might be to suggest that political parties should become international in their membership and operation. The model for such forms of global democracy might be the

European parliament, to which representatives are directly elected by the people of Europe rather than being delegates sent by governments. The existence of the EU with its parliament, which can override national parliaments on some matters, is taken to be a demonstration that such global institutions are viable.

The principle at issue in this proposal is the fundamental democratic idea that all those who are affected by a decision – especially if the effect is a potential harm – should have a say in the making of that decision. Given the global reach of the economy and of the political institutions of powerful nations, all members of the world community should play a democratic role in world governance. Representatives of nations pursue only the interests of those nations. Moreover, the representatives sent by governments to world bodies will not be truly democratic representatives of their peoples if those governments are themselves not democratic. Given the number of despotic governments in the world, a global body to which governments send delegates will be a clique of ruling elites acting without any democratic checks and balances on their capacity to order world affairs so as to secure their own benefit. Accordingly, many cosmopolitans argue for a form of global democracy that can bypass the system of nation-states. This echoes Kant's insistence that, for the sake of world peace, there should be a public space in which there is free and uncoerced discourse through which anyone is able to participate in debates on public policy and global justice.

Tolerance and pluralism

If cosmopolitans reject Rawls's form of political toleration in the context of the global community of peoples, they do not reject religious and cultural tolerance and an acceptance of a global pluralism of values. Aside from the political institutions through which people are ruled in various parts of the world, there is also a great variety of cultural practices and beliefs that cosmopolitans who stand in the tradition of the Western Enlightenment might call into question. Religious beliefs around the world are based on metaphysical beliefs and conceptions of the self that are not universally shared. By themselves, many of these are harmless enough and need not attract the attention of those concerned for human rights and global justice. People should be allowed to hold what beliefs they like. However, it is when those beliefs lead to practices that deny human rights or threaten justice that questions might be asked.

Christianity used to condone burning heretics at the stake and drowning witches, and we consider it to be an example of moral progress that we no longer do so. Today we would not tolerate such practices and feel ourselves justified in this intolerance. When we look around the world, however, we see many cases of injustice and the violation of human rights that seem to be condoned or even encouraged by deeply held beliefs. We see religious violence, such as mobs tearing down mosques and temples and attacking each other in the street. We see religiously inspired laws that condemn female adulterers to death while male adulterers go free. We see women forced to cover themselves head to foot. We see female genital mutilation, the burning of widows and an inflexible caste system based on ancient beliefs about reincarnation. In many societies, homosexuality is punishable by death, witchcraft is practised, children enslaved and animals systematically mistreated. Does the respect that cosmopolitans are urged to show for cultures other than their own require that such practices should be tolerated? Is cultural tolerance a cosmopolitan virtue?

Summarizing McKinnon (2006), we can describe the key structural features of the virtue of tolerance as involving:

(i) *Difference*: what is tolerated differs from the tolerator's conception of what should be done, valued, or believed.
(ii) *Importance*: what is tolerated by the tolerator is not trivial to her.
(iii) *Opposition*: the tolerator disapproves of and/or dislikes what she tolerates.
(iv) *Power*: the tolerator believes herself to have the power to alter or suppress what is tolerated.
(v) *Non-rejection*: the tolerator does not exercise this power.
(vi) *Requirement*: toleration is right or expedient, and the tolerator is virtuous, just, or prudent.

It might be suggested at the outset that (iv) does not apply to most cosmopolitans in the global context. While there might be domestic situations in which one person or a group of people has the power to prevent others from doing what they disapprove of, this does not normally apply in the global context. Certainly no individual – not even so eminent a moral leader as the Pope or the Dalai Lama – has the power to prevent others from doing what they deem immoral in other parts of the world. But even powerful states are limited in this power. There have been cases where a powerful state has placed conditions on medical aid that it was not to be used in the procurement of abortions, for example (USAID n.d.), but even if such states have the military capacity to impose their moral prejudices on other states or communities, the price of doing so measured in diplomatic, military or economic terms will be so great that the pragmatic stance advocated by Rawls and others should hold sway. One would have to be a superpower of grand proportions to be able to impose one's own moral predilections on the world. The history of the humanitarian interventions that have been endorsed by the international community through the UN shows how vulnerable even superpowers are in this context. So, even if there were individuals or states that believed themselves to have the power to suppress the perceived immoralities of others, it would seem that the actual power to prevent those practices of which one morally disapproves is largely lacking in the international arena. Accordingly, the question of whether tolerance is a cosmopolitan virtue is relatively moot. If (iv) does not obtain, then the conditions for the exercise of tolerance are not present.

There is still, however, an issue for cosmopolitanism. I have said that cosmopolitanism is a virtuous attitude. Let us focus then on the attitudes that both private individuals and public officials should adopt. Is tolerance a virtuous attitude (Engelen & Nys 2008)? Suppose an anti-Muslim bigot who had the power to deny a job to a Muslim applicant declined to do so; would we describe that person as displaying the virtue of tolerance? On McKinnon's account we would have to say that he was. He was opposed to a difference he saw in the other, took it to be important, had the power to act, but refrained from doing so. But this judgement will depend on our attitude to bigotry. Why was the difference important to him? For my part, I see no justification for the anti-Muslim attitude. Accordingly, I would not regard as virtuous a person who had such an attitude even if that person declined to act on it. Such a person is prejudiced even if his view is based on a rejection, for example, of the stoning of women adulterers. To have such an attitude is already a failure of virtue. What this argument shows is that (iii) is problematic. By what right do we disapprove of the moral practices or cultural beliefs of others? A truly tolerant or cosmopolitan person would show genuine respect for other cultures and not have any feelings of moral disapproval for their practices, no matter how different those practices were from the norms that that person adheres to (Appiah 2006: chs 4, 5).

The reason that this may seem difficult is that it involves morality. If your disapproval of the actions of others or the practices of other peoples is based on moral convictions, it is likely to be absolute, dismissive, condemnatory, self-righteous and vehement. It is likely to be moralistic (Coady 2006). It will usually involve no attempt to understand sympathetically the practice in terms of its cultural context and in terms of the understanding that its participants have of it. Indeed, McKinnon argues that there is a kind of existential contradiction between (iii) and (v). If you disapprove of something morally, why would it be virtuous to not act on that disapproval? Surely your moral feeling that a practice is morally wrong should lead you to oppose it to whatever limits of power you might have. That is what it means to disapprove of it morally. One cannot consistently disapprove of some practice morally and yet not be inclined to oppose it. But this is the impetus towards both moralism and fundamentalism. Fundamentalists take an absolute view of moral and religious matters and find it impossible to accept practices and beliefs that are different from their own. They are often militant in their opposition and enraged by what they see as the immorality or infidelity of those whose practices and beliefs are different from their own. This is a form of fanaticism. It condemns what it disapproves of out of moralistic indignation rather than out of compassion for the victims of the condemned practices. Our ability to understand others and enter sympathetically into their lives depends on our being able to imagine ourselves in their situation. It does not depend on there being one standard to which all must subscribe.

In this context it might be suggested that tolerance consists in the negation of (iii). That is, it consists in adopting an attitude of not condemning what others do on moral or religious grounds. There are a number of ways in which one might do this. One is to adopt an attitude of irony towards one's own convictions, much as I advocated an attitude of irony towards nationalism.[7] If one considers that one's own views are not so absolute and may be incorrect, or at least seen as strange by others, one will not be so inclined to insist on them or disapprove of those who think differently. Of course this may be difficult. It is in the very nature of moral views that we hold them with a high degree of conviction and commitment. They seem to us to be self-evident and unquestionable. Perhaps a better strategy therefore would be to seek to understand the moral and religious practices of others as sympathetically as we can.

What is striking about many of these practices and what is often most surprising to outside observers is that the apparent victims of these practices often approve of them. The burnt widow wanted to be burnt. The "victim" of genital mutilation considers that she would have been "unclean" if it were not done. The Muslim woman who wears the burqa sees herself as modest and socially acceptable. What needs to be understood is that none of these practices – any more than our own – are options laid out before a person as if they were goods in a cultural supermarket. As I noted earlier, many individualist philosophers seem to think that religious beliefs and moral convictions are a matter of choice. They are not. Even in liberal societies that valorize choice and autonomy, they are not. They are structures of identity. This is the point that communitarianism highlights and that Tan's stress on autonomy obscures. It is through your cultural practices that you define who you are. If you are a Muslim you will not eat pork and if you are a Muslim woman you will dress modestly. This is not a matter of choice. Nor is it merely a matter of conditioning or indoctrination through one's upbringing, although that is surely involved. It is a matter of identity (Appiah 2005). It is a matter of how you understand yourself and your place in the world. A Muslim would no more eat pork than you or I would eat a rat. Both foods are quite nutritional, but to eat them is, for the relevant communities, unthinkable.

Recognizing this should give us pause. If the participants in these practices can accept them, then perhaps there are ideas and beliefs involved that render them acceptable to those who participate in them even if they do not seem acceptable to me. This thought alone should serve to reduce the vehemence with which I am inclined to reject those practices. Studying the religious traditions and the histories of the moral practices of those peoples may also help.[8] However, it remains the case that it is difficult to sympathetically understand and adopt an attitude of approval towards many of the practices of which I have given examples. Value pluralism is endemic in the human condition. We must not expect that the whole world will converge on a single set of religious and moral beliefs. As Appiah puts it, "Cosmopolitans suppose that all cultures have enough overlap in their vocabulary of values to begin a conversation. But they don't suppose, like some universalists, that we could all come to agreement if only we had the same vocabulary" (2006: 57). The beliefs and practices of others may be seen as reasonable by those others no matter how strange or objectionable they may seem to us. We must not be intolerant of difference, no matter how secure we feel in the correctness or self-evidence of our own views.

A further step in taking moralism out of our attitude to foreign practices would be to think of them in terms of the real and demonstrable harm they might cause. If a practice results in physical injury or death – such as widow burning or many forms of female genital mutilation – then it can be condemned in terms that do not rely on moral concepts. Physical injury and death are harms that everyone wants to avoid, unless they see the latter as martyrdom or justified self-sacrifice. If we return to the kind of common-sense, reasonable and practical thinking that was exemplified by Nussbaum's list of capabilities, we can say that any practice that reduces those capabilities causes harm that should be avoided. We could even say that everyone has a right to not have those harms done to them and that societies have a duty to ensure that such harms do not occur within them. Indeed many individuals in the communities that engage in the kinds of practices we are considering have made this point and are opposing those practices from within those traditions. By identifying a practice as harmful within a common-sense or reasonable conception of what constitutes harm, we can oppose it without thereby seeking to impose our own moral convictions. We would be appealing to reasonableness rather than to our own moral commitments.

The least moralistic and most respectful way to express one's disapproval of harmful but culturally condoned practices, aside from trying to understand them and to respect them, is to encourage and protect the political space within the relevant communities that would be needed for members of those communities to voice their opposition to those practices themselves. This is why cosmopolitans need a stronger stance on political rights than is provided by Rawls's political liberalism. The liberalism that underpins the cosmopolitan attitude seeks to encourage those political conditions – freedom of speech and right of exit – that ensure that cultural practices and norms are not oppressively imposed on those who participate in them.

Conclusion

The concept of global community gives us a theoretical basis for combining the cosmopolitan themes of human rights, global justice, the pursuit of lasting peace and the embrace of values pluralism. The principle of humanity addresses each of us individually and asks of us that we respond to the misfortunes of others by rendering assistance. This principle, if accepted universally, would begin to constitute our globalized world as a community. But within a communitarian outlook a community would be seen as a body of people committed to reciprocity rather than just assistance for the needy. If one lives in a community, as opposed to a collection of individualists, one is obligated to help others in times of trouble and one is entitled to expect that one will be assisted in such times. The difference between suffering bad luck and suffering an injustice where the harm is the same in both cases is that, in the case of bad luck, no one could have prevented what happened. An injustice occurs when someone is able to prevent the harm or ameliorate its effects, has an obligation to do so but does not do so. It is only in a community that injustices can occur because a community is a system of mutual obligations. If a person is not part of any community, then no injustice can be done to them since no one has any obligations to them. The harms that befall them are therefore cases of bad luck. They are no less harmful for that and they frustrate the desires of the victim just as greatly, but the victim has no grounds for feeling aggrieved. Victims of misfortune have grounds for feeling aggrieved only if there were others who had an obligation to prevent or ameliorate the misfortune (Ci 2006). Only in a context of community would the victim have a right and a reason for complaint. It is when we recognize others – no matter where they live and no matter what their nationality, religion, race, caste or ethnicity – as fellow members in a global community that we shall see that we have an obligation in solidarity to stand by them in the pursuit of justice, and to defend their human rights. Even the greatest cultural differences between us do not expunge that obligation.

The nations of the world declared themselves to be such a global community and committed themselves to the cosmopolitan vision through the charter of the United Nations and the UDHR. All that remains now is for us to live up to that declaration.

Notes

Introduction

1. For useful anthologies, see Thomas Pogge and Darrel Moellendorf (eds), *Global Justice: Seminal Essays* (St Paul, MN: Paragon House, 2008), Thomas Pogge and Keith Horton (eds), *Global Ethics: Seminal Essays* (St Paul, MN: Paragon House, 2008), and Thom Brooks, *The Global Justice Reader* (Oxford: Blackwell, 2008). See also Gillian Brock, *Global Justice: A Cosmopolitan Account* (Oxford: Oxford University Press, 2009).
2. Ulrich Beck also uses this phrase but he does so in order to refer to a sociological methodology that transcends the framework of the nation-state; Ulrich Beck, "Cosmopolitical Realism: On the Distinction between Cosmopolitanism in Philosophy and the Social Sciences", *Global Networks* **4**(2) (2004), 131–46.
3. For further reading, see Timothy Brennan, *At Home in the World: Cosmopolitanism Now* (Cambridge, MA: Harvard University Press, 1997); Samuel Scheffler, "Conceptions of Cosmopolitanism", *Utilitas* **11**(3) (1999), 255–76, reprinted in his *Boundaries and Allegiances: Problems of Justice and Responsibility in Liberal Thought*, 111–30 (Oxford: Oxford University Press, 2001); Jeremy Waldron, "What is Cosmopolitan?", *Journal of Political Philosophy* **8**(2) (1999), 227–43; Carol A. Breckenridge, Sheldon Pollock, Homi K. Bhabha & Dipesh Chakrabarty (eds), *Cosmopolitanism* (Durham, NC: Duke University Press, 2002); Steven Vertovec & Robin Cohen (eds), *Conceiving Cosmopolitanism: Theory, Context, and Practice* (Oxford: Oxford University Press, 2002); Andrew Strauss, Daniele Archibugi, Mathias Koenig-Archibugi, Robin Blackburn *et al.* (eds), *Debating Cosmopolitics* (London: Verso, 2003); Seyla Benhabib, *The Rights of Others: Aliens, Residents, and Citizens* (Cambridge: Cambridge University Press, 2004); Tan Kok-Chor, *Justice without Borders: Cosmopolitanism, Nationalism, and Patriotism* (Cambridge: Cambridge University Press, 2004); Gillian Brock & Harry Brighouse (eds), *The Political Philosophy of Cosmopolitanism* (Cambridge: Cambridge University Press, 2005); Kwame Anthony Appiah, *Cosmopolitanism: Ethics in a World of Strangers* (New York: Norton, 2006).
4. This has also been referred to as "legal cosmopolitanism" or "institutional cosmopolitanism".
5. Mention should also be made of the work of John Hick in attempting to find a common spiritual core in all of the world's religions. See his *God and the Universe of Faiths* (New York: St Martin's Press, 1973).

6. See also Peter Gowan, "The New Liberal Cosmopolitanism", in A. Strauss *et al.* (eds), *Debating Cosmopolitics*, 51–64. Gowan argues that "the new liberal cosmopolitanism" is an ideology that serves the interests of American world hegemony.

1. Cosmopolitanism and patriotism

1. The terminology of "thick" and "thin" is also used by Michael Walzer, *Thick and Thin: Moral Argument at Home and Abroad* (Notre Dame, IN: University of Notre Dame Press, 1994).
2. A similar point is made by Michael Walzer, "Spheres of Affection", in Martha C. Nussbaum, *For Love of Country?: Debating the Limits of Patriotism*, J. Cohen (ed.) for *Boston Review* (Boston, MA: Beacon Press, 1996), 125–7.
3. For an alternative view see Kenneth Baynes, "Communitarian and Cosmopolitan Challenges to Kant's Conception of World Peace", in *Perpetual Peace: Essays on Kant's Cosmopolitan Ideal*, James Bohman & Matthias Lutz-Bachmann (eds), 219–34 (Cambridge, MA: MIT Press, 1997), who argues that political community and cultural community are distinct. One can be committed to procedural liberalism and also to community.
4. Another author who is suspicious of appeals to the concept of "humanity" is Cheng Cheah in his *Inhuman Conditions: On Cosmopolitanism and Human Rights* (Cambridge, MA: Harvard University Press, 2006).
5. This analogy was first used by the Stoic philosopher Hierocles to argue that our concern should extend from ourselves and our families to the whole human race. His account is reproduced and discussed in Tad Brennan, *The Stoic Life: Emotions, Duties, & Fate* (Oxford: Clarendon Press, 2005), 157ff.
6. For more on the expanding circle analogy see Steven Vertovec & Robin Cohen, "Introduction: Conceiving Cosmopolitanism", in Vertovec & Cohen (eds), *Conceiving Cosmopolitanism*, 1–22. See also, Peter Singer, *The Expanding Circle: Ethics and Sociobiology* (New York: Farrar, Straus & Giroux, 1981), who suggests that the circle should be expanded to include not just the whole of humanity, but also any animals that are capable of sentience and thus of suffering.
7. In his "Cosmopolitanism and Global Citizenship", *Review of International Studies* **29**(1) (2003), 3–17, Bhikhu Parekh argues that our membership of nations and of specific political communities should not be devalued just because it is historically contingent. Even accidents have ethical significance: the family I was born into for example. Political communities are central to the identity of peoples and national solidarity is both appropriate and consistent with global moral responsibility.
8. Kwame Anthony Appiah speaks of "rooted cosmopolitanism", which accepts such local loyalties while rejecting nationalism, in his *The Ethics of Identity* (Princeton, NJ: Princeton University Press, 2005), ch. 6.
9. This is not the same kind of irony as is advocated by Richard Rorty in *Contingency, Irony and Solidarity* (Cambridge: Cambridge University Press, 1989). Rorty's irony is based on the thought that one's views might be wrong. My irony is based on the thought that one's commitments might not be all that important.
10. This acknowledges the communitarian objections to Nussbaum's thesis of Amy Gutmann ("Democratic Citizenship", in Nussbaum, *For Love of Country?*, 66–71) and Gertrude Himmelfarb ("The Illusions of Cosmopolitanism", in Nussbaum, *For Love of Country?*, 72–7), who argued that the cosmopolitan needs a nation-state in order to learn how values of justice and human rights can be instantiated while advocating that the outlook so

developed be expanded to seek a global realization of the moral values learnt in a specific national community.

11. I intend, with this phrase, to echo the notion of "political liberalism" used by John Rawls, through which he articulated the idea of a pragmatic approach to political engagement free of commitments to values and conceptions of the good life not shared by all. (I discuss this further in Chapter 5.) In much the same way, I espouse a form of patriotism that is free of commitments to romanticized notions of the nation or of a commitment to ethnic, linguistic or religious communities. See John Rawls, *Political Liberalism* (New York : Columbia University Press, 1993). My concept is also akin to that of "constitutional patriotism" espoused by Jürgen Habermas, which refers to feelings of solidarity that grow out of democratic participation in political communities rather than out of commitments to romanticized notions of the nation or of ethnic, linguistic or religious communities. See Jürgen Habermas, "Appendix II: Citizenship and National Identity", in *Between Facts and Norms: Contributions to a Discourse Theory of Law and Democracy*, William Rehg (trans.), 491–515 (Cambridge, MA: MIT Press, 1996).
12. Nathan Glazer argues that nation-states must continue to exist because they are the organs that can establish and sustain rights.
13. Richard Falk criticizes Nussbaum for failing to take economic matters into account. He argues that nationalism is based on a sovereign state that provides for its citizens, which he calls the humane state. Without such provision, nationalism cannot grow because there is no social contract. But states are now woven into a global economic system that forces governments to lower taxes, open markets and reduce social services. As a result, sovereignty is reduced and, with it, the basis of nationalist allegiance. Globalization also threatens cosmopolitanism. It is being swamped by global capital, which is forging a global order in which the cosmopolitan ideal is seen as wishful thinking. The solution is citizen engagement through NGOs and UN conferences, which address both the problems of globalization and national priorities.
14. Even Kant was not immune from making such remarks about national characteristics and even about races. See Joris van Gorkom, "Immanuel Kant on Racial Identity", *Philosophy in the Contemporary World* **15**(1) (Spring 2008), 1–10.

2. Human rights

1. For the full text of the Universal Declaration of Human Rights, see www.un.org/Overview/rights.html (accessed March 2009).
2. For a general introduction to the philosophy of rights, see Robert Paul Churchill, *Human Rights and Global Diversity* (Upper Saddle River, NJ: Pearson Prentice Hall, 2006). See also R. K. M. Smith & C. van den Anker (eds), *The Essentials of Human Rights* (London: Hodder Arnold, 2005).
3. I prefer not to use the term "resentment", which is used by Peter Strawson ("Freedom and Resentment", in his *Freedom and Resentment, and Other Essays* [London, Methuen, 1974], 1–25) and Bernard Williams (*In the Beginning Was the Deed: Realism and Moralism in Political Argument*, Geoffrey Hawthorn [selected, ed. and intro.] [Princeton, NJ: Princeton University Press, 2005]), because of the connotations given this term by such writers as Friedrich Nietzsche and Max Scheler, who see it as an ignoble attitude expressive of envy and humiliation.
4. For more on the history of the concept of human rights, see William A. Edmundson, *An Introduction to Rights* (Cambridge: Cambridge University Press, 2004). See also M. A.

Glendon, *A World Made New: Eleanor Roosevelt and the Universal Declaration of Human Rights* (New York: John Wiley, 2001).

5. Tom Campbell speaks of "democratic positivism" in his *Rights: A Critical Introduction* (London: Routledge, 2006). The basic idea is that rights are grounded in legal arrangements or social rules that can be implemented and enforced and that are democratically agreed on. This abstracts from the question of what rights *should* exist in favour of the question of what rights *do* exist as a result of appropriate political processes.
6. See also John Tomlison, "Interests and Identities in Cosmopolitan Politics", in Vertovec & Cohen (eds), *Conceiving Cosmopolitanism*, 240–53. Michael Ignatieff defends the political character of rights and rejects any treatment of them in metaphysical or philosophical terms in his *Human Rights as Politics and Idolatry* (Princeton, NJ: Princeton University Press, 2001).
7. This is also the basis of Henry Shue's conception of "Basic Rights" in his *Basic Rights: Subsistence, Affluence, and US Foreign Policy*, 2nd rev. edn (Princeton, NJ: Princeton University Press, 1996), chs 1, 2.
8. Len Doyal distinguishes needs from wants by saying that needs are "goals" that are universalizable: goals that everyone could be conceived as having universally. Without the satisfier of a need, a person would suffer serious harm. "It follows that the search for objective basic needs becomes that for universalizable preconditions that enable nonimpaired participation both in the form of life in which individuals find themselves and in any other form of life that they might subsequently choose if they get the chance" ("A Theory of Human Need", in *Necessary Goods: Our Responsibilities to Meet Others' Needs*, Gillian Brock [ed.], 157–72 [Lanham, MD: Rowman & Littlefield, 1998], 158).
9. Two classic arguments for human rights that depend on the notion of autonomy are H. L. A. Hart, "Are there any Natural Rights?", in *Political Philosophy*, A. Quinton (ed.), 53–66 (Oxford: Oxford University Press, 1967), and Margaret MacDonald, "Natural Rights", in *Theories of Rights*, J. Waldron (ed.), 21–40 (Oxford: Oxford University Press, 1984).
10. One theorist who bases human rights directly on human dignity is Jack Mahoney, *The Challenge of Human Rights: Origin, Development, and Significance* (Oxford: Blackwell, 2007).
11. For another argument basing human rights on basic human needs, see David Copp, "Equality, Justice, and the Basic Needs", in *Necessary Goods: Our Responsibilities to Meet Others' Needs*, G. Brock (ed), 113–33 (Lanham, MD: Rowman & Littlefield, 1998).
12. I shall continue to use these two adjectives interchangeably.
13. Nussbaum is not alone in making such claims. Nigel Dower downplays the theoretical debates about a universal objective morality or the real existence of universal human rights in favour of a "pre-existing common core" of ethical commitments, which he describes as follows:

    > A global ethic is a set of values and norms that are, as a matter of fact, universally or generally accepted throughout the world. … The *Declaration toward a Global Ethics* of the Parliament of the World's Religions of 1993 came up with four leading ethical directives and many sub specifications of them. The four main ones are:
    >
    > - Commitment to a culture of non-violence and respect for life;
    > - Commitment to a culture of solidarity and a just economic order;
    > - Commitment to a culture of tolerance and a life of truthfulness;

- Commitment to a culture of equal rights and partnership between men and women.

(Hans Küng & K. J. Kuschel, *A Global Ethic: The Declaration of the Parliament of the World's Religions* [London: SCM Press, 1993], quoted in Nigel Dower, *An Introduction to Global Citizenship* [Edinburgh: Edinburgh University Press, 2003], 31)

For further discussions, see William M. Sullivan & Will Kymlicka (eds), *The Globalization of Ethics: Religious and Secular Perspectives* (New York: Cambridge University Press, 2007).

14. Nussbaum has put forward a newer version of the list in *Frontiers of Justice: Disability, Nationality, Species Membership* (Cambridge, MA: Harvard University Press, 2006), 76–7.
15. However, in the context of discussing the dilemma that liberals face in thinking about the religious bases of many of the practices that violate women's rights, Nussbaum does argue that "the liberty of religious belief, membership, and activity is among the central human capabilities"; see her "The Role of Religion", in her *Women and Human Development: The Capabilities Approach*, 167–240 (Cambridge: Cambridge University Press, 2000), 179.

3. Global justice

1. Peter Singer has recently updated his argument in his *The Life you Can Save: Acting Now to End World Poverty* (Melbourne: Text Publishing, 2009).
2. For a representative selection, see Deen K. Chatterjee (ed.), *The Ethics of Assistance: Morality and the Distant Needy* (Cambridge: Cambridge University Press, 2004).
3. Robert Audi, *Moral Value and Human Diversity* (Oxford: Oxford University Press, 2007) has suggested that moral value is one value among several, such as art, family and knowledge, which human agents should take seriously. See also Garrett Cullity, *The Moral Demands of Affluence* (New York: Oxford University Press, 2004), who argues that we are not obliged to deny ourselves a life enriched by various values in order to meet the needs of others.
4. Chris Goodmacher challenges Singer's argument on the grounds that special relationships are an ineliminable part of the ethical life and so cannot be weighed against the lives of distant others:

   > Valued personal relationships – such as those between parents/children, siblings, lovers, and friends – are ends in themselves, an inextricable part of our identities, and the principal source of our ability to care for others, even those beyond our personal circle. And to value these personal relationships requires us to be partial to those with whom we have these connections.
   >
   > (Chris Goodmacher, "Partiality and World Poverty", *Philosophy in the Contemporary World* **14**[2] [Fall 2007], 74–85, esp. 79)

5. Paul Ricoeur, *Oneself as Another*, K. Blamey (trans.) (Chicago, IL: University of Chicago Press, 1992), chs 7, 8, 9, has argued that when one thinks within the framework of justice, everyone is abstracted from their specific national, racial, caste, or ethnic identity and considered as a node in a reciprocal system of entitlements in which everyone is an "each" – as in "to each according to their due".
6. This term arises from the writings of Carol Gilligan and the debate she generated. See Carol Gilligan, *In a Different Voice: Psychological Theory and Women's Development* (Cambridge, MA: Harvard University Press, 1993), and Susan J. Hekman, *Moral Voices, Moral Selves: Carol Gilligan and Feminist Moral Theory* (Cambridge: Polity, 1995).

7. In this way it seems to support various forms of patriotism. This is the basis of the remarks of Benjamin Barber quoted in Chapter 2.
8. For a further example, see Singer, *The Expanding Circle*.
9. See the discussion of Martha Nussbaum's argument in Chapter 2; see also Martha C. Nussbaum, "Reply", in her *For Love of Country?*, 131–44.
10. This example is discussed by Lawrence A. Blum, *Moral Perception and Particularity* (Cambridge: Cambridge University Press, 1994), 91–2. It is also discussed by both James Q. Wilson, *The Moral Sense* (New York: Free Press, 1993) and Kristen Renwick Monroe, *The Heart of Altruism: Perceptions of a Common Humanity* (Princeton, NJ: Princeton University Press, 1996).
11. In the introduction to his book *World Poverty and Human Rights: Cosmopolitan Responsibilities and Reforms* (Cambridge: Polity, 2002), Thomas Pogge details the many ways in which we affluent Westerners hide these realities from ourselves.
12. I have argued for the compatibility of these differing kinds of motivation in *Understanding Virtue Ethics* (Chesham: Acumen, 2006), ch. 4.
13. More than 130,000 people died as a result of this tsunami in Indonesia alone, while at least 37,000 others remain missing. The exact number of victims will probably never be known. About 500,000 Indonesians were made homeless. In Sri Lanka, more than 31,000 people died and more than 4,000 have been reported missing. More than half a million people were made homeless. On the mainland of India, 8,850 people were confirmed dead, 7,983 of them in Tamil Nadu. It is estimated that almost 70,000 people were in relief camps or centres on the mainland. On islands in the Indian Ocean almost 1,900 islanders were confirmed dead from a population of some 400,000. More than 5,550 are still missing. In Thailand, 5,395 people were confirmed dead. They included about 2,400 foreigners from thirty-six countries. The number of people still missing exceeds 2,800. In the Maldive Islands, at least 81 people died. More deaths occurred in Malaysia, Burma and as far away as Africa. The BBC report from which these figures are taken ("At a Glance: Countries Hit" [report on the damage caused by the 2004 tsunami in south-east Asia], http://news.bbc.co.uk/2/hi/asia-pacific/4126019.stm [accessed April 2009]) also speaks of ongoing relief and rebuilding efforts that are still going on today, funded by governments and millions of generous individuals and organizations from around the world.
14. Des Gasper, *The Ethics of Development: From Economism to Human Development* (Edinburgh: Edinburgh University Press, 2004), makes the same point and then espouses an ethic in which the goals of development should focus on the meeting of basic human needs. He theorizes such needs as going beyond mere survival so as to include Maslow's hierarchy of needs. He also endorses Nussbaum's and Sen's use of the capabilities approach in defining what those needs are.
15. For example, William Easterly, *The White Man's Burden: Why the West's Efforts to Aid the Rest have Done so much Ill and so little Good* (Oxford: Oxford University Press, 2006), prefers small-scale development projects that are cost effective to large-scale development goals that are unresponsive to local conditions and costly because of the scale of planning and evaluation required.
16. For wide-ranging discussions of the demands of justice, see James P. Sterba (ed.), *Justice: Alternative Political Perspectives*, 4th edn (Belmont, CA: Wadsworth, 2003).
17. In *Frontiers of Justice*, Nussbaum contrasts Rawls's procedural conception of justice in which an outcome is just provided that it was arrived at through fair and impartial procedures with her own conception in which an outcome is just only if it provides the prerequisites for exercising the ten capabilities she has identified as necessary for a dignified human life.

18. This example is used by Iris Marion Young in her "Responsibility, Social Connection, and Global Labor Justice", in her *Global Challenges: War, Self-Determination and Responsibility for Justice*, 159–86 (Cambridge: Polity, 2007). In this essay Young argues that we all share responsibility for the injustices of the global labour market, especially in sweatshops in the garment industry. To argue this case she analyses the concept of structural injustice and also argues that the scope of justice extends beyond the borders of one's political community. She also distinguishes the notion of responsibility as liability from the notion of responsibility based on social connection. In the liability model we look for the person who is to blame or who should be held accountable. But there may not be any individual or group who is responsible. The problem might be institutional or collective. "The social connection model of responsibility says that all agents who contribute by their actions to the structural processes that produce injustice have responsibilities to work to remedy these injustices" (*ibid*.: 159).

    > *Structural injustice* exists when social processes put large categories of persons under a systematic threat of domination or deprivation of the means to develop and exercise their capacities, at the same time as they enable others to dominate or have a wide range of opportunities for developing and exercising capacities. Structural injustice is a kind of moral wrong distinct from the wrongful action of an individual agent or the wilfully repressive policies of a state. (*Ibid*.: 170)

19. The website for the UNHCR can be found at www.unhcr.org/cgi-bin/texis/vtx/home (accessed April 2009).
20. Radical proposals for completely open borders are put by Joseph H. Carens, "Aliens and Citizens: The Case for Open Borders", *Review of Politics* **49**(2) (Spring 1987), 251–73, and by Robert E. Goodin, "If People Were Money ...", in *Free Movement: Ethics Issues in the Transnational Migration of People and of Money*, B. Barry & R. E. Goodin (eds), 6–22 (University Park, PA: Penn State University Press, 1992).
21. For further references to this debate, see Jürgen Habermas, "Citizenship and National Identity: Some Reflections on the Future of Europe", *Praxis International* **12**(1) (April 1992), 1–19; David A. Hollinger, "Not Universalists, Not Pluralists: The New Cosmopolitans Find Their Own Way", in Vertovec & Cohen (eds), *Conceiving Cosmopolitanism*, 227–39; Desmond Manderson, "The Care of Strangers", *Res Publica* **10**(2) (2001), 1–4; Julian Burnside, "Ethics and the Outsider", *Res Publica* **12**(2) (2003), 1–6; Emma Larking, "Please Consider", *Res Publica* **12**(2) (2003), 7–12. Seyla Benhabib has written extensively on this topic. Her *The Rights of Others* argues for what she calls "porous boundaries" between states, while in *Another Cosmopolitanism* (Oxford: Oxford University Press, 2006) she questions the rights of states to define who will be citizens of that state when such decisions affect non-citizens and aliens. Given that they are affected, the principle of democracy would suggest they should be involved in the decision.
22. The UN's Millennium Development Goals can be found at www.un.org/millenniumgoals/ (accessed April 2009).

4. Lasting peace

1. Although this theory is often repeated, not everyone agrees with it. For example, Hilary Putnam suggests that only powerful democracies do not attack each other. The Vietnam War was a war against a government that had popular support and it was fought in defence of democracy. Moreover the USA unseated democratic governments in Chile and Costa Rica. British, French and Israeli attacks on Nasser's Egypt during the Suez

crisis were also attacks on a democracy. See Hilary Putnam, "Must We Choose between Patriotism and Universal Reason?", in Nussbaum (ed.), *For Love of Country?*, 91–7. Michael W. Doyle defends the thesis that democracies do not go to war with each other in his *Ways of War and Peace: Realism, Liberalism, and Socialism* (New York: Norton, 1997).

2. To highlight the link between Kant's arguments and democracy, David Held argues that "Universal hospitality is not achieved if, for economic, cultural, or other reasons, the quality of the lives of others is shaped and determined in near or far-off lands without their participation, agreement, or consent" ("Cosmopolitan Democracy and the Global Order: A New Agenda", in James Bohman & Matthias Lutz-Bachmann [eds], *Perpetual Peace*, 235–51, esp. 244).
3. Parekh, in "Cosmopolitanism and Global Citizenship", challenges the centrality of the notion of sovereignty. International interdependence and the existence of international treaties all limit state sovereignty. No state can quarantine itself from the wider world. Moreover, according to Benhabib, "The exercise of state sovereignty even within domestic borders is increasingly subject to internationally recognised norms that prohibit genocide, ethnocide, mass expulsions, enslavement, rape, and forced labor" (*Another Cosmopolitanism*, 29).
4. Another argument for the necessity of states in a cosmopolitan world is given in Steven Slaughter, "Reconsidering the State: Cosmopolitanism, Republicanism and Global Governance", paper presented at "Questioning Cosmopolitanism", the Second Biennial Conference of the International Global Ethics Association, Melbourne, 26–8 June 2008.
5. > Like dragons the causes of war sometimes sleep and sometimes wake but they will not go away unless men can change or modify their institutions and at the same time overcome – somehow! – the natural propensity to aggression lurking inside their heads.
   >
   > (Jenny Teichman, *The Philosophy of War and Peace* [Exeter: Imprint Academic, 2006], 16).
6. For a good introduction to the pacifist tradition see Mark Kurlansky, *Nonviolence: Twenty-five Lessons from the History of a Dangerous Idea* (New York: Modern Library, 2006).
7. As Bryan Turner puts it, "If human beings are to have the capacity to articulate their needs and interests, then cultural rights to language, religion, and identity are fundamental to the generic right to enjoy rights" (*Vulnerability and Human Rights* [University Park, PA: Penn State University Press, 2006], 45).
8. For a striking example of the damage caused by forced assimilation see Jonathan Lear, *Radical Hope: Ethics in the Face of Cultural Devastation* (Cambridge, MA: Harvard University Press, 2008).
9. See also Avashai Margalit & Joseph Raz, "National Self-Determination", *Journal of Philosophy* **87**(9) (1990), 439–61; Peter Jones, "Group Rights and Group Oppression", *Journal of Political Philosophy* **7**(4) (1999), 353–77.
10. This charge is also made in Daniele Archibugi, "Cosmopolitical Democracy", in Strauss *et al.* (eds), *Debating Cosmopolitics*, 1–25.

5. Towards a global community

1. Amartya Sen, *Identity and Violence: The Illusion of Destiny* (New York: Allen Lane, 2006) argues that identity is not a single all-embracing classification through which social actors

can be understood or through which they should be encouraged to see themselves. Our identities are multiple. I might be a Catholic, an Australian, of European descent, male and a Greens party voter. None of these "identities" implies any of the others and each interacts in complex ways with the others to express themselves in my behaviour. To suppose that I am predestined or morally obligated by any of them to act in a certain way is to ignore the all-important role of choice in my life. A truly multicultural society is not a collection of monocultures living in social federation, but a society of equal citizens who have, alongside their common citizenship, a variety of other group identifications and cultural practices.

2. Henry Shue has argued that "It is obvious nonsense to describe the international arena, as some self-styled 'realists' do, as an 'anarchy,' and mean thereby a complete free-for-all in which outcomes are determined entirely by the distribution of power, while attributing a right to sovereignty to any of the players in the arena" ("Conditional Sovereignty", *Res Publica* **8**[1] [1999]: 1–7, esp. 2). There would be neither rights nor duties in an anarchic world: a Hobbesian world without law. Accordingly, leaders cannot argue that the world is an anarchy and then also claim that they have sovereign rights. If they claim sovereign rights they must accept that the international sphere is not anarchic, and they must then accept the duties that go with the rights that they claim.
3. He is supported in this by Catherine Audard in her "Cultural Imperialism and 'Democratic Peace'", in *Rawls's Law of Peoples: A Realistic Utopia?*, R. Marttin & D. A. Reidy (eds), 59–75 (Oxford: Blackwell. 2006).
4. As Charles Taylor has put it "Humanity is something to be realized, not in each individual human being, but rather in communion between all humans. ... The fullness of humanity comes not from the adding of differences, but from the exchange and communion between them" ("Living with Difference", in *Debating Democracy's Discontent: Essays on American Politics, Law, and Public Philosophy*, A. L. Allen & M. C. Regan [eds], 212–26 [New York: Oxford University Press, 1998], 214).
5. Benhabib subscribes to a universal discourse ethics in the manner of Habermas. She argues that the "discursive scope" (*Another Cosmopolitanism*, 18) of discourse ethics is universal and embraces the whole of humanity.
6. See also D. Archibugi, D. Held & M. Köhler (eds), *Re-imagining Political Community: Studies in Cosmopolitan Democracy* (Cambridge: Polity, 1998); Torbjorn Tannsjo, *Global Democracy: The Case for a World Government* (Edinburgh: Edinburgh University Press, 2008); and Carol Gould, *Globalizing Democracy and Human Rights* (Cambridge: Cambridge University Press, 2004).
7. Such irony is also advocated by Richard Rorty in his "Justice as a Larger Loyalty". In *Cosmopolitics: Thinking and Feeling Beyond the Nation*, P. Cheah & B. Robbins (eds), 45–58 (Minneapolis, MN: University of Minnesota Press, 1998). See also his "Solidarity", in his *Contingency, Irony and Solidarity*, 189–98 (Cambridge: Cambridge University Press 1989).
8. For a good place to start, see Sullivan & Kymlicka (eds), *The Globalization of Ethics*.

Bibliography

Ackermann, W. 1931. "The Cosmopolitan Union", J. Zube (trans.). http://www.panarchy.org/zube/cosmopolitan.1931.html (accessed April 2009).

Ali, W. 2007. *People Like Us: How Arrogance is dividing Islam and the West*. Sydney: Picador.

Alkire, S. 2005. "Needs and Capabilities". See Reader (ed.) (2005), 229–51.

Amnesty International 2008. "Hu Jia Jailed for Three and a Half Years". www.amnesty.org/en/news-and-updates/news/chinese-activist-gets-jail-sentence-20080403 (accessed April 2009).

Amstutz, M. R. 1999. *International Ethics: Concepts, Theories and Cases in Global Politics*. Lanham, MD: Rowman & Littlefield.

Appiah, K. A. 1996. "Cosmopolitan Patriots". See Nussbaum (1996a), 21–9.

Appiah, K. A. 2005. *The Ethics of Identity*. Princeton, NJ: Princeton University Press.

Appiah, K. A. 2006. *Cosmopolitanism: Ethics in a World of Strangers*. New York: Norton.

Archibugi, D. 2003. "Cosmopolitical Democracy". See Strauss *et al.* (eds) (2003), 1–25.

Archibugi, D., D. Held & M. Köhler (eds) 1998. *Re-imagining Political Community: Studies in Cosmopolitan Democracy*. Cambridge: Polity.

Arendt, H. 1968, *Eichmann in Jerusalem: A Report on the Banality of Evil*, rev. edn. New York: Viking.

Armstrong, K. 2000. *The Battle for God: Fundamentalism in Judaism, Christianity and Islam*. London: HarperCollins.

Atack, I. 2005. *The Ethics of Peace and War: From State Security to World Community*. Edinburgh: Edinburgh University Press.

Audard, C. 2006. "Cultural Imperialism and 'Democratic Peace'". See Marttin & Reidy (eds) (2006), 59–75.

Audi, R. 2007. *Moral Value and Human Diversity*. Oxford: Oxford University Press.

Barber, B. R. 1996. "Constitutional Faith". See Nussbaum (1996a), 30–37.

Barry, B. 1982. "Humanity and Justice in Global Perspective". In *Nomos XXIV: Ethics, Economics and the Law*, J. R. Pennock & J. W. Chapman (eds), 219–52. New York: NYU Press.

Baynes, K. 1997. "Communitarian and Cosmopolitan Challenges to Kant's Conception of World Peace". See Bohman & Lutz-Bachmann (eds) (1997), 219–34.

BBC News 2005. "At a Glance: Countries Hit" (report on the damage caused by the 2004 tsunami in south-east Asia). http://news.bbc.co.uk/2/hi/asia-pacific/4126019.stm (accessed April 2009).

Beck, U. 2002. "The Cosmopolitan Society and its Enemies". *Theory, Culture & Society* **19**(1–2): 17–44.
Beck, U. 2004. "Cosmopolitical Realism: On the Distinction between Cosmopolitanism in Philosophy and the Social Sciences". *Global Networks* **4**(2): 131–46.
Beitz, C. 1975. "Justice and International Relations". *Philosophy and Public Affairs* **4**(4) (Summer): 360–89.
Beitz, C. 1979. *Political Theory and International Relations*. Princeton, NJ: Princeton University Press.
Beitz, C. 1999a. "International Liberalism and Distributive Justice: A Survey of Recent Thought". *World Politics* **51**(2) (January): 269–96.
Beitz, C. 1999b. "Social and Cosmopolitan Liberalism". *International Affairs* **75**: 515–29.
Benhabib, S. 2004. *The Rights of Others: Aliens, Residents, and Citizens*. Cambridge: Cambridge University Press.
Benhabib, S. 2006. *Another Cosmopolitanism*. Oxford: Oxford University Press.
Blum, L. A. 1994. *Moral Perception and Particularity*. Cambridge: Cambridge University Press.
Bohman, J. 1997. "The Public Spheres of the World Citizen". See Bohman & Lutz-Bachmann (eds) (1997), 179–200.
Bohman, J. & M. Lutz-Bachmann (eds) 1997. *Perpetual Peace: Essays on Kant's Cosmopolitan Ideal*. Cambridge, MA: MIT Press.
Boswell, C. 2005. *The Ethics of Refugee Policy*. Aldershot: Ashgate.
Braybrooke, D. 1987. *Meeting Needs*. Princeton, NJ: Princeton University Press.
Breckenridge, C. A., S. Pollock, H. K. Bhabha & D. Chakrabarty (eds) 2002. *Cosmopolitanism*. Durham, NC: Duke University Press.
Brennan, T. 1997. *At Home in the World: Cosmopolitanism Now*. Cambridge, MA: Harvard University Press.
Brennan, T. 2003. "Cosmopolitanism and Internationalism". See Strauss *et al.* (eds) (2003a), 40–50.
Brennan, T. 2005. *The Stoic Life: Emotions, Duties, & Fate*. Oxford: Clarendon Press.
Brock, G. (ed.) 1998. *Necessary Goods: Our Responsibilities to Meet Others' Needs*. Lanham, MD: Rowman & Littlefield.
Brock, G. 2005. "Needs and Global Justice". See Reader (ed.) (2005), 51–72.
Brock, G. 2009. *Global Justice: A Cosmopolitan Account*. Oxford: Oxford University Press.
Brock, G. & H. Brighouse (eds) 2005. *The Political Philosophy of Cosmopolitanism*. Cambridge: Cambridge University Press.
Brock, G. & D. Moellendorf (eds) 2005. *Current Debates in Global Justice*. Dordrecht: Springer.
Brooks, T. 2008. *The Global Justice Reader*. Oxford: Blackwell.
Burnside, J. 2003. "Ethics and the Outsider". *Res Publica* **12**(2): 1–6.
Campbell, T. 2006. *Rights: A Critical Introduction*. London: Routledge.
Campbell, T. 2007. "Poverty as a Violation of Human Rights: Inhumanity or Injustice?". In *Freedom from Poverty as a Human Right: Who Owes What to the Very Poor*, T. Pogge (ed.), 55–74. Oxford: Oxford University Press, in conjunction with the United Nations Educational, Scientific and Cultural Organization.
Caney S. 2005. *Justice Beyond Borders: A Global Political Theory*. Oxford: Oxford University Press.
Caputo, J. D. 2001. *On Religion*. London: Routledge.
Carens, J. H. 1987. "Aliens and Citizens: The Case for Open Borders". *Review of Politics* **49**(2) (Spring): 251–73.
Chandler, D. 2003. "International Justice". See Strauss *et al.* (eds) (2003a), 27–39.

Chatterjee, D. K. (ed.) 2004. *The Ethics of Assistance: Morality and the Distant Needy*. Cambridge: Cambridge University Press.

Cheah, C. 2006. *Inhuman Conditions: On Cosmopolitanism and Human Rights*. Cambridge, MA: Harvard University Press.

Christopher, P. 2004. *The Ethics of War and Peace: An Introduction to Legal and Moral Issues*, 3rd edn. Upper Saddle River, NJ: Pearson Prentice-Hall.

Churchill, R. P. 2006. *Human Rights and Global Diversity*. Upper Saddle River, NJ: Pearson Prentice-Hall.

Ci, J. 2006. *The Two Faces of Justice*. Cambridge, MA: Harvard University Press.

Cicero 1928. *On the Laws*. In *On the Republic, On the Laws*, C. W. Keyes (trans.) (Loeb Classical Library). Cambridge, MA: Harvard University Press.

Coady, C. A. J. (ed.) 2006. *What's Wrong with Moralism?* Oxford: Blackwell.

Coady, C. A. J. 2008. *Morality and Political Violence*. Cambridge: Cambridge University Press.

Cobban, A. 1969. *The Nation State and National Self-Determination*, rev. edn. London: Collins.

Commers, M. S. R., W. Vandekerckhove & A. Verlinden (eds) 2008. "Introduction". In their *Ethics in an Era of Globalization*, 1–10. Aldershot: Ashgate.

Copp, D. 1998. "Equality, Justice, and the Basic Needs". In *Necessary Goods: Our Responsibilities to Meet Others' Needs*, G. Brock (ed.), 113–33. Lanham, MD: Rowman & Littlefield.

Crocker, D. A. & T. Linden (eds) 1998. *Ethics of Consumption: The Good Life, Justice, and Global Stewardship*. Lanham, MD: Rowman & Littlefield.

Crocker, D. A. 2002. "Hunger, Capacity, and Development". In *Ethics in Practice: An Anthology*, 2nd edn, H. LaFollette (ed.), 591–603. Oxford: Blackwell.

Cullity, G. 2004. *The Moral Demands of Affluence*. New York: Oxford University Press.

Delanty, G. 2000. *Citizenship in a Global Age: Society, Culture, Politics*. Buckingham: Open University Press.

Diogenes Laertius 1925. *Lives of the Eminent Philosophers*, 2 vols, R. D. Hicks (trans.). Cambridge, MA: Harvard University Press.

Dower, N. 1998. *World Ethics: The New Agenda*. Edinburgh, Edinburgh University Press.

Dower, N. 2003. *An Introduction to Global Citizenship*. Edinburgh: Edinburgh University Press.

Doyal, L. 1998. "A Theory of Human Need". In *Necessary Goods: Our Responsibilities to Meet Others' Needs*, G. Brock (ed.), 157–72. Lanham, MD: Rowman & Littlefield.

Doyle, M. W. 1997. *Ways of War and Peace: Realism, Liberalism, and Socialism*. New York: Norton.

Drydyk, J. 1997. "Globalization and Human Rights". In *Global Justice, Global Democracy*, J. Drydyk & P. Penz (eds), 159–83. Winnipeg: Fernwood Publishing.

Easterly, W. 2006. *The White Man's Burden: Why the West's Efforts to Aid the Rest have Done so much Ill and so little Good*. Oxford: Oxford University Press.

Edmundson, W. A. 2004. *An Introduction to Rights*. Cambridge: Cambridge University Press.

Engelen, B. & T. Nys 2008. "Tolerance: A Virtue? Toward a Broad and Descriptive Definition of Tolerance". *Philosophy in the Contemporary World* **15**(1) (Spring): 44–54.

Etzioni, A. 1995. *New Communitarian Thinking: Persons, Virtues, Institutions, and Communities*. Charlottesville, VA: University Press of Virginia.

Etzioni, A. & M. Wenglinsky (eds) 1970. *War and Its Prevention*. New York: Harper & Row.

Falk, R. 1996. "Revisioning Cosmopolitanism". See Nussbaum (1996a), 53–60.

Falk, R. 1999. *Predatory Globalization: A Critique*. Cambridge: Polity.

Follesdal, A. & T. Pogge 2005. *Real World Justice: Grounds, Principles, Human Rights, and Social Institutions*. Dordrecht: Springer.
Fotion, N. 2007. *War and Ethics: A New Just War Theory*. London: Continuum.
Frankfurt, H. 1988. "Freedom of the Will and the Concept of the Person". In his *The Importance of What We Care About*, 11–25. Cambridge: Cambridge University Press.
Gaita, R. 1999. *A Common Humanity: Thinking about Love & Truth & Justice*. Melbourne: Text Publishing.
Gasper, D. 2004. *The Ethics of Development: From Economism to Human Development*. Edinburgh: Edinburgh University Press.
Giddens, A. 1985. *A Contemporary Critique of Historical Materialism, Vol 2: The National-State and Violence*. Cambridge: Polity.
Gilligan, C. 1993. *In a Different Voice: Psychological Theory and Women's Development*. Cambridge, MA: Harvard University Press.
Glazer, N. 1996. "Limits of Loyalty". See Nussbaum (1996a), 61–5.
Glendon, M. A. 2001. *A World Made New: Eleanor Roosevelt and the Universal Declaration of Human Rights*. New York: John Wiley.
Goodin, R. E. 1985. *Protecting the Vulnerable*. Chicago, IL: University of Chicago Press.
Goodin, R. E. 1986. "What is So Special About Our Fellow Countrymen?". *Ethics* **98**: 663–86.
Goodin, R. E. 1992. "If People Were Money ...". In *Free Movement: Ethics Issues in the Transnational Migration of People and of Money*, B. Barry & R. E. Goodin (eds), 6–22. University Park, PA: Penn State University Press.
Goodmacher, C. 2007. "Partiality and World Poverty". *Philosophy in the Contemporary World* **14**(2) (Fall): 74–85.
Gould, C. 2004. *Globalizing Democracy and Human Rights*. Cambridge: Cambridge University Press.
Gowan, P. 2003. "The New Liberal Cosmopolitanism". See Strauss *et al.* (eds) (2003a), 51–64.
Gutmann, A. 1996. "Democratic Citizenship". See Nussbaum (1996a), 66–71.
Habermas, J. 1973. *Legitimation Crisis*, T. McCarthy (trans.). Boston, MA: Beacon Press.
Habermas, J. 1992. "Citizenship and National Identity: Some Reflections on the Future of Europe". *Praxis International* **12**(1) (April): 1–19.
Habermas, J. 1993. *Justification and Application: Remarks on Discourse Ethics*, C. Cronin (trans.). Cambridge: Polity.
Habermas, J. 1996. "Appendix II: Citizenship and National Identity". In *Between Facts and Norms: Contributions to a Discourse Theory of Law and Democracy*, William Rehg (trans.), 491–515. Cambridge, MA: MIT Press.
Habermas, J. 1997. "Kant's Idea of Perpetual Peace, with the Benefit of Two Hundred Years' Hindsight". In *Perpetual Peace: Essays on Kant's Cosmopolitan Ideal*, J. Bohman & M. Lutz-Bachmann (eds), 113–53. Cambridge, MA: MIT Press.
Hart, H. L. A. 1961. *The Concept of Law*. Oxford: Oxford University Press.
Hart, H. L. A. 1967. "Are there any Natural Rights?". In *Political Philosophy*, A. Quinton (ed.), 53–66. Oxford: Oxford University Press.
Hekman, S. J. 1995. *Moral Voices, Moral Selves: Carol Gilligan and Feminist Moral Theory*. Cambridge: Polity.
Held, D. 1992. "Democracy: From City-States to a Cosmopolitan Order?". *Political Studies* (special issue) **40** (August): 10–39.
Held, D. 1995. *Democracy and the Global Order: From the Modern State to Cosmopolitan Governance*. Cambridge: Polity.

Held, D. 1997. "Cosmopolitan Democracy and the Global Order: A New Agenda". See Bohman & Lutz-Bachmann (eds) (1997), 235–51.

Held, D. & A. McGrew 2000. *The Global Transformations Reader: An Introduction to the Globalization Debate*. Cambridge: Polity.

Hick, J. 1973. *God and the Universe of Faiths*. New York: St Martin's Press.

Himmelfarb, G. 1996. "The Illusions of Cosmopolitanism". See Nussbaum (1996a), 72–7.

Hinsch, W. & M. Stepanians 2006. "Human Rights as Moral Claim Rights". See Marttin & Reidy (eds) (2006), 117–33.

Hobbes, T. 1651. *Leviathan, or The Matter, Forme and Power of a Common Wealth Ecclesiasticall and Civil*, section xiii. www.gutenberg.org/etext/3207 (accessed April 2009).

Hollinger, D. A. 2002. "Not Universalists, Not Pluralists: The New Cosmopolitans Find Their Own Way". See Vertovec & Cohen (eds) (2002a), 227–39.

Honneth, A. 1997. "Is Universalism a Moral Trap? The Presuppositions and Limits of a Politics of Human Rights". See Bohman & Lutz-Bachmann (eds) (1997), 155–78.

Howard, J. 2001. Election campaign speech, 28 October. www.australianpolitics.com/news/2001/01-10-28.shtml (accessed April 2009).

Huntington, S. P. 1996. *The Clash of Civilizations and the Remaking of World Order*. New York: Simon & Schuster.

Hurrell, A. & N. Woods (eds) 1999. *Inequality, Globalization, and World Politics*. Oxford: Oxford University Press.

Hutchings, K. & R. Dannreuther (eds) 1999. *Cosmopolitan Citizenship*. New York: St Martin's Press.

Hutchinson, J. & A. D. Smith (eds) 1994. *Nationalism*. Oxford: Oxford University Press.

ICISS 2001. *The Responsibility to Protect*. Report of the International Commission on Intervention and State Sovereignty, International Research Centre for ICISS, Ottawa. www.iciss.gc.ca (accessed April 2009).

Ignatieff, M. 2001. *Human Rights as Politics and Idolatry*. Princeton, NJ: Princeton University Press.

Ishay, M. R. 2004. *The History of Human Rights: From Ancient Time to the Globalization Era*. Berkeley, CA: University of California Press.

Jonas, H. 1984. *The Imperative of Responsibility: In Search of an Ethics for the Technological Age*. Chicago, IL: University of Chicago Press.

Jones, C. 1999. *Global Justice: Defending Cosmopolitanism*. Oxford: Oxford University Press.

Jones, P. 1999. "Group Rights and Group Oppression". *Journal of Political Philosophy* 7(4): 353–77.

Kaldor, M. 2002. "Cosmopolitanism and Organized Violence". See Vertovec & Cohen (eds) (2002a), 268–78.

Kant, I. 1928. *The Critique of Judgement*, J. C. Meredith (trans.). Oxford: Clarendon Press.

Kant, I. 1991. "Perpetual Peace: A Philosophical Sketch". In his *Political Writings*, 2nd edn, H. Reiss (ed. with intro. and notes), H. B. Nisbet (trans.), 93–130. Cambridge: Cambridge University Press.

Koshy, S. 1999. "From Cold War to Trade War: Neocolonialism and Human Rights". *Social Text* **58**: 1–32.

Küng, H. & K. J. Kuschel 1993. *A Global Ethic: The Declaration of the Parliament of the World's Religions*. London: SCM Press.

Kurlansky, M. 2006. *Nonviolence: Twenty-five Lessons from the History of a Dangerous Idea*. New York: Modern Library.

Lango, J. W. 2008. "The Security Council and the Use of Military Force: Disagreement and

Compromise about Applications of Generalized Just War Principles". Paper presented at "Questioning Cosmopolitanism", the Second Biennial Conference of the International Global Ethics Association, Melbourne, 26–8 June.

Larking, E. 2003. "Please Consider". *Res Publica* **12**(2): 7–12.

Lear, J. 2008. *Radical Hope: Ethics in the Face of Cultural Devastation*. Cambridge, MA: Harvard University Press.

Levinas, E. 1969. *Totality and Infinity: An Essay on Exteriority*, A. Lingis (trans.). Pittsburgh, PA: Duquesne University Press.

Locke, J. 1960. "An Essay Concerning the True Original, Extent and End of Civil Government". In his *Two Treatises of Government*, P. Laslett (ed.). Cambridge: Cambridge University Press.

MacDonald, M. 1984. "Natural Rights". In *Theories of Rights*, J. Waldron (ed.), 21–40. Oxford: Oxford University Press.

MacIntyre, A. 2002. "Is Patriotism a Virtue?". In *Patriotism*, I. Primoratz (ed.), 43–58. Amherst, NY: Humanity Books.

Maffettone, S. 2007. "Human Rights and Cultural Diversity". Paper presented at the Centre for Applied Philosophy and Public Ethics, University of Melbourne, 15 February.

Mahoney, J. 2007. *The Challenge of Human Rights: Origin, Development, and Significance*. Oxford: Blackwell.

Manderson, D. 2001. "The Care of Strangers". *Res Publica* **10**(2): 1–4.

Margalit, A. & J. Raz 1990. "National Self-Determination". *Journal of Philosophy* **87**(9): 439–61.

Maritain, J. 1986. *"Christianity and Democracy" and "The Rights of Man and Natural Law"*. San Francisco, CA: Ignatius Press.

Marttin, R. & D. A. Reidy (eds) 2006. *Rawls's Law of Peoples: A Realistic Utopia?* Oxford: Blackwell.

May, L. E. Rovie & S. Viner (eds) 2006. *The Morality of War: Classical and Contemporary Readings*. Upper Saddle River, NJ: Pearson Prentice-Hall.

McConnell, M. W. 1996. "Don't Neglect the Little Platoons". See Nussbaum (1996a), 78–84.

McGrew, A. 1997. "Democracy Beyond Borders? Globalization and the Reconstruction of Democratic Theory and Politics". In *The Transformation of Democracy*, A. McGrew (ed.), 231–66. Cambridge: Polity.

McKeogh, C. 2002. *Innocent Civilians: The Morality of Killing in War*. Basingstoke: Palgrave.

McKinnon, C. 2006. *Toleration: A Critical Introduction*. London: Routledge.

Mendus, S. 1989. *Toleration and the Limits of Liberalism*. London: Macmillan.

Mill, J. S. 1987. "Utilitarianism". In J. S. Mill & J. Bentham, *Utilitarianism and Other Essays*, A. Ryan (ed.), 272–338. Harmondsworth: Penguin.

Miller, D. 1999. "Justice and Global Inequality". In *Inequality, Globalization, and World Politics*, A. Hurrell & N. Woods (eds), 187–210. Oxford: Oxford University Press.

Monroe, K. R. 1996. *The Heart of Altruism: Perceptions of a Common Humanity*. Princeton, NJ: Princeton University Press.

Nagel, T. 1977. "Poverty and Food: Why Charity is Not Enough". In *Food Policy: The Responsibility of the United States in the Life and Death Choices*, P. G. Brown & H. Shue (eds), 54–62. New York: Free Press.

Nathanson, S. 1993. *Patriotism, Morality, and Peace*. Lanham, MD: Rowman & Littlefield.

Newton, L. H. 2003. *Ethics and Sustainability: Sustainable Development and the Moral Life*. Englewood Cliffs, NJ: Prentice-Hall.

Nickel, J. W. 2004. *Making Sense of Human Rights: Philosophical Reflections on the Universal Declaration of Human Rights*, new rev. edn. Oxford: Blackwell.

Nietzsche, F. [1886] 1966. *Beyond Good and Evil*, W. Kaufmann (trans.). New York: Random House.
Nussbaum, M. C. 1992. "Human Functioning and Social Justice: In Defence of Aristotelian Essentialism". *Political Theory* **20**(2): 202–46.
Nussbaum, M. C. 1996a. *For Love of Country?: Debating the Limits of Patriotism*, J. Cohen (ed.) for *Boston Review*. Boston, MA: Beacon Press.
Nussbaum, M. C. 1996b, "Patriotism and Cosmopolitanism". See Nussbaum (1996a), 3–17.
Nussbaum, M. C. 1996c, "Reply". See Nussbaum (1996a), 131–44.
Nussbaum, M. C. 1998. "Aristotelian Social Democracy". In *Necessary Goods: Our Responsibilities to Meet Others' Needs*, G. Brock (ed.), 135–56. Lanham, MD: Rowman & Littlefield.
Nussbaum, M. C. 1999. "Women and Cultural Universals". In her *Sex and Social Justice*, 29–54. Oxford: Oxford University Press.
Nussbaum, M. C. 2000. "The Role of Religion". In her *Women and Human Development: The Capabilities Approach*, 167–240. Cambridge: Cambridge University Press.
Nussbaum, M. C. 2006. *Frontiers of Justice: Disability, Nationality, Species Membership*. Cambridge, MA: Harvard University Press.
Office of the High Commissioner for Human Rights 1996. Fact Sheet No. 2 (Rev. 1): The International Bill of Human Rights. www.unhchr.ch/html/menu6/2/fs2.htm (accessed April 2009) or www.ohchr.org/Documents/Publications/FactSheet2Rev.1en.pdf (accessed April 2009).
O'Neill, O. 1986. *Faces of Hunger: An Essay on Poverty, Justice and Development*. London: Allen & Unwin.
O'Neill, O. 1998. "Rights, Obligations, and Needs". In *Necessary Goods: Our Responsibilities to Meet Others' Needs*, G. Brock (ed), 95–12. Lanham, MD: Rowman & Littlefield.
O'Neill, O. 2000. *Bounds of Justice*. Cambridge: Cambridge University Press.
Oldenquist, A. 1982. "Loyalties". *Journal of Philosophy* **79**: 173–93.
Parekh, B. 2003. "Cosmopolitanism and Global Citizenship". *Review of International Studies* **29**(1): 3–17.
Pettit, P. 1997. *Republicanism: A Theory of Freedom and Government*. Oxford: Oxford University Press.
Pettit, P. 2006. "Rawls's Peoples". See Marttin & Reidy (eds) (2006), 38–55.
Pinsky, R. 1996. "Eros against Esperanto". See Nussbaum (1996a), 85–90.
Pogge, T. 1989. *Realizing Rawls*. Ithaca, NY: Cornell University Press.
Pogge, T. 1992. "Cosmopolitanism and Sovereignty". *Ethics* **103**(1) (October): 48–75. Reprinted in *Political Restructuring in Europe: Ethical Perspectives*, C. Brown (ed.), 89–122 (London: Routledge, 1994) and in *Global Justice: Seminal Essays*, T. Pogge & D. Moellendorf (eds), 355–90 (St Paul, MN: Paragon House, 2008).
Pogge, T. 1998. "A Global Resources Dividend". In *Ethics of Consumption: The Good Life, Justice, and Global Stewardship*, D. A. Crocker & T. Linden (eds), 501–10. Lanham, MD: Rowman & Littlefield.
Pogge, T. 2002a. *World Poverty and Human Rights: Cosmopolitan Responsibilities and Reforms*. Cambridge: Polity.
Pogge, T. 2002b. "The Bounds of Nationalism". In his *World Poverty and Human Rights: Cosmopolitan Responsibilities and Reforms*, 118–45. Cambridge: Polity.
Pogge, T. 2005. "Real World Justice". In *Current Debates in Global Justice*, G. Brock & D. Moellendorf (eds), 29–53. Dordrecht: Springer.
Pogge, T. 2006. "Do Rawls's Two Theories of Justice Fit Together?". See Marttin & Reidy (eds) (2006), 206–25.

Pogge, T. (ed.) 2007a. *Freedom from Poverty as a Human Right: Who Owes What to the Very Poor*. Oxford: Oxford University Press, in conjunction with UNESCO.

Pogge, T. 2007b. "Severe Poverty as a Human Rights Violation". In *Freedom from Poverty as a Human Right: Who Owes What to the Very Poor?*, T. Pogge (ed.), 11–54. Oxford: Oxford University Press, in conjunction with UNESCO.

Pogge, T. & K. Horton (eds) 2008. *Global Ethics: Seminal Essays*. St Paul, MN: Paragon House.

Pogge, T. & D. Moellendorf (eds) 2008. *Global Justice: Seminal Essays*. St Paul, MN: Paragon House.

Pollis, A. & P. Schwab 1979. "Human Rights: A Western Construct with Limited Applicability". In *Human Rights: Cultural and Ideological Perspectives*, A. Pollis & P. Schwab (eds), 1–18. New York: Praeger.

Pollock, S. 2002. "Cosmopolitanism and Vernacular in History". In *Cosmopolitanism*, C. A. Breckenridge, S. Pollock, H. K. Bhabha & D. Chakrabarty (eds), 15–53. Durham, NC: Duke University Press.

Primoratz, I. 2008. "Patriotism and Morality". *Journal of Moral Philosophy* **5**(2): 204–26.

Primoratz, I. & A. Pavkovic (eds) 2007. *Patriotism: Philosophical and Political Perspectives*. Aldershot: Ashgate.

Putman, H. 1996. "Must We Choose between Patriotism and Universal Reason?". See Nussbaum (1996a), 91–7.

Rawls, J. 1972. *A Theory of Justice*. Oxford: Oxford University Press.

Rawls, J. 1993. *Political Liberalism*. New York : Columbia University Press.

Rawls, J. 1999. *The Law of Peoples*. Cambridge, MA: Harvard University Press.

Reader, S. (ed.) 2005. *The Philosophy of Need*. Cambridge: Cambridge University Press.

Ricoeur, P. 1966. *Freedom and Nature: The Voluntary and the Involuntary*. Evanston, IL: Northwestern University Press.

Ricoeur, P. 1992. *Oneself as Another*, K. Blamey (trans.). Chicago, IL: University of Chicago Press.

Rorty, R. 1989. *Contingency, Irony and Solidarity*. Cambridge: Cambridge University Press.

Rorty, R. 1998. "Justice as a Larger Loyalty". In *Cosmopolitics: Thinking and Feeling Beyond the Nation*, P. Cheah & B. Robbins (eds), 45–58. Minneapolis, MN: University of Minnesota Press.

Rousseau, J.-J. 1968. *The Social Contract. Book One*, M. Cranston (trans. and intro.). Harmondsworth: Penguin.

Sandel, M. J. 2005. *Public Philosophy: Essays on Morality in Politics*. Cambridge, MA: Harvard University Press.

Sassen, S. 2003. "The State and Globalization". *Interventions* **5**(2): 241–8.

Sassen, S. 2006. *Territory, Authority, Rights: From Medieval to Global Assemblages*. Princeton, NJ: Princeton University Press.

Scheffler, S. 1999. "Conceptions of Cosmopolitanism". *Utilitas* **11**(3): 255–76. Reprinted in his *Boundaries and Allegiances: Problems of Justice and Responsibility in Liberal Thought*, 111–30 (Oxford: Oxford University Press, 2001).

Sen, A. 1999. *Development as Freedom*. New York: Random House.

Sen, A. 2006. *Identity and Violence: The Illusion of Destiny*. New York: Allen Lane.

Shapcott, R. 2001. *Justice, Community, and Dialogue in International Relations*. Cambridge: Cambridge University Press.

Shue, H. 1996. *Basic Rights: Subsistence, Affluence, and US Foreign Policy*, 2nd rev. edn. Princeton, NJ: Princeton University Press.

Shue, H. 1999. "Conditional Sovereignty". *Res Publica* **8**(1): 1–7.

Singer, P. 1972. "Famine, Affluence and Morality". *Philosophy and Public Affairs* **1**(3): 229–43.

Singer, P. 1981. *The Expanding Circle: Ethics and Sociobiology*. New York: Farrar, Straus & Giroux.

Singer, P. 2002. *One World: The Ethics of Globalisation*. Melbourne: Text Publishing.

Singer, P. 2009. *The Life you Can Save: Acting Now to End World Poverty*. Melbourne: Text Publishing.

Slaughter, S. 2008. "Reconsidering the State: Cosmopolitanism, Republicanism and Global Governance". Paper presented at "Questioning Cosmopolitanism", the Second Biennial Conference of the International Global Ethics Association, Melbourne, 26–8 June.

Smith, A. 1976. *An Inquiry into the Nature and Causes of the Wealth of Nations*, R. H. Campbell & A. S. Skinner (eds), W. B. Todd (textual ed.). Indianapolis, IN: Liberty Classics.

Smith, R. K. M. & C. van den Anker (eds) 2005. *The Essentials of Human Rights*. London: Hodder Arnold.

Sparrow, J. 2008. "Oh, What a Lovely War". *The Age Features*, 21 June: 14.

Sterba, J. P. (ed.) 2003a. *Justice: Alternative Political Perspectives*, 4th edn. Belmont, CA: Wadsworth.

Sterba, J. P. (ed.) 2003b. *Terrorism and International Justice*. New York: Oxford University Press.

Stiglitz, J. E. 2002. *Globalization and its Discontents*. Harmondsworth: Penguin.

Stiglitz, J. E. 2006. *Making Globalization Work: The Next Steps to Global Justice*. Harmondsworth: Penguin.

Stocker, M. 1976. "The Schizophrenia of Modern Ethical Theories". *Journal of Philosophy* **73**(14) (August): 453–66.

Strauss, A., D. Archibugi, M. Koenig-Archibugi, R. Blackburn *et al.* (eds) 2003. *Debating Cosmopolitics*. London: Verso.

Strawson, P. F. 1974. "Freedom and Resentment". In his *Freedom and Resentment, and Other Essays*, 1–25. London: Methuen.

Sullivan, W. M. & W. Kymlicka (eds) 2007. *The Globalization of Ethics: Religious and Secular Perspectives*. New York: Cambridge University Press.

Tan Kok-Chor 2000. *Toleration, Diversity, and Global Justice*. University Park, PA: Penn State University Press.

Tan Kok-Chor 2004. *Justice without Borders: Cosmopolitanism, Nationalism, and Patriotism*. Cambridge: Cambridge University Press.

Tan Kok-Chor 2006. "The Problem of Decent Peoples". See Marttin & Reidy (eds) (2006), 76–94.

Tannsjo, T. 2008. *Global Democracy: The Case for a World Government*. Edinburgh: Edinburgh University Press.

Taylor, C. & A. Gutmann 1994. *Multiculturalism: Examining the Politics of Recognition*. Princeton, NJ: Princeton University Press.

Taylor, C. 1989. "Cross-Purposes: The Liberal–Communitarian Debate". In *Liberalism and the Moral Life*, N. L. Rosenblum (ed.), 159–82. Cambridge, MA: Harvard University Press.

Taylor, C. 1996. "Why Democracy Needs Patriotism". See Nussbaum (1996a), 119–21.

Taylor, C. 1998. "Living with Difference". In *Debating Democracy's Discontent: Essays on American Politics, Law, and Public Philosophy*, A. L. Allen & M. C. Regan (eds), 212–26. New York: Oxford University Press.

Taylor, P. W. 1986. *Respect for Nature: A Theory of Environmental Ethics*. Princeton, NJ: Princeton University Press.

Teichman, J. 2006. *The Philosophy of War and Peace*. Exeter: Imprint Academic.

Tharoor, S. 1999/2000. "Are Human Rights Universal?". *World Policy Journal* **16**(4) (Winter): 1–7.
Tomlison, J. 2002. "Interests and Identities in Cosmopolitan Politics". See Vertovec & Cohen (eds) (2002a), 240–53.
Traub, J. 2006. *The Best Intentions: Kofi Annan and the UN in the Era of American Power*. London: Bloomsbury.
Turner, B. S. 2000. "Cosmopolitan Virtue: Loyalty and the City". In *Democracy, Citizenship, and the Global City*, E. F. Isin (ed.), 129–47. London: Routledge.
Turner, B. S. 2006. *Vulnerability and Human Rights*. University Park, PA: Penn State University Press.
United Nations 2004. *A More Secure World: Our Shared Responsibility*, report of the High-level Panel on Threats, Challenges and Change (HPTCC). New York: United Nations.
United Nations 2005. General Assembly Resolution A/60/L.1, 2005 World Summit Outcome. http://stdev.unctad.org/docs/a60l1.pdf (accessed April 2009).
United Nations 1948. Universal Declaration of Human Rights. www.un.org/Overview/rights.html (accessed April 2009).
USAID n.d. "USAID's Family Planning Guiding Principles and U.S. Legislative and Policy Requirements". www.usaid.gov/our_work/global_health/pop/restrictions.html (accessed April 2009).
van der Veer, P. 2002. "Colonial Cosmopolitanism". See Vertovec & Cohen (eds) (2002a), 165–79.
van Gorkom, J. 2008. "Immanuel Kant on Racial Identity". *Philosophy in the Contemporary World* **15**(1) (Spring): 1–10.
van Hooft, S. 1995. *Caring: An Essay in the Philosophy of Ethics*. Niwot, CO: University Press of Colorado.
van Hooft, S. 2006. *Understanding Virtue Ethics*. Chesham: Acumen.
van Hooft, S. 2007. "Cosmopolitanism as Virtue". *Journal of Global Ethics* **3**(3) (December): 303–15.
Vertovec, S. & R. Cohen (eds) 2002a. *Conceiving Cosmopolitanism: Theory, Context, and Practice*. Oxford: Oxford University Press.
Vertovec, S. & R. Cohen 2002b. "Introduction: Conceiving Cosmoplitanism". See Vertovec & Cohen (eds) (2002a), 1–22.
Vincent, R. J. 1992. "The Idea of Rights in International Ethics". In *Traditions of International Ethics*, T. Nardin & D. R. Mapel (eds), 250–69. Cambridge: Cambridge University Press.
Viroli, M. 1995. *For Love of Country*. Oxford: Clarendon Press.
von Clausewitz, C. 1976. *On War*, M. Howard & P. Paret (eds and trans.). Princeton, NJ: Princeton University Press.
Waldron, J. 1999. "What is Cosmopolitan?". *Journal of Political Philosophy* **8**(2): 227–43.
Wallerstein, I. 1996. "Neither Patriotism Nor Cosmopolitanism". See Nussbaum (1996a), 122–4.
Walzer, M. 1981. "The Distribution of Membership". In *Boundaries: National Autonomy and Its Limits*, P. G. Brown & H. Shue (eds), 1–35. Lanham, MD: Rowman & Littlefield.
Walzer, M. 1983. *Spheres of Justice*. Oxford: Blackwell.
Walzer, M. 1992. *Just and Unjust Wars*, 2nd edn. New York: Basic Books.
Walzer, M. 1994. *Thick and Thin: Moral Argument at Home and Abroad*. Notre Dame, IN: University of Notre Dame Press.
Walzer, M. 1996. "Spheres of Affection". See Nussbaum (1996a), 125–7.
Walzer, M. 1997. *On Toleration*. New Haven, CT: Yale University Press.

Westermarck, E. 1912. *The Origin and Development of the Moral Ideas*, 2nd edn. London: Macmillan.

Wiggins, D. 2005. "An Idea we Cannot do Without: What Difference Will it Make (eg. to Moral, Political and Environmental Philosophy) to Recognize and Put to Use a Substantial Conception of Need?". See Reader (ed.) (2005), 25–50.

Williams, B. 2005. *In the Beginning Was the Deed: Realism and Moralism in Political Argument*, G. Hawthorn (selected, ed. and intro.). Princeton, NJ: Princeton University Press.

Wilson, J. Q. 1993. *The Moral Sense*. New York: Free Press.

Wiredu, K. 1990. "An Akan Perspective on Human Rights". In *Human Rights in Africa*, A. Ahmed, An-Na'im & F. M. Deng (eds). Washington, DC: Brookings Institution.

Young, I. M. 2007a. *Global Challenges: War, Self-Determination and Responsibility for Justice*. Cambridge: Polity.

Young, I. M. 2007b. "Power, Violence, and Legitimacy: A Reading of Hannah Arendt in an Age of Police Brutality and Humanitarian Intervention". See Young (2007a), 79–104.

Young, I. M. 2007c. "Responsibility, Social Connection, and Global Labor Justice". See Young (2007a), 159–86.

Zubaida, S. 2002. "Middle Eastern Experiences of Cosmopolitanism". See Vertovec & Cohen (eds) (2002a), 32–41.

Index